YOUR TOWNS & CITIE

EDINBURGH

AT WAR 1939-45

YOUR TOWNS & CITIES IN WORLD WAR TWO

EDINBURGH
AT WAR 1939-45

CRAIG ARMSTRONG

Pen & Sword
MILITARY

AN IMPRINT OF PEN & SWORD BOOKS LTD.
YORKSHIRE - PHILADELPHIA

First published in Great Britain in 2018 by
Pen & Sword Military
an imprint of
Pen & Sword Books Ltd
Yorkshire – Philadelphia

ISBN 978 1 47387 9 638

A CIP catalogue record for this book is
available from the British Library.

Printed and bound in England by CPI Group (UK) Ltd, Croydon, CR0 4YY
Typeset by Aura Technology and Software Services, India

Pen & Sword Books Limited incorporates the imprints of Atlas, Archaeology, Aviation, Discovery, Family History, Fiction, History, Maritime, Military, Military Classics, Politics, Select, Transport, True Crime, Air World, Frontline Publishing, Leo Cooper, Remember When, Seaforth Publishing, The Praetorian Press, Wharncliffe Local History, Wharncliffe Transport, Wharncliffe True Crime and White Owl.

For a complete list of Pen & Sword titles please contact
PEN & SWORD BOOKS LIMITED
47 Church Street, Barnsley, South Yorkshire, S70 2AS, England
E-mail: enquiries@pen-and-sword.co.uk
Website: www.pen-and-sword.co.uk

Or

PEN AND SWORD BOOKS
1950 Lawrence Rd, Havertown, PA 19083, USA
E-mail: Uspen-and-sword@casematepublishers.com
Website: www.penandswordbooks.com

Contents

CHAPTER 1

1939

As the situation in Europe deteriorated the government began planning air raid precautions in earnest. In Edinburgh this resulted in a recruiting campaign for the proposed ARP services, especially the Wardens Service. In mid-April the local press ran a number of features giving advice on measures which could be taken to decrease the risk from air raids. The ARP services already in place in Edinburgh were also given a series of lectures, instructional talks and demonstrations to sharpen the wardens' skills and to assess how efficient the organisation was and where improvements could be made.

There had been some confusion over the issue of air raid sirens for the city. The city authorities had initially requested that forty be issued to the city but the government had reduced this number by half. After the first test of the sirens it became clear that more were required and the government agreed to furnish a further 12, bringing the total to 32 across the city; this was later increased to 53. There was some confusion over who was responsible for the sirens. It was decided that the request for sirens to be sounded would be the responsibility of the RAF locally; the sounding of the sirens was the responsibility of the police; and the installation and maintenance of the sirens and equipment was the responsibility of the Post Office. The police were given the responsibility of sounding the sirens due to the fact that all police boxes and stations in the city were linked by telephone to the headquarters (which would actually sound the sirens) and it was felt that it would be too expensive to construct another new telephone network. Unfortunately this also made this system vulnerable as, if the police headquarters was hit, the alarm system would be compromised. This unnecessarily cumbersome system of operation was later to prove ineffective and spark much criticism in the city of Edinburgh.

As of April the city had 6,000 wardens recruited and under training. More than 1,000 were still required to bring the service up to wartime strength. Recruitment drives were launched, focusing on the George Square and St. Leonard's wards of the city as warden recruitment had been particularly poor in these areas.

Demolition squads were also being recruited (later renamed rescue squads, both heavy and light) who would have responsibility for demolishing structures which had been damaged and rendered dangerous and also in extricating those who had been trapped beneath rubble. They were based at the various engineering depots scattered throughout the city.

One of the more highly qualified fields within the ARP service was the gas detection and decontamination squads. These were made up of trained personnel, mainly chemists, and would be responsible, under the auspices of the Inspector of

Lighting and Cleansing, not only for the detection of gas but also for 'dispersing and rendering innocuous poison gases'.[1] By mid-April over eighty per cent of the city's adult population had been fitted for and issued with gas-masks (respirators) and the issuing of masks to children was still proceeding.

One of the main sources of concern amongst the authorities was the threat of a gas attack being launched on the general population. This was despite the fact that at this stage in the war the Luftwaffe had almost no means of delivering such an attack. Gas masks were a sensible precaution but, despite official urging, people seem to have been reluctant to carry them at all times as advised. ARP training was also adversely affected by this paranoid fear of gas attack. For example, while Edinburgh Electricity Department had trained more than 1,200 of its staff in various ARP procedures, there was a huge imbalance. While 500 of its staff had been trained in gas decontamination procedures only 60 had been trained in first aid and a further 60 in fire-fighting operations. The authorities fitted yellow gas detection boards in the streets and the tops of post boxes were coated in gas detecting paint. For some ARP workers there was the issue of gas-proof coats which had been made from oilskins. While these were largely unpopular there was further uproar over the news that approximately 5,000 of these inflammable coats had been stored in cramped conditions in a room which was above the switching room of an electricity sub-station.

Of all the problems facing the ARP authorities was the fact that the city, like most other Scottish cities, had areas of crowded tenement buildings which were exceptionally vulnerable to fire. The ARP services looked for alternative supplies of water in the event of an incendiary attack and it was agreed between the local authority and the LNER that the water in the Union Canal would be made available during emergencies. The LNER insisted on a payment of 10s per annum.

The canal itself was something of an ARP concern as fears had been expressed that in the event of bombing the canal banks could be breached between Sighthill and Leamington Bridge resulting in the inundation of a significant part of the city. It was decided that the construction of three cotter dams was necessary to provide flood protection.

Along with every other authority, those in Edinburgh expected air raids to result in mass casualties far above what proved to be the reality. Dozens of first aid posts were set up across the city while 21 church halls, in addition to the greyhound stadium at Stenhouse, were set up as makeshift mortuaries to be opened during heavy raiding. Accompanying and working alongside these facilities would be 22 information centres, under the Council for Social Services.

The local authorities had undertaken a survey of almost every basement and cellar in the city to assess their viability for use as air raid shelters but had run into numerous problems. Many were not suitable and some owners were proving reluctant in approving the use of their properties in this manner. Nevertheless, a list of suitable properties had been sent to the Home Office for approval and the authorities were willing to commandeer them if it proved necessary. The subject of providing public shelters through construction projects was still under consideration at this stage.

A census of all children, expectant mothers and other especially vulnerable people was also undertaken at this time so that they could be offered a place in the evacuation scheme that the government was preparing. It had been agreed that accommodation for people who wished to be evacuated would be in the south of Scotland, no further north than Perthshire (approximately 37,000 signed up to the evacuation scheme).

Under the Defence Act employers were ordered to provide ARP training for workers and to ensure that there was adequate shelter provision for their workforces. This would prove extremely costly and the government had set aside more than £25,000,000 for this in addition to a number of grants. Some Edinburgh firms were ahead of the game and immediately began fortifying their offices and places of business, securing training materials and organising training programmes.

Many Edinburgh contractors saw gilt-edged opportunities in the provision of ARP materials and the local press was inundated with adverts for myriad items which were claimed to be vital for protecting oneself and one's family. Frost's of Shandwick Place, for example, claimed to stock every item to gas-proof a room. Their anti-gas home protection outfit, available for 35s or 45s, consisted of curtains and lining materials along with a large booklet explaining how to seal a room against gas. It was claimed that this could be done in 15-20 minutes. The enterprising firm, which in peacetime described itself as decorative furnishers, also sold items necessary to comply with blackout regulations.

Advert for Frost's
(Edinburgh Evening News)

Messrs Calder of Leith, meanwhile, described themselves as being specialists in equipment for the blackout. As contractors to the Admiralty, the Office of Works and several local authorities they claimed to be well-placed to provide materials and to offer expert advice on all manner of situations related to the blackout. The firm was willing to submit offers for any size of work saying that it could provide estimates for contracts for a single blind through to 'complete equipment of blinds for barracks, hospitals, or large factories'.[2] The company also advertised other items including its ambulance stretchers, camp beds, blankets and sandbags.

The Liberton quarrymasters Messrs J.B. Alexander advertised sandbags ready for immediate use and in any quantity. Its adverts informed prospective customers that the sandbag was an essential defence, that it had been proven effective in the First World War and the Spanish Civil War and that there was no comparable method of providing extra defence for buildings and air raid shelters.

Advert for Calder's (EEN)

Advert for Alexander's (EEN)

Messrs James Grey & Sons of 89 George Street claimed to have been one of the first to appreciate the importance and the necessity of ARP works and were offering what they described as an easily erected and affordable 'Fortress Toolshed' which gave protection against bomb splinters, blast and shrapnel. The firm offered these shelters in two different sizes capable of seating six or twelve adults and advised that they be partially buried underground where they could be disguised under a rockery. They seem to have been an early and unofficial form of the highly effective Anderson Shelter.

The Castle Street building contractors firm of Thomas Graham Ltd offered an aerocrete (cellular concrete) shelter which, once again, could be buried under a rockery and offered protection against extremes of temperature. Adverts for the company claimed that they were specialists in the construction of this type of shelter. A great number of building contractors were anxious to obtain ARP business including that of J & W Henderson Ltd of 18 York Place who offered aggregates, cement and all necessary materials for the construction of ARP shelters. Henderson's described themselves as 'an old-established Scottish firm' with over a century's history.[3] They had branches in four other locations (Ayr, Dundee, Glasgow and London) and were War Office and Admiralty contractors as well as undertaking projects for the Royal Ordnance Factory, several Scottish airfields and Lanark Barracks.

Advert for James Grey & Sons (EEN)

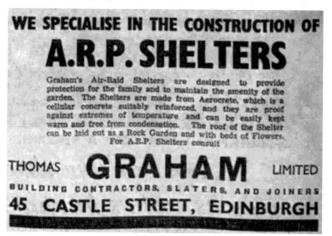

Advert for Thomas Graham (EEN)

Advert for J.W. Henderson's (EEN)

Advert for John Glen (EEN)

The Bathgate firm of John Glen & Co described themselves as being pioneers and the leading experts in the construction of ARP trenches and prided themselves on being the only Scottish firm on the list of Home Office approved list of designs for trench shelters. In their advertising they mentioned how they had provided the concrete ribs for the trench shelters constructed at East Meadows and that 'In addition to the erection of numerous private shelters, they are at the present time undertaking large protection schemes for municipalities and industrial concerns'.

Millets of Leith Street offered protective clothing and equipment. The company also offered steel helmets, stretchers, and blankets suitable for the sealing of refuge rooms against gas. Fleming's Stores, which was a household ironmongers with premises on Grey Street, Home Street and St. John's Road, Corstorphine, also offered a wide range of ARP and firefighting equipment including stirrup pumps, corrugated steel air raid shelters and blackout supplies. They were joined in this enterprise by D.M. Munro of 25 Paties Road. Publishers also got in on the act with E & S Livingstone of Teviot Place offering customers, at a price of 6d, a newly published booklet by Halliday Sutherland MD, entitled *Sutherland's First Aid to the Injured and Sick* complete with a new section on gas warfare described as being 'Indispensable to Every Citizen'.

Above left: Advert for Millet's *(EEN)*

Above right: Advert for Fleming's *(EEN)*

Above: Advert for Munro's *(EEN)*

Right: Advert for Livingstone's *(EEN)*

Wireless engineering firm Rossleigh Ltd of 6 Queensferry Street advised customers that during these times of national emergency keeping in touch with developments through official radio announcements would be vitally important but that in the event of heavy raiding it was possible that mains supplies would be knocked out and thus the possession of a battery operated wireless set might prove to be a necessity. The company offered choices from eight different makers and price ranges from £7.7s.

There remained fundamental problems with the city's ARP scheme. In July the Labour MP for East Edinburgh said in the House of Commons that the provision of air raid shelters for those who lived in the city's tenement buildings was completely inadequate and asked if something was going to be done about it. Lord Privy Seal, Sir John Anderson, replied that he was aware of the problem and that he had ordered one of his senior advisors to make a special visit to the city to discuss the matter with the local authorities.

The commercially-supplied concrete surface shelters varied greatly in their quality with some firms using shoddy materials and construction techniques. Several shelters had to be demolished when it was discovered they were inadequate. One firm, For and Torrie Ltd, went so far as to offer to construct one shelter for free to demonstrate their high levels of workmanship to the authorities.

By October, 6,190 public shelters had been built in the city along with 19,095 trenches while almost 800 closes had been provided with sandbag blast walls. Large public shelters were built at St. Stephen's Church in St. Vincent Street (capacity of 400), the basement of the YMCA in St. Andrew Square (200) and the basement of Morrison's Garage at Roseburn Bridge (100). Perhaps the most ingenious shelters used the store rooms under the terrace at the Southern Cemetery. After being strengthened, having the windows bricked up and a ventilation system fitted they provided shelter for large numbers. There was also a plan to dig a deep tunnel shelter from Waverley Bridge to the Grassmarket using an abandoned railway tunnel which ran from Waverley Market to Scotland Street, but this was eventually shelved as being too expensive and the tunnel was instead used for the growing of mushrooms!

Advert for Rossleigh (EEN)

Despite this flurry of activity the authorities were forced to admit in October that there was currently only shelter provision for approximately one third of the population (140,000 people).

The blackout had already proved contentious with prosecutions for various breaches of the regulations causing resentment towards the ARP wardens who were responsible for their enforcement. Sometimes the official attitude towards the blackout bordered on paranoia with warnings appearing in newspapers during November stating that smoking a cigarette outside in the hours of darkness could be viewed as a breach of the regulations.

One Edinburgh resident complained to the council that the white lines which had been painted on the corner of his house so that people would see it during the blackout amounted to vandalism and demanded their removal. But numerous injuries were caused by collisions with motor vehicles, walls, trees, people falling off kerbs and tripping over obstructions such as the emergency water supply pipes which had been laid in some places.

One area in which Edinburgh was well prepared for the coming emergency was in the strength of its Auxiliary Fire Service. By early 1939 the service had 28 stations in the city and when it was mobilised in September 1,193 of its established strength of 1,200 reported for duty. This was the best record of any AFS in Scotland, and largely put down to the leadership and enthusiasm of its commandant, Councillor A.H.A. Murray. Murray had set about his task with commendable vigour and developed a reputation as being a friend to the service. This had been strengthened by his vehement opposition to a Scottish Office request in the first weeks of the war to reduce the strength of the Edinburgh AFS by 700 men. He was successful in part and managed to convince the Scottish Office to reduce the strength by only 500 men.

During the first days of September 1939 the government put into action its evacuation plans. There were extensive arrangements to be overseen to facilitate the movement of thousands of children and others out of the city. Over the first two days of September some 30,000 people left Edinburgh. The authorities in reception areas had made provision for 100,000 evacuees and even though 30,000 seems a huge number it was still 7,000 less than the total number that had signed up for the scheme. A total of 78 schools were amongst those evacuated with the majority (45) leaving on 1 September. The authorities declared that they were disappointed by the numbers involved and estimated that over half of Edinburgh's children remained in the city. Enquiries by the authorities revealed that the main reason was that people felt that their children were as safe at home as anywhere.

Craigmillar School demonstrates the experience of a large school. Approximately 3,000 people were expected to be evacuated under the school's scheme and they arrived in a steady stream to be sorted into two groups: children accompanied by their mothers; and those who were unaccompanied. By far the greater percentage was those who were accompanied. The evacuees were then divided into groups of twenty and it became clear that there would be problems as mothers attempted to ensure they were accompanied by friends. Observers commented on the numbers of extremely large families, but this was partially because some mothers had taken children 'under their wing' from multiple families, probably those of neighbours. Many had ignored instructions to bring only essentials and had turned up with heavy and awkward luggage. Some mothers were struggling with luggage, prams and babies and the police on duty were praised for their cheerful attitudes and willingness to help the evacuees. One policeman, helping a young mother, was thanked and the young woman explained how she had 'four children and the oldest is only five'.[4] Others were assisted by anxious fathers, some in uniform, but the press commented that there were few emotional scenes as trains left Duddington Station at regular intervals.

For the children from the Broughton area the gathering point was London Street School, which evacuated 676 people including teachers, helpers, mothers, children and almost 200 unaccompanied children. As the groups were to be evacuated from Waverley Station it was important that they were well organised, hence the large numbers of helpers. Many of the children were curious as to what was happening, and observers reported parents disinclined to talk, standing quietly in small groups with sad expressions. One little girl ran away and had to be returned tearfully, while one mother on seeing the queues hurried home to 'waken "Wee Alec" saying she had forgotten all about the evacuation until she saw the crowds'! Most of the children here were aged 8-10 although there were a number of older children who were accompanying younger siblings, many of them toddlers. Before the groups were marched off to the station each child was given a glass of milk and a banana to sustain them on their journey.

Blackhall School was the base for 140 evacuees from a variety of schools and had prepared for the event by holding a rehearsal the day before (only ninety had turned up). Once again, before being marched off to the station the youngsters were fed; this time with biscuits, a banana and milk. Most were of school age but, once more, there were a number of boys aged over 16 who were escorting younger siblings.

The James Gillespie Girls' School on Bruntsfield Links evacuated 65 pupils and a number of teachers and helpers, while the Boys' School at Marchmont Crescent evacuated 105 including 57 school children and 15 pre-schoolers (the youngest being 6 months old). The number of evacuees who turned up was only a third of that expected but helpers commented on the coolness shown by both the children and parents in the face of the great stress and anxiety of the situation.

At the Flora Stevenson School there was a similarly disappointing turnout with fewer than half of the 1,000 people who had turned up for a previous rehearsal. There were some tearful scenes which helpers and teachers attempted to calm before the little groups left for their departure station. The police were kept busy as they directed anxious mothers and children, carried milk and food for the youngsters, and one embarked on a successful search for a small boy's shoe which had fallen off as he was carried into the school.

At Portobello 300 children and their helpers departed for Berwickshire from Tower Bank School. Before the children left they attended a short service of prayer and song led by the Rev W.L. Fraser. They were seen off on their way to the railway station by Lord Provost Steele.

At Leith the take-up of the offer of evacuation seems to have been more popular with the Links School, Lochend Road School and St. Mary's School all reporting satisfactory turnouts with many of the evacuees arriving at the schools an hour before the scheduled time. Observers commented on the large number of adult women who were present.

At Prestonfield there were similar scenes as large numbers of children assembled at Preston Street School, although still only a third of those expected, before their departure to Newington Station and various border parishes. There was an amusing scene here as an anxious mother scanned the crowd trying to locate her son Johnnie who apparently could not bear to be parted from his school friends and, despite not being officially evacuated, had taken it upon himself to join the throng anyway! Johnnie was eventually located and handed back to his mother who was admonished to 'keep your eye on him this time. He's been here half a dozen times this morning.'

The organisation of the evacuation scheme seems to have worked with surprising smoothness in Edinburgh, and the education officer, J.B. Frizell, could afterwards reflect that all, or nearly all, had gone well. Mr Frizell stated that the plans which they had put in place could have coped with five times the number of evacuees and said that anyone who had previously registered could be accommodated. He said that in view of the smaller than expected numbers who had been evacuated it would be necessary to bring back some of the teachers so that those who remained behind could continue to receive an education. Perhaps in an effort to assuage parental

Edinburgh Evacuees at Station (EEN)

More Edinburgh evacuees wait anxiously at station (EEN)

concerns Mr Frizell commented on reports of extremely warm welcomes being given to evacuees in the billeting areas. A humorous story was relayed of a mother with her three children who objected to being billeted in the largest mansion in the area as it looked too much like a poorhouse, and instead asked to be homed in a cottage.

One party of evacuees witnessed an unnerving incident when their train was passing through Leuchars Junction. An unattended baggage cart fell onto the line in front of the train which was going 40 mph at the time. The train struck the cart with a loud bang and drew up slightly beyond the station. The cart had contained, amongst other items, a crate full of carrier pigeons; the birds were all killed and strewn along the platform. There was no damage to the train and it set off on its way again a short time later.

Mothers-to-be were also eligible for evacuation. In Edinburgh those pregnant women who had registered for evacuation were informed that they should assemble at the agreed places on the morning of 3 September.

On the weekend war was declared, the people of Edinburgh who were not taking part in the evacuation attempted to put aside their anxieties over the international situation, and the theatres and cinemas did a brisk trade. For the owners and staff of these establishments it was a worrying time as they had been told that the police might order the closure of places of entertainment to limit the dangers of casualties from bombing.

Customers had a variety of theatrical performances to choose from. The Royal Lyceum hosted a performance of *The Rising Generation*, a comedy play performed by the Howard & Wyndham Repertory Company. It was about two children who come home with friends to find that they have to look after the house. As the evacuation of 30,000 people (mainly children) was taking place at the same time one can see the connection that people made between reality and comedy. In Southside the Empire Theatre was hosting a show by Carroll Levis and several of his 'radio discoveries'.[5] Levis had begun his radio career in the USA and had become renowned as a talent spotter who toured with groups of unknown performers (a sort of forerunner to Simon Cowell) and his travelling shows had proven to be widely popular. There were also several summer shows which were still drawing the crowds. On Leven Street the King's Theatre featured Dave Willis in *Half Past Eight*; the Theatre Royal offered Jack Radcliffe in a summer show; and the Palladium also offered a summer show (it was its final week).

For those visiting the cinema there was a huge choice ranging from the relatively high-brow *Mikado* which was showing at the New and New Victoria cinemas to *The Lambeth Walk* which was the main feature at the Playhouse. This was a film version of the musical *Me and My Girl* and starred Lupino Lane in the leading role. At the Regal and the Ritz customers could enjoy James Stewart in *Made for Each Other* and at the Rutland and St. Andrew Square the main feature was *The Hound of the Baskervilles* starring Basil Rathbone and Nigel Bruce.[6] A grittier gangster drama, *Too Dangerous to Live*, starring Sebastian Shaw and Greta Glyn was the main feature at the Caley.

Edinburgh and Leith Cinemas, 2 September 1939

Cinema	Main Feature
Alhambra	*The Girl Downstairs*
Astoria	*Youth Takes a Fling*
Blue Halls	*What a Woman*
Broadway	*Vacation from Love*
Capitol	*Society Lawyer*
Carlton	*Persons in Hiding*
County	*Room Service*
Dominion	*39 Steps*
Embassy	*Stand Up and Fight*
Gaiety	*City Streets*
Grand	*The Great Man Votes*
King's Cinema	*Peck's Bad Boy at the Circus*
Leith Palace	*Brother Rat*
Lyceum	*Ambush*

Cinema	Main Feature
Palace	*Idiot's Delight*
Poole's	*Stagecoach*
Picturedrome	*Blondie*
Regent	*Society Lawyer*
Roxy	*39 Steps*
Salisbury	*The Challenge*
Salon	*Comet Over Broadway*
Savoy	*Brother Rat*
State	*Roman Scandal*
Tivoli	*What a Woman*

On Sunday 3 September at 11 am many of the people of the Edinburgh area were close to a wireless set listening to the Prime Minister, in a rather doleful and less than inspiring broadcast, announce that Britain was once again formally at war with Germany. Fears of an immediate aerial onslaught seemed to have come true when, just as Chamberlain had finished speaking, the air raid sirens over much of central and southern Scotland sounded. This proved a false alarm caused by some aircraft flying off the Dutch coast being spotted on radar and another flight of aircraft suddenly appearing over central Scotland. This second flight was two Spitfires of 602 (City of Glasgow) squadron on a flight from their home base at Abbotsinch to inspect their wartime airfield at Grangemouth.[7] Thus Squadron Leader A. Douglas Farquhar and Flight Lieutenant Sandy Johnstone were unwittingly partly responsible for the first alert of Scotland's war.

One of the larger industrial employers in Edinburgh was the North British Rubber Company which had a large factory at Castle Mills. The firm had links with Edinburgh dating back to 1856 and during the First World War had produced over a million boots for the British Army along with pneumatic tyres and other vital items of equipment. At the outbreak of the Second World War orders for Wellington boots for the forces again rose dramatically. Contracts for gas masks, tyres, and fabric for barrage balloons also swelled the company's order books.

At Leith the shipbuilders Henry Robb Ltd (locally known as Robbs) specialised in the construction of small and medium sized vessels such as tugs and dredgers. The war proved a great financial boon to this company with naval orders pouring in throughout the war. Amongst the orders received in the first year was one for three Bird-class corvettes for the Royal New Zealand Navy.

Rosyth was an important military staging base as well as naval dockyard and Leith an important east coast port. Both would have to be strongly protected along with the sea lanes of the coast. In September the Royal Navy took over the Granton Hotel at Granton Harbour and commissioned it as HMS *Claverhouse*. The base was used mainly for reserve training.

The defences put in place were extensive and included minefields both at the mouth of the Firth of Forth and along its southern banks. Some of the mines could be detonated via an electrical signal from Inchkeith. On 21 November the cruiser HMS *Belfast* was sailing through the Firth when a German magnetic mine exploded underneath her, injuring twenty-one of her crew. The damage to the modern vessel (she had been in service for just over a year) was severe and it was thought at first that the mine might have broken her back. After being towed back to Rosyth inspections revealed that her keel had been warped by the blast and there had been extensive damage to the engine room and boilers. It was thought that the cruiser would have to be scrapped but after further consideration it was decided to make repairs. After the initial repairs were completed at Rosyth the ship sailed for Devonport where she had to be practically rebuilt. She did not return to service until November 1942.

Edinburgh and much of the east coast was seen as a prime target for the Luftwaffe with the naval units stationed in the Firth being of key strategic importance. Edinburgh was protected by several squadrons and airfields, most notably RAF Turnhouse (now Edinburgh International Airport), RAF Grangemouth, RAF Drem and RAF East Fortune. There was also RAF Donibristle which served a dual purpose as a shore base for Fleet Air Arm aircraft and as an aircraft repair base.

After a series of false alerts the first real enemy attack of the war developed on 26 September when a group of radar contacts were obtained over the North Sea heading for the Firth of Forth. The reaction to the air raid sirens was perhaps influenced by the series of false alarms and many people simply took no heed and went on with their business. It was later reported that postmen had continued making their deliveries. Others found that there was not room for them in the public shelters and trenches. Across the river in Dunfermline air raid wardens had to order curious crowds of onlookers off the streets.

Others did heed the warnings. It was claimed that some banks emptied their tills before taking to the vault shelters, and students at Dalkeith High School were escorted by teachers to the basement air raid shelter. ARP wardens rushed to their posts and first aid stations were hurriedly manned. The warnings proved, in some ways, to be another false alarm as the enemy aircraft were attacking shipping and did not stray inland. In Edinburgh questions were asked in the press, as the alarms had rung on three separate occasions during the morning causing significant disruption to local business.

Shortly after 11 am two sections of 603 (City of Edinburgh) Squadron were scrambled from RAF Turnhouse with orders to patrol to the east of May Island where it was believed that the anti-aircraft escort destroyer HMS *Valorous* was under attack by Heinkel HE111 and Junkers JU88 bombers. Upon arriving on station the RAF fighters immediately found themselves being fired upon by the destroyer which was assigned to convoy escort duties with Rosyth Force. Luckily no hits were scored on the RAF fighter but there was no decisive combat contact made with the enemy either.[8]

Following several further false alarms, one involving a flight of geese, the enemy launched its first raid on British soil on 16 October. The action began shortly before

HMS Valorous
(Public Domain)

10 am when the Observer Corps reported sighting an unidentified aircraft flying over Dunfermline in the direction of Rosyth. There was no confirmation via radar as the station at Drone Hill had reported a malfunction and was out of order for most of the day. Spitfires of 603 (City of Glasgow) Squadron were scrambled to intercept and just after 10.20 am Flight Lieutenant George Pinkerton, a farmer from Renfrewshire, who was leading Blue Section, spotted a Heinkel flying a reconnaissance mission to photograph the dockyards at Rosyth. Pinkerton thus became the first pilot to go into action against the Luftwaffe during the war. Calling the 'tally-ho', Pinkerton and his wingman, Flying Officer Archie McKellar, followed the Heinkel as it fled into cloud and established another first for themselves as they became the first RAF airmen to fire on an enemy aircraft during the war. The Heinkel, from Kampfgeschwader 26 (KG26), escaped and fled back across the North Sea.[9]

The reconnaissance flight was obviously the portent for further action and there were repeated sightings of high-flying unidentified aircraft during the morning along with radio intercepts which showed that the Luftwaffe was indeed engaged on active reconnaissance over Scotland. Shortly after 11 am another reconnaissance Heinkel was spotted over RAF Drem and the commanding officer of 602 (City of Glasgow) Squadron reported the sighting only to be told somewhat casually that he would investigate if he thought it necessary. Squadron Leader Farquhar immediately scrambled Red Section which gave chase after spotting the Heinkel circling over the radar masts of Drone Hill. Unfortunately the Spitfires had been scrambled too late and the high-flying Heinkel was able to make good its escape. The morning was a story of frustration for the RAF pilots who were eager to come to grips with the Luftwaffe bombers. The failure of the radar at Drone Hill meant that they were reliant upon the Observer Corps and there seem to have been many, often contradictory, sightings reported. Confusion over headings was also a problem with several flights of fighters being sent on courses directly away from the enemy aircraft they had been sent up to pursue. By lunchtime activity had died down and most RAF fighters were recalled to base with only a few standing patrols left flying.

Unbeknownst to Fighter Command the action was not over. Analysis of photos taken during the morning had revealed to the Luftwaffe the presence of a large warship at Rosyth. The Luftwaffe wrongly identified the ship as the *Hood* (it was in fact HMS *Repulse*) and orders were quickly passed to Hauptmann Helmut Pohle, the commanding officer of KG30, to launch an immediate attack on the ship. KG30 was the first Luftwaffe unit to be equipped with the fast and long range JU88 bomber and the men of KG30 were anxious to prove themselves. Like their British opponents the early experience of wartime flying was a testing one for the men of KG30 and by 2.15 pm Pohle's formation was crossing the North Sea but in a somewhat scattered and loose formation.[10]

Early warning of the incoming raid was again impossible. The radar equipment at Drone Hill had been repaired but suffered another breakdown when the public electricity supply was disrupted and the lack of provision of emergency generators meant that the entire site was rendered inoperable. Once again it was the men and women of the Observer Corps who found themselves in the front line and they passed on a warning of enemy aircraft over the East Lothian area at around 2.20 pm. Flight Lieutenant George Pinkerton again led his Blue Section off the ground to intercept at 2.23 pm. Meanwhile on the ground there was further confusion. An anti-aircraft battery stationed in Dalmeny Park had been practising loading drills when they sighted a JU88 flying upriver. The battery commander requested permission to fire when the bomber was directly over the Forth Bridge. Astonishingly, indecision continued and it took over ten minutes for the battery to be given the order to go into action; by this time some bombs had already been dropped.

At RAF Turnhouse two sections of Spitfires from 603 (City of Edinburgh) Squadron were scrambled to intercept the enemy bombers which were now reported to be over the Forth Bridge and Dalkeith. Yellow Section, led by Flight Lieutenant

HMS Hood (PD)

HMS Repulse (PD)

George Denholm, quickly found the enemy; indeed, they ran into a flight of three JU88s just after take-off. Denholm led his section into the attack and a running fight developed during which the enemy bombers scattered. The fight, which began over Threipmuir Reservoir, was watched from the ground by a number of interested witnesses, amongst them Roslin police officer James Henderson who saw a bomber being chased by Denholm's section and heard machine-gun fire. At nearby Langhill Farm Joseph Thomson also heard the fire and upon looking up found himself showered with spent shell casings from the machine guns of the Spitfires. One of the bombers was seen to be fleeing from the fight in a north-easterly direction but this unlucky aircraft, piloted by Oberleutnant Hans Storp, ran into Red Section of 603 (City of Edinburgh) Squadron and came under renewed attack. On sighting the three Spitfires the JU88 turned left and headed for the Forth but Flight Lieutenant Patrick Gifford led his section into the attack and ground observers were treated to the sight of the fire from the three fighters knocking pieces off the German bomber and putting one engine out of action. At Port Seton, fisherman John Dickson and his two sons were sailing back to port aboard their boat the *Day Spring* and witnessed the final moments of the combat. As Flight Lieutenant Gifford attacked, once again smoke poured from the JU88 which climbed steeply before falling into the sea.

Despite being initially reluctant to rescue the German airmen, Dickson and his sons did the right thing and investigated the crash site. They found and rescued three survivors (rear gunner Obergefreiter Krämer was never found) who had, despite some sensationalist press claims, suffered only minor injuries, and brought them ashore at Port Seton half an hour later. The three airmen, Storp, Feldwebel Hans Georg Hielscher and Feldwebel Hugo Rohnke, were taken to the local police station where they were attended to by the local GP before being sent under escort to a military hospital within Edinburgh Castle.

At the same time as this action was taking place another section of five JU88s approached Rosyth from the south-west of Edinburgh. The first three bombers

John Dickson and his sons after rescuing three Luftwaffe airmen (EEN)

HMS Southampton (PD)

launched divebombing attacks on HMS *Southampton* and scored at least one direct hit. This bomb penetrated the armour of the ship and emerged through the ship's hull just above the waterline before exploding and sinking a pinnace and the Admiral's barge which were moored to the cruiser.[11]

It was fortunate that the enemy aircrew had been ordered not to attack civilian targets as at the time of this attack a train was crossing the Forth Bridge and, although this gave the passengers an amazing view of the first attack of the war, it would have made a prime target which, if hit, would have resulted in many casualties.

Meanwhile the commanding officer was still searching unsuccessfully for HMS *Hood*. Keenly aware that he had been ordered not to bomb any ship that was docked in case of causing civilian casualties he instead targeted two cruisers which he spotted lying moored in the Forth. As he initiated his divebombing attack his cockpit canopy came loose and flew off hindering him somewhat. Pohle still managed to drop two bombs and then circled so he could assess the results of the attacks of the rest of his squadron. At 2.38 pm other aircraft came into attack and the frustrated men of the anti-aircraft battery at Dalmeny Park were finally authorised to open fire. They were quickly joined by other anti-aircraft batteries, at Dalmeny village, Donibristle, Mire End and Primrose Farm.

Again the attack was witnessed by many on the ground. Men building air raid shelters under the arches of the Forth Bridge at South Queensferry saw the JU88s attacking the shipping and, as the raid spread and anti-aircraft fire erupted in the skies above south-east Edinburgh, shrapnel fell onto cars that had been halted by police on the Hawes Brae. Windows were broken across a wide area of Edinburgh and one tram passenger at Portobello had a narrow escape when a large chunk of shrapnel smashed through his tram narrowly missing him. HMS *Repulse* now joined in with the anti-aircraft fire and the barrage from the battlecruiser added to the amount of shrapnel falling over the city. It was even reported that the Territorials who were guarding the bridge were forced to take cover behind the parapet. At Alma Street the first casualty occurred when a dog was hit by shrapnel and subsequently had to be put down. At Dalmeny Station a woman was standing waiting for a train when a red hot piece of shrapnel fell from the sky into her coat pocket and set it on fire. Meanwhile a farm worker, Peter McGowan, was injured slightly by falling shrapnel and Aberdour farmer's wife Mrs Milne was injured by shrapnel which came through the roof of her farmhouse. Amongst the more serious pieces of hardware crashing to earth were the brass and lead shell caps from anti-aircraft shells. Unexploded shells also caused much concern across Edinburgh as they fell to earth, sometimes exploding on impact.

Edinburgh housewife hands over shell cap to policeman (EEN)

The barrage was largely ineffective and was hindered by a lack of fire control and by the presence of a number of training aircraft from RAF Donibristle which remained in the area during the early part of the raid.

We have already heard how Flight Lieutenant George Pinkerton and two comrades from 602 Squadron had been scrambled to search for intruders. At 2.23 pm the three Spitfires were at 20,000 feet over Dalkieth when they sighted what they believed were enemy aircraft and gave pursuit only to find that they were Sea Skua training aircraft from RAF Donibristle. Twenty minutes later they found the real enemy and Pinkerton gave a joyous cry over the radio before moving his section into attack. The JU88 which they had picked out was that of Helmut Pohle. After the first attack one of Pinkerton's wingmen became lost but the other two Spitfires took up positions either side of the JU88 and launched a series of attacks. As Pohle made for the sea the attacks by the Spitfires continued, damaging both engines and a wingtip, killing two crewmen and seriously wounding another. A missing cockpit canopy added to Pohle's difficulties and when Pinkerton made another attack he managed to knock out both engines. Pohle just had time to pull up to avoid a coaster before the stricken JU88 dropped heavily into the sea. The member of Pinkerton's section who had got lost came across another two JU88s and successfully chased them off before returning to base.

Pohle, suffering from a fractured skull and other injuries, was plucked from the water by the coaster which he had narrowly avoided before being transferred to the destroyer HMS *Jervis*. He was taken to sick bay and before he lost consciousness was interrogated by a German-speaking officer of the crew. After being landed ashore, Pohle was transferred to the naval hospital at Port Edgar where, after remaining unconscious for several days, he was treated for over a month before he was well enough for transfer south to a PoW camp in Westmoreland. There he was reunited with Hans Storp, and the two captive airmen were later visited by both Pinkerton and Gifford.

Just minutes after Pohle had crashed a third wave of bombers was spotted and a further six Spitfires of 603 (City of Edinburgh) Squadron were scrambled from Turnhouse but there was some confusion over where to send them. At first ordered to patrol at just 3,000 feet by the Turnhouse sector controller the order was quickly and bad-temperedly changed by 13 Group to a far greater altitude which would give the Spitfires a tactical advantage in the attack.

With 13 Group convinced that this was a concerted attack on the naval units at Rosyth, 602 (City of Glasgow) Squadron was ordered to put up three Spitfires, and Red Section was scrambled to patrol over RAF Drem at 2.50 pm. Ten minutes later Flight Lieutenant Dunlop Urie inconclusively attacked and gave chase to a bomber off Kirkcaldy. Shortly after 3 pm Pilot Officer Norman Stone attacked another JU88 over Gullane and drove the bomber off to the east.

The aircraft chased off by Pilot Officer Stone came under further attack by three Spitfires of 603 Squadron shortly after but survived, largely because two of the Spitfires nearly collided during the attack. The situation continued to be confused and this was not helped by the arrival of a convoy in the Forth which became another target of opportunity.

Meanwhile thirty miles to the north, Green Section of 602 (City of Glasgow) Squadron were refuelling at the Coastal Command station at RAF Leuchars following an uneventful earlier patrol. It appears that someone at 13 Group suddenly remembered that they were there and ordered them into action as the three pilots (Douglas Farquhar, Sandy Johnstone and Ian Ferguson) were contentedly eating sandwiches and watching what they thought was a flight of Blenheim bombers flying southwards down the coast. Farquhar went over to the mess to enquire what was happening and returned at a run yelling to the other two that the 'Blenheims' were in fact JU88s and that a force was bombing Rosyth as they sat there. The three pilots ran to their aircraft which were already running, with the admonishments of the Coastal Command base commander ringing in their ears.

Unfortunately they became separated at once as Sandy Johnstone's Spitfire overheated, backfired and suffered engine failure. The other two took off while Johnstone got off some eight minutes later. Farquhar and Ferguson roared over the Forth Bridge but did not spot any enemy aircraft. Shortly after this the JU88s arrived and launched an attack on the convoy and its escorts. One of the bombs fell beside HMS *Mohawk* narrowly missing the destroyer and damaging it badly. It was at this point that Sandy Johnstone came onto the scene and launched a long range attack on one JU88 despite being under intense anti-aircraft fire from the convoy and its escorts. Aboard HMS *Mohawk* the first lieutenant, three other officers and thirteen crewmen were dead while the captain, Commander Richard Jolly, was badly wounded in the abdomen. Aware that his ship was damaged and that many of his crew were injured Jolly repeatedly refused to leave his bridge to seek medical treatment and instead brought his ship into port at Rosyth while telling those who attempted once more to get him to leave the bridge to see to the other injured men. The passage into port took over an hour with Jolly losing strength all the time; so much so that his orders had to be repeated down the voice tubes by the wounded navigation officer. When the destroyer made port Jolly and the rest of the injured were taken off but the brave commanding officer died of his injuries five hours later.[12]

HMS Mohawk (PD)

After climbing up and assessing the tactical situation Douglas Farquhar noticed enemy aircraft being shelled by anti-aircraft fire and went to the attack along with his wingman. A long chase developed with both Spitfires and anti-aircraft batteries taking it in turns to engage the JU88 (which had been forced to jettison its bombs harmlessly). Several people were injured along the route of the pursuit as bullets entered properties and broke windows. Over Leith the JU88 dropped lower and began flying around the roofs of tall buildings to try to shake off his pursuers. The chase ended over Portobello as Ian Ferguson fired his last bursts at the JU88 before it headed out to sea.

At around 4 pm there was further action as three Spitfires of 603 (City of Edinburgh) Squadron made two separate interceptions. In the first, Flying Officer Boulter chased a bomber out to sea off Aberdour. In the second Pilot Officers Robertson and Morton attacked a JU88 which was flying at very low altitude. Once again there was considerable danger to those on the ground as the fight developed into a running battle over built-up areas of Edinburgh. At the Royal Scots Club in Abercromby Place a meeting was interrupted when the JU88 roared overhead prompting the chairman to exclaim 'My God, that's a Jerry!' before calling the meeting to order once more.

When the fight was over Portobello the aircraft had dropped even lower with the JU88 being observed at rooftop height. Two painters were at work on Abercorn Terrace and witnessed the fight. After the aircraft had passed over, one of them, Joe McLuskie, turned to his friend and said that he had been hit. He was immediately rushed to hospital where it was discovered he had been hit in the stomach by a bullet.

By 4.30 pm the action was over and most of the Spitfires returned to their bases where their excited pilots made out their combat reports. Typically they were overly optimistic in their claims: eleven pilots submitted positive combat reports, and several bombers were claimed shot down and others damaged and heading out to sea. The intelligence officers sorted out the claims and reduced them to three bombers destroyed and at least one damaged. Aircraft recognition was proved to be very poor. Not only had several pilots misidentified JU88s as British Blenheim bombers, they had also submitted claims for Heinkel HE111s and a Dornier Do215. The pilots also mentioned that the camouflage of the JU88s was far more effective than that of the RAF and on several occasions RAF pilots had only spotted enemy bombers after they had been bracketed by anti-aircraft fire.

Other tactical problems that the raid highlighted included the unfamiliarity of some of the pilots with the Spitfire,[13] poor tactics which had been more suited to the pre-war days of slower biplane aircraft, the ineffectiveness of RAF fighter area attacks (which had been drilled into the pilots) during a confused action, the unreliability of early radar systems, poor control procedures and pilots opening fire from too long a range.[14]

Sixteen members of the Royal Navy had been killed in the attack with almost fifty injured, while the true Luftwaffe losses amounted to two aircraft shot down, four crew members killed and four taken prisoner.

Despite the problems, the response to the attack, at least by the RAF and officialdom, was portrayed as one of a triumph of British pluck and skill over the much-vaunted Luftwaffe. Eager to reinforce this perception, two of the victorious pilots, Flight

Lieutenants Gifford and Pinkerton, were awarded the DFC for their actions on this day. This seems to have been in contrast to the treatment of Commander Jolly who was awarded the George Cross despite his wounds having been at the hands of the enemy.

The official story of a British triumph was not easily swallowed by many in the Edinburgh area and there were complaints about the initial failure of the sirens to sound and the subsequent confusion when they sounded repeatedly and seemingly without any accuracy as to the presence of the enemy. Lord Provost Henry Steele made an official complaint about the failure of the siren system; possibly partially motivated by the fact that his house had been sprayed by machine-gun fire during the raid. Steele was aware that many people had not heeded the sirens when they did sound and that some of the people of the area were treating the situation as a bit of a joke, but did not let this stop him from venting his views. He demanded an explanation saying that 'The civil population … are probably very fortunate not to be facing serious effects of such an experience … I am very annoyed, and determined that I shall get to the bottom of the mystery.'[15] Despite his determination his complaint got nowhere as the Regional Commissioner, the local police and even the Scottish Office had no answers.

The next day the editorial columns of the Scottish newspapers were almost wholly critical. The *Glasgow Herald* commented that the lack of warning given to the people of Edinburgh and the surrounding area was completely unacceptable and had placed them in great danger, while *The Scotsman* blamed flaws in the system, especially in the liaison between the relevant authorities, and although it acknowledged that on this occasion no great harm had been done, it pointed out that things could have been far more serious.

Bullet holes in Lord Provost Steele's home (window and mirror) (EEN)

The recriminations highlighted some confusion in the operation of the air raid warning system. It was revealed that despite the siren sounding in the Port Seton area the Fife Council members who were in a meeting at the time ignored the advice of the police and did not take to the shelter during the alert. Chief Constable W.B.R. Morren said that 'the police could not accept responsibility for sounding the siren on their own suspicions'.[16] Morren went on to describe how he was in the street when the anti-aircraft shells began bursting over the city, that he had immediately gone to the offices of the Regional and District Commissioners to ascertain what was happening, but that it was a full ten minutes before any official information could be provided.

Indeed, the higher echelons of both the council and the ARP seem to have been reluctant to accept that any recriminations were necessary, or that if things had gone wrong, it was nothing to do with them. Mr Tom Johnston of the Scottish Regional Defence Commissioners only stated that 'The warning system is under the control of the Air Ministry' while the District Civil Defence Commissioner for the south-east of Scotland, W.Y. Darling, asked a rather unconcerned and even facetious question: 'Do the people of Luxembourg receive air raid warnings when aerial engagements take place in the vicinity of the Duchy? Do we have sirens sounding when there is a battle in the North Sea? People should ask themselves these questions.'[17] This was an attempt to deflect blame. The events which had taken place over Edinburgh and the surrounding area had placed members of the public in unnecessary danger due to the failure of the warning system. The battle did not, largely, take place over the North Sea but over the city and more should clearly have been done to get people into the shelters.

Enquiries revealed further flaws in the system and exposed a rather lax approach by some. It was established that no warning at all sounded in Dalkeith even though aircraft flew over the town at low altitude. And it emerged that Leith Customs House had received a raid warning at noon but had disregarded it and failed to pass it on as it was believed that it was probably a test warning. The chief warden at the customs house admitted, 'we did not take it as a real warning, considering it just a normal test, such as we have had in the past.' He said that they had stopped normal work until the all-clear was received half an hour later. 'Nothing happened at all during that time to make us think it was anything but a test and I am convinced it had nothing to do with the raid that came later in the afternoon.'

This lax attitude was not only reflected in the attitudes of officialdom. Many of the civilian population also seem to have taken the matter lightly. It was reported that 'most of the populace thought that it was only a mock attack'. The response of the city council was ambivalent with Councillor J.I. Falconer stating that 'Clearly there was no raid on the city', but that aircraft had attempted to attack a nearby location and had been driven off over the city.[18] This was quite correct but that did not lessen the risk to the public. Councillor Falconer was keen to stress this, telling the public that lessons must be learned from the attack. The key lessons were that people should not remain in the streets or look out of windows but should take shelter if for no other reason than to lessen the strain on the medical services.

The explanation was in reality quite simple. The air raid warning system was largely dependent upon the radar chain to provide advance warning of incoming raids and when this failed it had to fall back onto the Observer Corps who could only give warnings over the unreliable telephone system when they spotted enemy aircraft and this was usually as they crossed the coast or even when they were already over land. *The Edinburgh Evening News* presumed that 'in this case … the Air Force did not give the necessary warning to the civil defence organisations'. While this was true, there were also significant flaws in the system, one being the lack of emergency generators at radar stations.

Not all members of the public treated the matter lightly. *The Edinburgh Evening News* stated that although the attitude during the raid had been one of calm this had quickly turned to one of sincere concern over the failure of the ARP system: the 'Edinburgh man-in-the-street' would like his question answered and his concerns addressed. A full-page article went on to give several examples of the concerns expressed. A railway engine driver believed that the ARP services were placing 'too much faith in the infallibility of the sirens'. 'Someone slept somewhere', he wrote. He was concerned that people could not tell the difference between British and German aircraft, and added, 'Thank goodness they were over to bomb naval objectives, and not the open city!'[19] He thought it had been 'a smart piece of work by the Germans' but expressed his frustrations that the raid had not been intercepted sooner and that more German aircraft had escaped than had been shot down. But he praised the pilots of the RAF saying that the Spitfires 'had the heels of the Germans absolutely'. He had seen two Spitfires attacking a JU88 (obviously he had also failed to take shelter!) and judged that against the Spitfires 'the German had no chance'. He concluded with a warning, however, saying, 'the Germans might do better than that next time'.[20]

An Edinburgh taxi driver agreed that the British airmen had done well but said that the raid would make people realise that no matter how good the defences were some bombers would always get through and that some of those who did would also escape. A porter in a Princes Street shop said that the raid began just as he finished lunch and he was surprised how calm everyone remained even when shrapnel was falling but said that it might have been a different story had the sirens sounded whereupon he believed people would have run for the shelters.

A lorry driver demonstrated the rather naïve and lax attitude that had prevailed when he admitted that 'he never dreamt it could happen … I certainly did not think it was an actual raid at first'. He had changed his mind when he had found a piece of shrapnel lying in Hanover Street. After expressing his admiration for the spirit shown by the general public he qualified this by saying that he believed that this was largely because 'they were caught so completely unawares that they did not properly understand what was happening'. A young waitress continued the theme saying that because the sirens did not go off people thought it was a mock raid but that in her opinion the 'defences were very good indeed' and that the shooting down 'of four enemy planes was splendid work by our airmen…It was one up for the British!'[21]

A letter to the paper by someone signing himself 'Anxious Citizen, well known in church circles' stated the opinion that the 'Lord Provost and our capable Chief Air Warden' had an absolute duty to provide the people of Edinburgh with an explanation for the failure of the siren system; this 'grave omission is too serious to be glossed over'. The writer highlighted the intense feelings that this had aroused in the citizenry and raised the spectre of public unrest saying, 'surging agitation all over the city last night might have led to demonstrations but for the black-out and the innate loyalty that restrains in the long run.'[22]

Some tales of amazing escapes began to emerge. The grounds of Brunstane Tennis Club were sprayed with bullets when a JU88 pursued by two Spitfires flew low overhead. The event could have ended in tragedy as the club usually hosted a large group of Edinburgh schoolboys who played football at this time. For some reason the boys had decided to switch venue that day to Portobello Golf Club. The golf course too was sprayed with bullets, and the boys took shelter under trees, but nobody was hurt.

At 26 Morton Street Mrs Forgan reported how 'a beautiful shining new bullet' had come through a window frame and landed on her duvet. A number of houses in this street were also hit, as were properties in Bedford Terrace and Hamilton Street with bullet holes in walls, windows, bedding and, in at least one case, a pram. One of the talking points around the city concerned the novelty of police officers wearing steel helmets during the raid.

The next day the press came up with a variety of suggestions. The diplomatic correspondent of the *Edinburgh Evening News* claimed that the raid was part of a grander plan involving the attack on the Saar front and the arrival of Hitler at his new HQ behind the Siegfried Line. He claimed that the raid on Rosyth was intended to provide proof of Germany's airpower 'by the wholesale sinking of the ships of the British Navy'. He went on that this plan had backfired as the attack on the Saar had been a costly defeat and 'his air raiders had bad luck'.[23]

The following day the people of Scotland received a blow to their morale when it was formally announced that in the early hours of 14 October the battleship HMS *Royal Oak* had been sunk while at anchor in Scapa Flow. The obsolescent battleship had been struck by four torpedoes launched from a German U-Boat which had somehow managed to penetrate the defences of the fleet anchorage. Amongst the 833 dead from the 909 strong crew was Acting Leading Stoker Joseph White (30) of 61 Fifth Street, Newtongrange. Joseph had been a keen supporter of the boy scout movement, had been a piper in the Arniston Pipe Band and, before joining the Navy (in which he had served for

Bullet hole in pillow (EEN)

HMS Royal Oak (PD)

Leading Stoker White (EEN)

ten years), had worked at Arniston Colliery. Joseph left behind a widow, Mitchell Sneddon Gilmour Hunter White.

   After all the criticisms and recriminations, the authorities were eager to reassure the population that the ARP system in Edinburgh was able to do its job effectively. The campaign of reassurance was aided and abetted by the press, and the Regional Commissioner for Scotland, Mr Tom Johnston, undertook a well-publicised tour of a number of key ARP sites. On 19 October, accompanied by his deputy the Earl of Airlie, Lord Provost Henry Steele and the Moderator of the General Assembly of the Church of Scotland (Right Reverend Professor Archibald Main), Mr Johnston visited the first-aid depot at the Royal High Preparatory School. The visit seems to have focused on the possibility of mass casualties from gas attacks. This was a common fear at this stage of the war after the widespread use of poison gas on the western front during the First World War. Also, the emergency services and the ARP seem to have undergone a widespread training and exercise regime at this time.

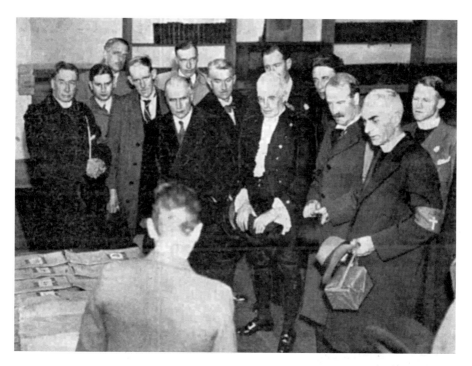

Above: Regional
Commissioner tours first
aid depot (EEN)

Right: AFS demonstrate
life saving techniques
at Albion Road School,
1939 (EEN)

At 11.30 am on 20 October the sirens wailed again. Some Edinburgh residents, despite the experience of previous days, ignored the sirens and went about their business normally, but others did take notice and packed the public shelter system to capacity. In the shelter at West Princes Street Gardens there was not enough room for everyone. Postmen were reported as having carried on with their deliveries during the alert.

Again there was confusion, with the all-clear sounding prematurely on two occasions causing some people to take shelter no less than three times. The first warning sounded minutes after aircraft had been heard overhead and a salvo of anti-aircraft fire had been heard over the city. The authorities confirmed that German aircraft were over the city heading north. Large numbers of people gathered in the streets to watch the spectacle although the only positive sighting of low flying aircraft was of three British fighters heading east. In a number of public gardens groups of soldiers and sailors remained in the open to watch any raid that might develop. Half an hour after the all-clear had sounded, the air raid siren went off again and people took cover once more; flights of RAF fighters were seen heading south at high speed and anti-aircraft guns again were heard. At this point an electrical fault resulted in one siren sounding the all-clear prematurely and people left the shelters even though the warning was in fact still in effect. This resulted in a third alert having to be sounded, much to people's bemusement and frustration.

Details of the causes of the warnings were scarce but the Air Ministry and Ministry of Home Security announced later in the day that the sirens had been precautionary as unidentified aircraft had been spotted flying high above the Forth and RAF fighters had been scrambled. No bombs were reported and it would appear that these German aircraft were again flying reconnaissance missions to identify possible targets for future raids.

Again the greatest danger to those who had remained in the open was from shrapnel from anti-aircraft shells, but there were no reported injuries or serious damage. At the Sheriff's Court the ARP system seems to have worked well with

Motorists watching air raid, 20 October 1939 (EEN)

People leave shelter at West Princes Street Gardens after false all-clear, 20 October 1939 (The Scotsman)

People leave shelter after the real all-clear sounds, 20 October 1939 (EEN)

those present filing down to the shelter in an orderly manner. Some people still seem to have been struggling to grasp the realities of the situation however, with 'one busy lawyer' wanting to know why the authorities had not fitted telephones in the shelters and many expressing 'annoyance that their "timetable" had been upset' as lunchtime approached. The women who worked in the canteen restaurant were reported to have been more concerned with the soup, tea and coffee which was going to waste as they waited for the all-clear and 'the restaurant did brisk business' when the all-clear did sound as hungry lawmakers descended upon it.[24]

A couple of hours after the all-clear, the first six funerals of those who had been killed aboard HMS *Mohawk* in the attack of 16 October took place. The canteen at Rosyth dockyard had been converted into a mortuary and in the time the bodies were stored there the floor had been covered with floral tributes. The coffins of the victims were of plain oak with brass fittings and each had a simple brass plaque which noted the name, rank and age of the deceased. The funeral ceremony was attended by representatives from every vessel which was in dock at the time and eight men from HMS *Mohawk* acted as pallbearers for their erstwhile comrades as they carried the Union Jack-draped coffins to the transports which were to take them to the cemetery. The crowd which formed to observe this sad journey included parties from the navy and army alongside the dockyard police and labourers. They were joined by a large crowd of the general public, and Able Seaman Mason's parents, brother and sister and a friend, all of whom had travelled from Birmingham, were also present. As the cortège moved away from the docks each truck was escorted by two sailors carrying wreaths on either side of the transports. The procession was headed by an RN bugler along with a firing party of twelve Royal Marines in dress uniform.

The three senior service chiefs in Scotland attended the funeral along with a large number of naval officers while an RAF aircraft flying overhead created a reminder of the circumstances in which the men had lost their lives. Four of the men, all Church of England, were buried in a communal grave while Able Seaman Jones and Chief Petty Officer Dent were buried separately as they were Catholic and Methodist respectively. A large number of wreaths were placed at the gravesides including one from Lady Sybil Gray which bore the message, 'With the sorrow and sympathy that every woman in Scotland is feeling today.'[25]

Sailors Buried on 20 October 1939

Rank	Name	Age
Chief Petty Officer	Frederick Alfred Dent	38
Able Seaman	Charles Victor Whatley	34
Able Seaman	George William Hatcher	20
Able Seaman	Lewin John Jones	37
Ordinary Seaman	Bernard Roebuck	18
Ordinary Seaman	Charles Thomas Mason	19

A few hours after the funeral of the naval personnel, another military funeral took place, that of two of the German airmen who had been killed during the raid on the Forth, Unteroffizier Kurt Seydel (19) from Leverkusen and Gefreiter August Schleicher (17) from Abtsroda, Hessen. Their bodies, which had been recovered from the sea, were laid in St. Phillip's Church, Portobello, until later in the afternoon when they were taken on an RAF trailer to their funeral service at Portobello cemetery. The coffins were draped in the Nazi flag (swastika and iron cross in black and red on a white background) and an estimated ten thousand people turned out to line the streets as the cortège passed. Present were Lord Provost Steele, the Regional Commissioner, Air Vice-Marshal Richard Saul (Officer Commanding 13 Group) and representatives from both 602 and 603 Squadrons. As the cortège wound its way towards the cemetery at Portobello the pipe band of 603 Squadron played *Over the Sea to Skye*. On the communion table in the church where the coffins were initially laid was a card which read, 'With the deepest sympathy of Scottish mothers'. Amongst the crowds gathered outside the church was a small group of wounded servicemen (from the First World War) from Edenhall. The press commented on how their presence was a reminder to people that the inter-war years 'had been little more than an extended armistice'. As the cortège proceeded on its way to the cemetery the large crowd was absolutely respectful with men removing their caps as the coffins passed. *The Scotsman* described the procession as 'a spectacle at once chivalrous and moving ... Not an untoward note or a bitter look disturbed it.'[26] At the cemetery large crowds gathered, they had begun assembling over an hour before the cortège arrived, necessitating the closing of the gates at one point. When questioned by the press many of those who had gathered said that they were aware the funeral was for German airmen but that they were paying the same respect to the young Luftwaffe airmen that they had already heard the Germans had done for British airmen who had been killed. Upon arrival at the graveside the two coffins were borne down from the trailer by NCOs of the RAF (neither German was an officer). After the coffins were lowered into the graves, the Reverend Rossie Brown, 603 (City of Edinburgh) Squadron's chaplain, who during the raid had been observed firing a Lewis gun at a German bomber, began the burial service. Following Rev. Brown's address another chaplain, the Rev. Lewis Sutherland gave the benediction. Then a volley of three shots was fired over the graves, after which the firing party fixed bayonets and presented arms as two buglers from a Highland Regiment played *The Last Post* and a piper played a lament. Large numbers of wreaths were placed on the graves, including two from two anonymous women. One of these bore the same message as that which had been on the card on the communion table, while the other read, 'To two brave airmen from the mother of an airman.'[27] The ceremony concluded with each officer present marching to the graves individually and saluting. Following the funerals, Rev. Brown wrote to the parents of the two airmen assuring them that they had been buried with full military honours.[28]

Naval ratings inspect wreaths at funeral of comrades (TS)

Naval funeral procession (TS)

Funeral of Luftwaffe airmen killed during the attack on the forth (TS)

Chaplains at funeral of German airmen (TS)

Funeral of Luftwaffe airmen (Unknown)

Right: Funeral of Luftwaffe airmen (Unknown)

Below: Funeral of Luftwaffe airmen (Unknown)

Despite the recent raids and alerts it is clear that some people and organisations remained determined to go on with life as normal. On the same day as the funerals for the British sailors and German airmen the Council of the Edinburgh Musical (Competition) Festival met and decided that they would go ahead with the twentieth annual festival which was scheduled for May 1940. The council decided that lighting restrictions would not be a problem during May but also said that there would be no mass performance of school choirs due to the danger and the impact of evacuation.

Although the schooling system had been badly dislocated by the evacuation scheme and by the closure of many schools as they were taken over by ARP services, some remained determined to stay open. Daniel Stewart's College and George Watson's Boys' College both reopened in October after a short closure but only for the tuition of senior pupils of Merchant Company Schools.

Sport remained popular and, despite football league fixtures being abandoned on 13 September for the duration of the war, friendly matches continued to attract crowds despite the attendant dangers. On 14 October a substantial crowd watched Heart of Midlothian defeat Celtic by five goals to two at Tynecastle. This was the third wartime friendly which had taken place there: Hearts had been defeated 2-4 by derby rivals Hibs on 23 September and had beaten Partick Thistle 4-2 on 7 October. The friendlies were the build-up to the beginning of the Emergency League 1939-40 (the league was divided into two divisions each of sixteen teams and divided into east and west leagues) which began on 21 October when Hibs were victorious 1-2 away to Dundee and Hearts began with a 2-3 defeat to Falkirk at Tynecastle. The Emergency League East provided the chance for Edinburgh's third team, St. Bernard's FC, to play competitive derby games against local rivals Hearts and Hibs. These fixtures attracted

Pupils of Daniel Stewart's College arriving for lessons (EEN)

substantial crowds as St. Bernard's reputation for flair and attacking football attracted the crowds eager to see goals.[29] On 4 November Hearts drew 2-2 with St. Bernard's at Tynecastle with a large crowd being entertained to some exciting football to take their minds of the crisis facing Britain.

It was clear that a system of rationing of certain items, including food, fuel, clothing, etc, would have to be imposed due to the war. Petrol was rationed from mid-September, with motorists having to present their licence to be issued with a bi-monthly ration card. Systems were put in place under the guidance of a Divisional Petroleum Officer and anyone asking for extra supplies above their ration had to apply to the petroleum officer giving convincing reasons. For those who depended on vehicles for their business, especially farmers and hauliers, regional groups were set up to facilitate adequate supplies. Motorists faced further restrictions due to the blackout when they were ordered to paint bumpers white and to fit hoods to their headlights. There were initial complaints from private vehicle hire businesses that the rationing system would severely curtail their businesses. By mid-October it had been agreed that so long as such businesses could prove they had been renting vehicles for at least six months before the start of the war, they could be granted a larger ration.

An early result of the petrol rationing in Edinburgh was a rise in the cost of motoring. In mid-October the Petroleum Board announced that the government had agreed to increase the cost of petrol to 1s 8d per gallon (an increase of 2d per gallon). Edinburgh motorists complained that this meant that for a motorist using a 10-12hp vehicle the typical cost of running was 1s per mile. One of the most noticeable effects of this was a rapid decline in the number of private vehicles on the roads of Edinburgh. The motor taxation office in the city reported that for the quarter covering the first months of the war the number of licences taken out declined by 33 per cent.

Hearts scoring against Celtic in friendly match, October 1939 (EEN)

One of the main concerns for the government was the possibility of Britain being starved out of the war by a sustained submarine campaign. Britain imported a huge quantity of food every year, especially wheat and oats, and would not be able to continue the war if it could not grow more of its own produce. To that end the government planned to ask landowners to plough up meadows and other lands for the production of cereals and vegetable produce. The farming community and other patriotic landowners embraced this. In early October Mrs Jane H. Murray (80) agreed to plough up the beautiful lawn at her home, Dundarach, in Craiglockhart Park, Edinburgh, for the planting of potatoes and other vegetables.

It was agreed that a system of food rationing be brought in by January 1940. This caused a great deal of extra administrative work for local authorities at a time when they were already stretched. In Edinburgh the writing up of food rationing cards for every resident was a monumental task. The convenor of the Food Control Committee, Councillor G.D. Brown, relied upon a small army of civilian volunteers and by the end of October the task had been completed. Councillor Brown thanked the volunteers profusely, as did Mr George White, who had been largely responsible for the initial organisation of the volunteers, while the Rev. D.W.P. Strang praised the work of the many volunteers from church organisations who had undertaken a large share of the work in various church halls. At the end of the meeting, to thank the volunteers a collection was taken with the proceeds going to the Red Cross.

The Red Cross was an extremely popular organisation during the first months of the war, with a variety of Edinburgh groups mounting charitable drives to raise funds. A number of depots were set up throughout the Edinburgh area and these supplied a variety of items to members of the armed forces directly and to the government.

Lawns at Dundarach being ploughed up (EEN)

These included the folding, rolling and packing of bandages and other medical supplies, and the local authorities made a series of visits to the depots to inspect the ongoing work to bolster and maintain morale amongst the volunteers and to publicise the efforts of the organisation.

In mid-October a concert show was held at the Theatre Royal in Edinburgh to raise funds for the Edinburgh branch of the Red Cross with the principal artiste being Sir Harry Lauder. The show proved very popular and a substantial sum was raised for the charity. The civic leaders of Edinburgh were, once again, eager to demonstrate their enthusiasm and the Lord Provost, Henry Steele, played an active role.

On 17 October the Red Cross was able to announce that almost £18,000 had already been raised by the people of Edinburgh even though the society's wartime fundraising efforts had not been in place for a month. The society stated that it had received donations of £250 from local brewers William Murray & Co. Ltd, £100 from a Mr L.L. Midgley of South Lauder Road, and £50 from Miss Ford of Murrayfield. Local societies and sports clubs were key contributors to the fund with the golfers of the Kingsknowe Club, for example, donating £2 2s in October. The club was also working with others to organise a fundraising exhibition match featuring the double Open winning champion Henry Cotton.[30]

Local rugby clubs also got in on the act with an exhibition match in aid of the fund between the Watsonians and a scratch team from Edinburgh Academicals and Edinburgh Wanderers at Myreside being organised for late October.

Another organisation which made a substantial early contribution to the welfare of the men and women who were in service to Britain was the YMCA movement. The YMCA had quickly swung into action upon the outbreak of war by making

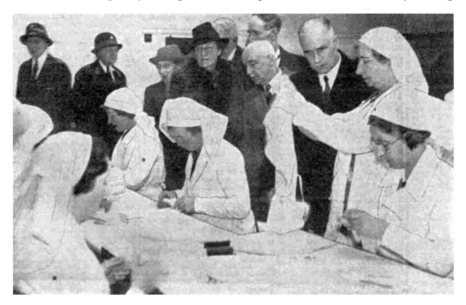

Provost Steele and Councillors visit Red Cross Depot in Edinburgh (EEN)

Sir Harry Lauder, Lord Provost Steele and Mr Jack Radcliffe during an interval at show (EEN)

its facilities available to servicemen, enabling them to find a place to rest, eat and to write home to family. By the middle of October the YMCA had recognised that the feeding system which was in place for the many servicemen passing through Edinburgh's Waverley Station was inadequate, even though the Women's Voluntary Service (WVS), led by Lady Sybil Grant, ran a canteen at the nearby New Carlton Hotel which was open seven days a week from 7 am until 10 pm. This service had not been well advertised and it was not until mid-October that a sign was erected in the station advising service personnel of the canteen. The YMCA agreed to open up its own canteen in the station which would be open 24 hours every day of the week for the use of the many servicemen and women who arrived in the city, often after hours of travel on the wartime rail network.

As the war became a reality for the people of Edinburgh some men who were not in the services became acutely aware of the glamour which attached to the men who were in arms. While the men of the Merchant Navy faced a grim and dangerous task which required great courage and skill, they did not receive much glory, and for some this rankled. There was a rash of cases of men from the service pretending to be in the RN which were dealt with by the courts, including that of Robert Bird, aged 39. Bird, a first mate in the Merchant Navy, was accused of impersonating a commander in the RN in order to fraudulently obtain goods from a naval outfitters and two Edinburgh jewellers. All of the offences were committed on Princes Street. At the outfitters Bird had purchased a trunk and a number of items of clothing telling the manager to charge the items to his naval pay account. At the first jewellery shop he had again convinced a member of staff of his RN credentials before purchasing two rings, a pair of sleeve links and a drinks flask. At the second jewellers he had convinced the proprietor that he was about to be married and purchased an engagement ring with a fraudulent cheque for £135 before also obtaining two more rings on probation which he failed to return. The court heard how the items, all of which were recovered, had been valued at £267 (over £16,000 today, adjusting for retail price inflation) and, after he admitted to four previous convictions dating back to 1922, Bird was sent to the High Court for sentencing. Five days later, at the High Court, his counsel told the court how he had been a chief officer in the Merchant Navy but was convicted of a crime in England in 1927 and had lost his certificate; this had resulted in him finding it very hard to find a job, but since returning to the merchant service he 'had a remarkably good record as a seaman'.[31] However, the court also heard that Bird had in fact been convicted on six previous occasions and the Lord Justice Clerk said that it was difficult, given the circumstances, not to impose a custodial sentence upon the accused. Mr Bird, who was an Edinburgh native, was subsequently sentenced to eighteen months in prison.

With the lack of an aerial onslaught many Edinburgh evacuees were brought back to the city by parents who would far rather have their children with them, and by mid-December it was estimated that 65 per cent of Edinburgh evacuees had returned to schooling within the city. Councillor the Rev. Dr. W.A. Guthrie, however, reported anxiously that there was a worrying trend of absenteeism within the schools system in the city with 3,000 children absent from school 'either on their own free will or by the will of their parents'. Councillor Guthrie reported that it was nothing short of a disgrace that there were many children running around the streets when they should be at school. The problem was a complex one, however, as the lack of teachers and facilities had exacerbated this problem, with many schools having been converted into rest centres, etc. Such were these shortages that corporation schools across the city were to open on a half-day system after Christmas. The city authorities remained determined to ensure that education did not suffer in the event of a lengthy war and approached the Scottish Education Department to obtain compulsory attendance powers which would enable them to enforce attendance at school for all children aged over 7. The council was overwhelmingly in favour of obtaining these powers as, according to one councillor the council should be alarmed over 'the number of parents who consider it of no great importance whether their children got any education or not. There are far too many children running about the streets and making no attempt to go to those classes being organised in houses.'[32]

A further hinderance was that every school had to have adequate shelter facilities. The authorities were attempting to progress with this work as quickly as possible, and the council could report on 18 December that 182 shelters had been constructed at schools in evacuation areas of Edinburgh with 86 partially completed and a further 18 being started immediately.

There was some dissension over the half-day system with two councillors (Murray and Cormack) arguing that representations should be made to the government to allow schools to open normally as pupils would be expected to undertake examinations as normal with only half the time available for tuition. Other councillors pointed out that many schools were being used for other purposes. One possible solution could be the cutting of what were seen as unnecessary things from the curriculum. Councillor Lamb said that he shared the concerns of his colleagues, and said that he had been informed that a board of assessors would be convened to take into account particular circumstances of individual children with regard to their examinations. Dr Guthrie replied that he feared that a long war would result in the educational system in the city being badly upset but that it was impossible to return to peacetime standards during the war and that the half-day system was the best that could be achieved during the crisis.

CHAPTER 2

1940

On 2 January Edinburgh Sheriff Court heard a case of theft. The accused, Patrick Kelly (49), was a married man who had nineteen previous convictions dating back to 1909. On 16 December he and an associate had been on a tramcar in Princes Street when the passenger in front of them, an elderly bookkeeper, got up. They also got up, and jostled him. A young woman on the tram saw Kelly put his hand in the bookkeeper's pocket and he realised his purse (containing £1) had gone. The tram conductor gave chase into South St. David Street and spotted Kelly throw away the purse. Despite pausing to pick up the purse the conductor still managed to capture Kelly and turned him over to the police. Kelly pleaded guilty to the charge and his solicitor (from Glasgow) pleaded for mercy saying that his client had a fine record in the last war serving with the Seaforth Highlanders, being wounded on three occasions and also being decorated three times. He also testified that Mr Kelly had tried to re-join his old regiment but had been turned down and had instead volunteered for minesweeping duties which he was expected to take up shortly. The Fiscal, however, stated that Kelly had a 'very bad criminal record of offences of this nature'. Sheriff Robertson agreed but said that, in view of Kelly being about to join the minesweeping service, he would modify the sentence and sentenced Kelly to three months imprisonment.

In the New Year many Edinburgh emporiums offered sales. Large adverts were placed in the local newspapers, many shops emphasising the importance of their wares in wartime conditions. For example, R.W. Forsyth, tailors, on Princes Street offered 10 per cent discount on civilian suits, overcoats and military officers' uniforms.

R.W. Forsyth's Annual Sale advert (TS)

Accidents caused by the blackout remained a serious problem and some areas became renowned as black-spots. Amongst these was the railway crossing on Commercial Street in Leith. This crossing became such a problem that it was proposed to allow it to be lit when it was known that a train was crossing. However, the proposal became bogged down when there was an unseemly and lengthy row over who was to be responsible for paying for the electricity. The Corporation, Dock Commission and LNER all argued that it should be the responsibility of the others and, with patriotism and safety apparently not as important as balancing the books, the argument dragged on for months.

The year had opened with two deaths on 2 January where the blackout was ruled as a causal factor. David Thomson Christie (37) of 104 Stenhouse Crescent slipped and fell while walking home on the night of 31 December and died as a result of head injuries. On the 28th Alexander Grierson (70) of 2 Haddington Place died instantly when he was struck by a tram car in Elm Row just after 8 pm. The next day Mrs Mary Herring (54) of Duddington Road West died in hospital after being knocked down by a van in Peffermill Road.

As a result, the Council of the Scottish Motor Trade Association urged the government to launch a campaign to educate pedestrians in taking care crossing roads during blackout conditions. The council argued for a 20 mph speed limit in built-up areas and placed the blame for the accidents, perhaps unfairly, on the motorist.

In the first week of February three fatalities due to accidents in the blackout were reported. The first had actually occurred on 1 December 1939 but Charles Brown Davidson Kelt (71), who had been knocked down by a Royal Mail van on Princes Street shortly before 6 pm, did not die until three weeks after the accident. There were two fatalities during the first two days of February. William Harkins (64) was killed when he was struck by a tramway car in London Road shortly after 6 pm on the night of 1 February and on the following night a tramcar struck and killed Alexander Walls in Wardie Road, Granton.

Just over a month later there was another tragic death suffered as a result of the blackout. Peggie Matheson McKerlich (20) was from Ben Fraoch in the Kyle of Lochalsh but was staying with friends in Northfield Road while she studied at Edinburgh Art College. On the night of 10 March, Peggie decided to take a walk in the King's Park but became disorientated in the blackout and fell off the north end of Dunsappie Rock suffering a fractured spine and breaking both of her legs. She died of her injuries three weeks later in Edinburgh Royal Infirmary.

On 27 March there was another fatal accident when retired civil servant John Alexander (68) of 16 Keir Street collided in the blackout with another pedestrian on Lauriston Place. Mr Alexander suffered a broken leg and despite being treated at Edinburgh Royal Infirmary he died on 9 April as a result of his injury.

On 10 August a car driving in the direction of London Road during a blackout was in collision with two men, killing one and injuring the other. The car did not stop and inquiries by the police failed to locate the culprit.

The accidents continued to be an almost ever-present feature of news in the local press with Peter Keelan of Craigmillar Castle Terrace dying in the

Edinburgh Royal Infirmary on 4 November after being hit by a van on Princes Street two days previously.

The problems of negotiating the blackout were not helped by some careless and, in some cases, criminal driving. In the same edition of *The Scotsman* in which the news of Mr Keelan's death appeared was a report on an Edinburgh taxi driver who had been fined £4 and suspended from driving for one year after being caught so drunk behind the wheel of his car that he could not maintain control of the vehicle. It was Henry Grant's (48) second such offence, having been fined £7 in 1935 for a similar offence.

On the morning of 21 February there was a lucky escape for a Mrs Cairns of 118 Salamander Street and her two children when an errant artillery shell badly damaged their Leith house. The battery commander at Inchkeith noticed that an RN trawler had strayed from the path which had been cleared of mines and so ordered his battery to fire a single six-inch practice shell across the trawler's bow. While this had the desired effect the shell had been fired at a flat trajectory and ricocheted off the surface. The shell, which weighed 100 lbs, carried on for a distance of 3½ miles before penetrating the tin roof of Neptune Mills in Leith and then hitting Mrs Cairns' house across the road. It penetrated the front wall of the house before smashing through the living room, then through a door and ripping out the kitchen sink before carrying on out of the rear wall and smashing a shed in the back garden. It finally came to rest against sandbags which protected the family air raid shelter. It caused devastation in the house 'smashing pieces of furniture into matchwood, throwing other pieces into indescribable heaps, and, besides dislodging heavy stones from the outside wall, tearing plaster and flooring in the interior'. The flight and impact of the shell was heard across the neighbourhood and was the cause of 'much excitement'. There was 'much speculation as to its cause' which was resolved when Scottish Command released a statement.[1]

Just how lucky the family had been was revealed when the full tale of their escape was made public in the press. The shell had torn a large hole in the front wall of the house and had caused a heavy wardrobe to fall onto a bed occupied by 3-year-old Robert Cairns. A party of workmen from the nearby mill were amongst the first on the scene and they assisted Mrs Cairns to escape from a window. Meanwhile, showing great presence of mind and courage, 11-year-old Janet Cairns had dashed to her brother's bedroom and rescued him. She passed him through another window to neighbours before escaping herself. One of the neighbours reported how she had been cooking before she heard a tremendous explosion and saw a cloud of dust and lime rising from the back of Mrs Cairns' house. She immediately went to assist and was one of those who helped Janet from the house. After being rescued Janet then had the presence of mind to run to the nearby factory where her father worked to fetch him. Upon arriving at his home Mr Robert Cairns found his home practically wrecked. He found his raincoat, which had been hanging on a peg, torn to shreds by the shell. Mrs Cairns and her son had, by this time, been taken to hospital. She had a nasty cut on her scalp while little Robert was physically unhurt but suffering from shock. The house was part of a group of three and although it was the only one damaged the residents of the other two were also in shock. They included two women who were recovering in bed from an illness and a man in his 70s who was also confined to bed.

Entrance and exit damage from shell at Salamander Street, Leith (TS)

Although thoughts were largely with the BEF in France, some in Britain had already been giving thought to how the country could be defended against enemy raids. The British army was woefully ill-prepared for this. Many of its best units had been dispatched to France which meant that most of the better equipped and most mobile army units were absent from Britain.[2] By March the defence of the Lothians area fell to one infantry battalion (in training at Glencorse), a cavalry training regiment which was still using horses (the 3rd Cavalry Training Regiment at Redford), two reserve regiments of artillery (at Edinburgh and Dreghorn), an artillery training regiment (Aberlady), a signals training regiment at Redford, and an officer training unit at Dunbar. So severe was the lack of transport that on several occasions the Royal Army Service Corps (RASC) personnel who were ordered to assist in the movement of various units had to resort to hiring vehicles from private contractors. Lack of modern artillery and ammunition was also in crippling deficit and after the invasion alert of late May it was discovered that there were fewer than 20 rounds available for each of the 24 field guns in the whole of Scotland.

We have already seen how Councillor A.H.A Murray, in his capacity as Commandant of the Edinburgh AFS, had helped to develop the city's AFS units and had fought the Scottish Office when it tried to cut the number of men in the service from 1,200 to 500. Throughout 1940 Councillor Murray continued his energetic work for the AFS. He toured areas of England which had suffered bombing and had been present in London during several raids. He used this experience and knowledge to make improvements in the Edinburgh AFS, altering some ways in which the control room functioned, obtaining fire-floats for use on the Firth of Forth, organising the collecting and distribution of thousands of sandbags throughout Edinburgh, encouraging the training of extra groups of volunteer fire parties and organising the distribution of 8,000 stirrup pumps for them. Tests and drills showed the fruits of Councillor Murray's endeavours when the Edinburgh control room earned a reputation as one of the best in the country.

Despite the war, crime continued to prove a headache for the police and on 12 January a particularly audacious robbery was committed at the sub-post office at Chapel Street. Shortly before the shop closed at 6 pm a man, who appeared to be a street hawker, entered the shop and made a purchase before moving to a writing desk and appearing to write something on an envelope. The sub-post mistress, Miss Niven, noticed a powerful smell in the shop but thought that the man might have had a cold and was sucking some sort of lozenge. Noticing nothing else out of the ordinary she went about her tasks. When turning around she noticed that the man had left the shop, or so she thought. Miss Niven then went about closing the shop but when she got to the front door the man, who had hidden himself behind a blackout curtain, stepped out and placed a handkerchief soaked in ether over Miss Niven's face. Before falling unconscious Miss Niven saw an accomplice enter the shop. Some five minutes later she regained consciousness and cried out, attracting the attention of a passing woman. She immediately phoned the police who arrived in less than ten minutes and it was established that the day's takings, amounting to approximately £130, had been taken. Despite the speed of the police response and the detailed description given by Miss Niven no-one was apprehended.

The press played an increasingly important role in maintaining morale as people became somewhat nonplussed by the lack of action which was a feature of the phoney war period (or bore war as some called it at the time). Although the people of Edinburgh had already witnessed some action both on sea and in the air the lack of ground combat perplexed many. Alongside press coverage as a means to boost morale was the frequent visits of VIPs, all of which were, of course, extensively covered in the press. At the end of February the Queen paid a weekend visit to the city during which she made a tour of civil defence, medical, military and civilian sites. This was Her Majesty's first visit to the city since war had been declared and crowds quickly assembled once word had got out. The Queen, wearing Air Force blue and accompanied by lady-in-waiting Lady Katherine Seymour, arrived at Waverley Station shortly before 7.30 am where she was met by Lord Elphinstone and other dignitaries. The party made a brief tour of the city before lunching at the City Chambers where Her Majesty was presented with a spray of white orchids. After this the party first visited the Regional Commissioner's room where the Queen was introduced to those responsible for organising and commanding the civil defence forces of the country. From here Her Majesty proceeded to St. Mary's Cathedral School where she inspected a parade of civil defence units, including a detachment of Women's Auxiliary Police assembled in the playground. The Queen was heard to remark to Chief Constable Morren that the work done on civil defence was 'simply splendid … It reflects great credit on Edinburgh.'

The party went on to tour the Coates Gardens headquarters of the Scottish Women's Voluntary Service (SWVS), and it was noted that during this visit Her Majesty wore the silver badge of this organisation. She was presented with several gifts by Lady Balfour, including a book on emergency cookery, and took the time to speak to all members of staff who were present. The next visit on the itinerary was

Queen inspects Women's Auxiliary Police (TS)

Above: *Queen inspects men of a decontamination squad (TS)*

Right: *Queen talks to Chief Constable Morren after inspecting ARP (Daily Record)*

a visit to the King George and Queen Elizabeth Victoria League Club in Princes Street. A large crowd had by this time assembled along the route and outside the club, and when the royal car pulled up at around 1 pm the crowd surged forward to get a glimpse of the Queen and there was loud cheering. Shortly after entering the club, the Queen witnessed an RAF tender passing by outside carrying the wings of a recently shot-down German aircraft. When she was escorted into the lounge by Admiral Backhouse she encountered seven servicemen (from Australia and Canada) who had obviously not been told to expect such a visitor. The men immediately sprang out of their chairs and leapt to attention before they were introduced. The Queen took the time to talk with all of them and shared a joke with Canadian Pipe Major Essen (from Vancouver) with both laughing heartily. The modest Canadian afterwards refused to reveal the joke to the press saying, 'Not while I'm in Scotland … That's a secret!'[3] After Her Majesty had shaken hands with the sixth man in line, Pipe Major A. MacDonald from Toronto, she was asked to pose for a picture with the servicemen and gracefully agreed. Following the photo Admiral Backhouse was about to introduce her to the final man in the line-up but was interrupted by Her Majesty who said that she had not yet spoken to the sixth man and insisted on doing so before she was introduced to the final man, Able Seaman F.J. Ryan. This man was an Australian from Sydney. Amongst the others who were introduced to the Queen, who was wearing a diamond brooch in the shape of a maple leaf for the visit, was another Australian, Leading Aircraftman Thornton. The young airman commented to the Queen that he found Scotland very cold after his homeland but had enjoyed the trip over and was making the most of his leave in Edinburgh.

After this visit the party proceeded to tour the 41 Charlotte Square depot of the Midlothian branch of the SWVS and Voluntary Aid Detachment (VAD), where Her Majesty inspected the knitted goods that were donated for personnel serving in the Royal Navy (especially those aboard minesweepers). She asked if many of the garments were found unsuitable but was told that the women of Scotland were skilled knitters and there had been few problems. During this visit the Queen was accompanied by Lady Elphinstone who was present as the county organiser of the SWVS.

Queen meets Australian and Canadian Servicemen, 1940 (TS)

This visit was followed, in what seems to have been a hectic schedule, by one to the Astley Ainslie Institution where Her Majesty spoke to as many of the 200 patients there as possible. She commented especially on the layout of the facility, the scenery visible from the wards and on the numbers of patients who were outside. In explanation of the latter query Her Majesty was told by the superintendent of nurses, Miss Lockie, that 'open-air treatment' was a feature of the institution. One of the men the Queen spoke to during this visit was Flying Officer D.A. Willis who was recovering from a ground accident. Willis had been the co-pilot to Wing Commander William Staton during the first RAF Bomber Command raid on Berlin and the Queen was able to converse with him over the fact that her husband had presented his erstwhile pilot with the DSO just days before.[4] Before leaving the institute Her Majesty was introduced to the principal assistant secretary, Mr G.H. Henderson, who revealed that he had been taken prisoner during the First World War alongside the Queen's brother the Honourable Michael Bowes-Lyon. Her Majesty replied that she was very glad to have met Mr Henderson and that she would tell her brother of the meeting.

Queen talking to injured soldier at Ainslie Institute (TS)

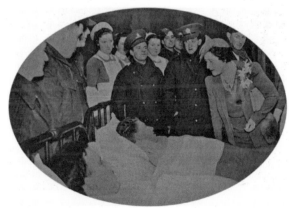

Queen talking to wounded servicemen (Illustrated London News)

The lengthy visit to the institution was followed by a visit to the Central Work Depot of the Edinburgh branch of the Red Cross at 5 George Square. Again the royal visitor was met by a crowd of several hundred outside the depot and once inside was introduced to many of the 150 volunteers who were present.

There were many stops during the tour of Edinburgh with the Queen inspecting several groups of civil defence and ARP workers, taking time to talk to members of the public and servicemen.

On Sunday morning the Queen attended church at St. Peter's Episcopal Church at Musselburgh alongside several members of the Elphinstone family. The occasion was that of the confirmation service of the Queen's own niece the Honourable Margaret Eplhinstone. During the afternoon Her Majesty, joined now by the King, visited an ARP post at Musselburgh where she was introduced to several of the local ARP commanders. Outside, an honour guard of members of the Auxiliary Fire Service had been drawn up and was inspected by the royal guests. After this the King and Queen were introduced to former prisoners of the *Altmark* and discussed their maltreatment aboard that vessel before the royal party departed for Pinkie House.

Pinkie House, the home of Lady Mary Hope, had been converted into a mixed clearing station, refuge and hospital for evacuees who might be rendered homeless due to enemy bombing. The house was capable of holding eighty inmates and had separate men's, women's and children's wards along with a volunteer staff and medical facilities to cope with minor injuries. The Queen was introduced to Lady

Queen visits Red Cross Depot (TS)

Above: Queen
talks to AFS
at Palmerston
Square (ILN)

Right: Queen
leaving church at
Musselburgh (TS)

Queen leaving Drill Hall at Musselburgh (TS)

King and Queen talking to Altmark survivors (ILN)

Hope, Miss L. Bruce and Mrs Greenlees and expressed an interest in viewing both Prince Charlie's bedroom and the picture gallery before she concluded her visit.

The royal party then travelled to Newbattle where a new YMCA canteen hut was inspected and Her Majesty was introduced to several army officers. Moving on to Dalkeith she visited the former Conservative Rooms which had been converted into a YMCA centre. There were 200 men present in the canteen or in the 'quiet' room writing letters to family. Her Majesty was informed that approximately 1,000 letters per week were being sent from the building. The vast majority of the men were young soldiers from England but there were some Scots present. Upon noticing an older soldier with the Mons Star the Queen immediately went over to speak with him.

Health care for the civilian population remained a concern and there were efforts to raise funds for such services throughout the year. A familiar property to many residents of Edinburgh, Dalmeny House (the home of the Earl of Rosebery) opened parts of its beautiful gardens to the public in March to raise funds for the Scottish branch of the Queen's Institute of District Nursing. Of particularly note was the magnificent display of snowdrops which blanketed the banks of Mons Hill.

March also welcomed news that the butter ration was to be doubled. For the grocery trade in the city this was welcome news as they had been calling for an adjustment to the ration for some time. They argued that this new arrangement would not affect supplies as they felt that many in the working-class areas of the city would not take up the full ration as they had already made the adjustment to margarine and found this quite suitable for most tasks.

Queen visits YMCA Hut at Newbattle (TS)

Snowdrops at Dalmenny House (TS)

As we have already seen the North British Rubber Company made a significant contribution to the war effort and, because of both the loss of male workers to the forces and the increased demand for its products, it became necessary to take on extra workers. The work was often unpleasant and hazardous, with the pungent stench of rubber, sulphur and soapstone used in the manufacturing processes. The machinery also presented a danger to inexperienced or inattentive workers. Many of the new workers at the mill were women who came from Edinburgh and the surrounding areas. The war was good news financially for the company which had been struggling for several years and had failed to pay an ordinary dividend for the previous eleven years. Indeed, such was the upturn that the company was not only able to pay a share dividend of 5 per cent in April 1940 but it could also pay off four years' arrears of second preference dividend.

With the risks of air raid a continuing threat, R.W. Forsyth Ltd of Princes Street and a Mr J.H. Stroud came up with an idea to improve the aircraft recognition skills of the general public. Mr Stroud, who had previously worked for Imperial Airways, constructed several dioramas which were put on display in the window of Forsyth Ltd. One of these was a re-creation of the raid on the Firth of the previous year and featured a model of the Forth Bridge and naval vessels along with models of aircraft from the two nations suspended above. A second diorama was of the attack on Kiel and featured a paper model of the battleship *Gneisenau* and U-Boats in the harbour with attacking RAF bombers above and a backdrop which showed barrage balloons against a starlit sky.

The blackout continued to be a cause for concern. On 16 March a 75-year-old man, John Johnston of 65 Comely Bank Avenue, was killed when he was struck by a bus on St. Andrew Street shortly before 11 pm. Such accidents were becoming almost commonplace and despite warnings from the city authorities it was clear that some drivers were acting in a dangerous manner during the blackout while some pedestrians were not taking adequate precautions in the dark conditions.

The rationing of some foodstuffs which had come into effect in January had an immediate impact on the civilians of Edinburgh and by April the Ministry of Food was warning of an impending shortage of eggs which was expected to hit in autumn and winter. Although eggs were currently available the prices had increased to 2s 3d per dozen. As supplies from Denmark had been cut off it was thought that it might become necessary to ration eggs when the local supplies began to dry up. There were concerns being expressed by Edinburgh housewives that the price of eggs might soar in the event of a shortage, while it had become common for residents to leave the city at weekends for country areas to secure supplies. However, a leading Edinburgh egg retailer was keen to reassure the public that there was little likelihood of a price rise and that supplies were available from northern Scotland and from Ireland.

The closure of the Danish market had also led to a shortfall in the supply of bacon and butter, but the ministry was keen to reassure the public that there were no plans in place for the rationing of lard, cooking fats or cheese.

During April the press attempted, despite heavy censorship, to keep the public apprised of the progress of the Norwegian campaign. Much of the reporting, however, was later proven to be overly optimistic. Typical of this was a report in *The Scotsman* on 30 April when the newspaper's military correspondent, Major General Sir Charles Gwynn, reported on how 'the danger to the allied forces in the Trondhjem [sic] region had passed'. General Gwynn reported how enemy attacks in the Gudbrands valley had been met with stubborn resistance. He perhaps betrayed his own doubts when talking about the arrival of British reinforcements saying that these would hopefully include anti-tank guns and artillery, but he assured the public that it should now 'be possible to consolidate a formidable defensive position'.[5] Major General Gwynn also believed that the enemy's attempt to outflank the British positions would fail as the Norwegians would be able to hold the mountain passes against them. The General sought to scotch the rumour that British forces in Norway were poorly equipped saying that this was largely down to the exaggerated reports of enemy successes and to the problems of unloading equipment at ports which were under aerial attack.

Many Edinburgh residents, however, seem to have been doubtful of such attempts at reassurance and distrusted both the press reporting and, particularly, the War Office and Ministry of Information. It is easy to see why when one looks at some of the communiqués which were being issued to the press and the public. For example, alongside the above report in *The Scotsman* was a short communiqué issued by the

War Office which simply stated that there had been no change in the Gudbrands valley despite heavy attacks, that heavy enemy air attacks had been carried out on two towns, that there had been enemy patrols in the Namsos area and that there was nothing to report from Narvik.

We have already seen how the RN had set up HMS *Claverhouse* at the Granton Hotel. The motor launches used by the local coastal forces were based here and from April the base also held Merchant Navy defence courses. The vital east coast convoys which sailed between the Forth and the Thames (coded FN or FS, depending on whether they were north or southbound) were an important national lifeline and the convoys were constantly targeted by aerial attack, mines, submarines and, especially after the fall of Denmark and Norway, E-boats. With the fall of France the convoys passing through the English Channel became even more dangerous and an alternative route around the north of Scotland was introduced for some convoys (these sailed between the Forth and the Clyde and were coded EN or WN depending on whether they were east or westbound).

HMS *Claverhouse* was also the base of several air sea rescue launches – fast motor boats used to recover airmen who had come down in the sea. The boats on the Firth were exceptionally busy during the year putting out to rescue downed airmen of all nationalities as well as seamen who had got into difficulties.

To help combat the threat from E-boats and submarines motor torpedo boats (MTBs) and motor gun boats were based here and were also used to launch their own raids on German shipping. These fast, agile and heavily armed boats attracted great interest as they were seen as being involved in exciting work. In March *The Scotsman* highlighted the work of these vessels under the headline 'Mosquito Patrol'. The article claimed that 'a warm welcome' awaited the enemy from these boats which were 'armed with torpedoes, depth charges and anti-aircraft multiple machine guns'.[6]

MTB off East Coast of Scotland (TS)

Anti-Aircraft guns on
MTB (TS)

The end of the phoney war came with the Blitzkrieg which smashed through France and the Low Countries. On 10 May the Germans launched their initial attacks.

With public and press campaigns for greater restrictions to be placed on those of German or Austrian descent becoming intensified, and exaggerated reports of a fifth column, the government felt pressured to act. On Sunday, 12 May, police across the eastern half of Britain were ordered to arrest all such male enemy aliens between 16 and 60 and transport them to local police stations from where they would be transferred to internment camps. In Edinburgh plain clothes police officers drove to the residences of male enemy aliens and placed them in custody before they were taken to the central police station. The arrests began at 8 am and by noon almost 100 men had been taken to the station. Smaller numbers were also arrested in Midlothian and East Lothian (especially around the Whittinghame area which was hosting many refugees).

Further to these draconian measures, male enemy aliens who lived outside the listed counties were forbidden to enter the east of the country under any circumstances. All other male aliens (whatever their nationality) between 16 and 60 living in these areas were required to report to a police station on a daily basis, to not make use of any motor vehicle or bicycle other than public transport, and were forbidden to be outside between 8 pm and 6 am. This curfew had a direct impact on the hundreds of foreign students who were studying at Edinburgh University and also affected the foreign seamen who lived or docked in the port.

Tales of parachutists and fifth columnists brought an immediate reaction in Edinburgh (and other towns and cities) with the police and army manning strategic points, parties of armed soldiers patrolling, and barbed wire blockades in some parts of the city. The local authorities in Edinburgh became somewhat paranoid, perhaps encouraged by General Ironside's erroneous and alarmist comments that a number of plots had already been foiled (including the preparation of landing fields for German paratroopers). The corporation announced that anglers were no longer to be allowed to fish in the reservoirs and lochs in case fifth columnists disguised themselves as anglers to poison the city's water supply.

Censorship of the press meant that reports of German gains were quickly hushed up and the Edinburgh public mostly read of German losses and allied victories. On 13 May *The Scotsman* featured a lengthy article on the progress of the battle under the headlines 'BATTLE SPREADS ALONG WESTERN FRONT', 'Germans Launch Assaults on Advance Posts of Maginot Line', and 'DRIVE IN BELGIUM AND HOLLAND SLOWED UP', along with a sub-headline telling of '130 Enemy Planes Reported Shot Down'.[7] The article described a 'Terrific' Luftwaffe bombing campaign on Belgium and admitted that the Belgians had lost ground. It relayed tales of Dutch troops and police fighting and killing German spies and parachutists in The Hague. Some of the headlines must have reminded some readers of the previous war and those reporting a British communiqué stating that British 'Cavalry Gain Advantage' seem to have come from that era and would not have been terribly reassuring. For those who looked beyond the encouraging headlines, the reports did give some clue as to the unfolding disaster. The above article, for example, included the admission that German troops had 'at various points crossed the Rivers Maas and Yssel' and that frontier troops had been forced to withdraw. The report also included the ominous news that the northern Dutch provinces 'which had no defences, have been entered by the Germans'. Reporting on the underhandedness of the Germans, the people of Edinburgh were told how the Germans were using civilians as human shields.

They were also being given mixed news on the progress of the battle in France. Headlines in *The Scotsman* of 24 May informed readers that the allies were making preparations for a counter-attack and that the RAF had made successful attacks on a number of vital objectives including a power station at Leipzig, ammunitions trains and mechanised columns of the German army. Readers were told how RAF Blenheims had successfully attacked armoured columns by daylight in 'an almost continuous assault with bombs and machine guns' while night-flying Hampdens, Wellingtons and Whitley bombers hammered lines of communication. In fact the attacks had been largely ineffectual and the Blenheim (and Fairey Battle) forces had suffered heavy losses for little effect.

However, alongside these headlines were those which hinted at disaster in France and the Low Countries. On the same page as the above, readers were told that German forces had reached Amiens, were poised to enter Boulogne, and had made advances of 200 miles. The situation was described as being 'Grave But Not Desperate' in one headline and readers were informed of the highly effective role being played by German bomber aircraft and heavy tanks in the campaign. In an apparent admission that the British and her allies had been both outfought and outmanoeuvred the report went on to inform readers that 'the German faith in lightning movement ... has been justified', although this was qualified as being 'momentarily'. Other German innovations to be revealed to a widely believing public were motorcycle 'suicide brigades' who, despite almost total losses, raided everywhere behind the lines using machine guns and incendiary bombs to 'spread havoc wherever they go', dressed in leather helmets and overalls which covered up their uniforms.[8] There was also criticism of civilians who had been terrified by German propaganda and, despite urging from their government, were choking roads and making the situation worse.

We have already seen how the authorities attempted to enforce the blackout regulations, so it must have come as something of a blow to them when they were informed by the Chief Constable that he had been told by an RAF pilot that Princes Street was lit up like Wembley Stadium when seen from above at night. The enforcing of blackout regulations combined with the limited nature of enemy raiding led to many people viewing the ARP wardens with derision. By April Edinburgh had more than 7,000 enrolled and trained wardens (20 per cent of whom were women) and there were complaints that they were being ridiculed by members of the public. Their job was a tough one with wardens being expected to expose themselves to the dangers of air raids and to be out on duty during the winter months. This was particularly onerous during the winter of 1940/41 as it was common for temperatures to dip below minus ten degrees.

There were concerns over the levels of anti-war sentiment, and the investigators of the Ministry of Information were reporting that the regular meetings of the Peace Pledge Union and the Women's Peace Movement were attracting large crowds. This began to change when Norway fell and there was a marked sense of depression in Edinburgh caused by the shock of British defeats. With the danger of invasion becoming very real, most people in Edinburgh saw little choice but commitment to the war effort. The Church of Scotland was giving a lead, and a motion to hold a peace conference at the Church of Scotland Assembly on 25 May was heavily defeated.

Early support for the Communist Party began to wane at this point although there was still enough to worry the Ministry of Information and the local authorities. On 29 April a large rally was held in Edinburgh where the key speakers were Willie Gallacher MP and Harry Pollitt, general secretary of the British Communist Party. Worried Ministry observers reported back that the crowd was enthusiastic and numbered approximately 2,400. But by the end of May they were able to report that support for the Communist Party was waning and confined to hardliners.

The decision to make arrests of prominent British fascists found widespread support. Amongst those arrested and interned alongside Oswald Mosley and eight of his lieutenants in the British Union of Fascists was Captain Archibald Henry Maule Ramsay MP (Peebles and South Midlothian). Ramsay was a leading member of the Right Club and was described as its president. He was arrested and interned after his contact with American-born suspected spy Tyler Kent became known to the authorities. It was already common knowledge that Ramsay was anti-Semitic: he had a motion on the order paper of the Houses of Commons at the time which decried the political and press bias 'against any nationalist cause, Christian or Mohammedan, and favours internationalists and Jews'.[9] A well-known figure in Edinburgh, there was concern when Ramsay was described in the House of Lords as being Hitler's candidate for Gauleiter of Scotland in the event of a successful invasion.

Captain A.H. Maule Ramsay, MP (TS)

Anti-alien sentiment was running high in Edinburgh and the substantial Italian population was the particular target of ire. From the end of May there were a number of attacks on Italian-owned premises. On 10 June, after much speculation, Italy declared war on Britain. The government reacted by announcing the rounding up of Italians, and public feeling, already febrile, broke into widespread demonstrations and criminal behaviour. While the police rounded up Italian subjects, many in Edinburgh took to the streets in 'an orgy of window-breaking and looting in different parts of the city'.[10] Crowds attacked Italian-owned (or what they assumed were Italian-owned) fish and chip shops and ice-cream parlours and it was necessary to bring in police reinforcements to contain the situation. Eighteen arrests were made, and at least six civilians suffering head injuries from thrown stones required hospital treatment (three of them women). In Leith Street and Union Place a crowd of over 1,000 assembled and youths began throwing stones and smashing the windows of the many Italian-owned businesses in the area. The police had to resort to baton charges and scuffles broke out with policemen having helmets knocked off and the crowd singing patriotic songs as those who had been arrested were put in the back of vans.

Elsewhere in the city there were attacks in Abbeyhill, Dalry, Portobello, the South Side and Stockbridge while windows were also smashed at a café in Princes Street and at a shop just yards away from the police headquarters in High Street. The police had to occupy an Italian premises in Picardy Place after it had been looted and the fire brigade had to extinguish a small fire. In the early hours another arson attack took place at an ice-cream shop at 9a Antigua Street.

While all of this was going on the police were also engaged in the rounding up of some of the estimated 380 Italians who lived in Edinburgh. Many were well-established families and many had brought up children in the city and were fully naturalised. It was the 100 or so Italians who were relatively recent residents who were initially rounded up on this night and taken to the police station for transfer to internment camps.[11] The roundups continued the next morning and by mid-morning some 200 had been arrested.

As Edinburgh awoke it became clear that the damage to Italian-owned property from the previous night had been extensive. At many premises there was not a pane of glass left while cigarette machines had been looted and wrecked along with other expensive catering equipment. The rioting had also taken place in Leith where many shops were looted and some completely stripped of all their stock. Many of the occupants of the shops were in fact naturalised British subjects. The local press reported how one well-known restauranteur whose premises was badly damaged had in fact fought in a Scottish regiment throughout the First World War while another had two sons who were currently serving in the Black Watch.

The eighteen men who had been arrested on the previous night appeared before Edinburgh Burgh Court the next morning. The first was a serving soldier, Frank Slaven, who admitted kicking and breaking a glass window in a shop owned by Nicola Valentino at 158 High Street. An officer appeared to defend Slaven saying that he had a good record as a soldier and that he believed that he had acted from an overly-exuberant show of national and patriotic zeal; Slaven was fined £1. The next nine cases were on charges of looting with eight men pleading guilty and being remanded in custody and one pleading not guilty. The next two cases involved men who, at the height of the disturbances, had admitted to assaulting police officers. The two, James Paton and William McLaren (both of 3 North St. James's Street), were fined £2 with the option of twenty days' imprisonment if they failed to pay. George McNicoll (18) of 39 Prestonfield Road admitted throwing a stone through a café window in Leith Street and was fined £1 or ten days' imprisonment. A similar sentence was passed on Andrew Doyle (21) of 31 Milton Street after he admitted to breaking a window in Union Place. Five juveniles also appeared in private after being accused of stealing sweets from ransacked shops and were informed that they would have to appear before the Juvenile Court.

The Regional Commissioner for Civil Defence for Scotland strongly criticised the rioting which had taken place in Edinburgh saying that rioting and mob violence was contrary to everything that Britain was struggling for. He added that the police could be depended upon to do whatever was necessary and local ratepayers would be liable for damage claims.

One of the results of the arrests was the discovery of an illegally held automatic pistol and almost 100 rounds of ammunition. It was in a safe in the home of restaurateur Primo Bosi at 6 Union Place. Mr Bosi was brought before the Burgh Court on the same day as those who had been tried for rioting and was remanded in custody. Appearing before the Sheriff Court just over a week later Bosi pleaded guilty to the offence but in mitigation said that he had bought the pistol for his own protection over two years ago from an old schoolfriend (a Scotsman) who was now in the forces. The police traced the man who verified Bosi's account. Mr Bosi was typical of the Italians who were caught up in the round-up in that he was in fact British-born (his parents had been resident in Britain since the beginning of the century). He had recently registered himself for national service and was expecting to be called up shortly.

Mr Bosi's defence said that he had no intention of ever using the weapon and there was no sinister motive behind his ownership of the weapon; the only sinister thing here was in fact his foreign name. Sheriff Jameson said that he understood that there were a great many Italians in the country who were above suspicion and that he had Italian friends but while he understood that many people owned some weapon as a relic of the last war he did query the ownership of such a large quantity of ammunition. Mr Bosi's defence said there was no reason for it and it was a stupid action. The depute-fiscal made the point that Bosi was 'a member of the Italian Fascisti in Edinburgh' but admitted that he had not yet been interned and that his possession of the pistol had no known connection with his alleged political affiliations. The depute-fiscal could only suggest that Bosi, who owned a substantial business and often had large sums of money on the premises, had bought the pistol as a means of protection. At this Sheriff Jameson expressed sympathy for the 'poor Italians' saying that they needed some form of protection 'after these cowardly assaults of last week'. He said he would not 'make it any harder for him because he has a foreign name' but, curiously, fined him £1 despite saying the usual fine was 10 shillings.[12]

By the end of May the BEF was in desperate straits and planning and organisation was beginning to break down. Along with many others the 1st Royal Scots found themselves isolated and expected to hold a badly prepared line of defence against overwhelming opposition including armoured units of the Wehrmacht. The line of defence was situated along several canals and units were instructed to hold at all costs to aid the withdrawal from Dunkirk. By the early hours of 27 May the battalion was occupying positions near Le Paradis and was informed that it could expect to face an attack on its flanks that morning. By 8 am the battalion was engaged and casualties were mounting, especially in A and C companies. It also lost its commanding officer which resulted in Major Watson MC taking over until 10 am when his headquarters was hit and he too was killed. Shortly after this A and C companies were overrun despite the former destroying several enemy tanks with hand grenades.

During this fighting the C Company commander Captain Edward Ian Cameron Elliott was killed. Captain Elliott was a 21-year-old native of Edinburgh (his parents, William and Katherine, lived at 20 Greenhill Gardens), had attended Edinburgh Academy and Sandhurst and had been with his regiment from when they were first posted to France. Like many killed during the chaotic fighting around the fall of France and evacuation from Dunkirk, Captain Elliott has no known grave and is commemorated on the Dunkirk Memorial.

Another Edinburgh officer to be killed during this desperate action was 2nd Lieutenant Ronald Somerville Turcan of A Company (indeed the young officer was commanding the company due to earlier casualties). His parents, Charles and Mary, received the news that their 23-year-old son was missing after Dunkirk but it was not until November that they received the news that he had in fact been killed. He is buried at the Mont-Bernanchon churchyard.[13]

B Company retreated and merged with the remnants of D Company under the command of an officer from the Norfolk Regiment. This composite unit resisted further enemy attacks until it was overwhelmed and captured at approximately 4 pm. The battalion HQ and HQ Company maintained their positions for a couple of days as they had been told there would be a counter-attack, but when this did not develop they too retreated only to be taken prisoner at Merville on 30 May.

Another of the casualties of the fighting on 27 May was Lance Corporal John Patrick Brannon McCabe of Edinburgh. McCabe was a married man aged 28 and was subsequently buried at Mont-Bernanchon churchyard.

One of those who had initially been posted missing in action during the fall of France was Second Lieutenant Edward Thomas Gollogly, Highland Light Infantry

(City of Glasgow Regiment). Edward was a resident of Edinburgh, where his parents, Edward and Agnes, still resided and had attended the Royal High School where he had excelled in sports being in the rugby team for many years. He was captain during 1939/40 but his army duties meant that he did not actively captain a match. He played three-quarter for the Edinburgh inter-city team and took part in the Red Cross matches against Glasgow in 1939. He was also a member of the Edinburgh Northern Harriers and excelled at field events. After being initially posted missing his parents had been informed that he had in fact been taken prisoner. But, tragically, they later received word that their 26-year-old son had died of peritonitis while in captivity in Germany on 24 July. He was buried in the Durnbach War Cemetery, Bavaria.

As in other communities across Britain, those Edinburgh men who were, for one reason or another, ineligible for military service had been agitating for the chance to play a role in the war effort. On the night of 14 May the government gave in to this pressure and Anthony Eden, in a BBC broadcast, asked for men aged between 17 and 65 who were ineligible for military service to come forward and volunteer their time for a newly created defensive force. The force was to be named the Local Defence Volunteers and would be organised along army lines. However, there were significant doubts over the precise role the LDV would play. The War Office and the army viewed the LDV as simply an armed version of the police force which would play a defensive role in guarding certain sites as well as observing and reporting on German troop movements in the event of an invasion or enemy raiding. This minor role was partly due to the lack of uniforms, equipment and weaponry, which had been exacerbated by the loss of equipment at Dunkirk. The volunteers saw themselves as having a far wider role and wished to be an active and effective part in the defence of Britain; in short, the volunteers saw the LDV as being an extension of the army, an officially recognised militia.

The first recorded patrols by members of the Edinburgh LDV were mounted on 29 May by the fifty volunteers who had formed B Section of 4th Company, City of Edinburgh LDV. This unit was largely made up of members of Braid Hills Golf Club and, with the only source of communication being the telephone in the clubhouse, the members of the section had to signal to an appointed orderly who sat at a clubhouse window using torches. This of course led to a series of complaints and reports to the authorities that people were signalling using torches at night and fears of an active fifth column.

At first the force was woefully ill-equipped with no uniforms, equipment or modern arms. The experience of A Company, 8th Battalion, Edinburgh Home Guard, was typical of this. The company was forced to train with antique rifles which were the property of Edinburgh Academy and operationally the company could only muster a single Boer War-era Mauser rifle and the pistol which was owned by its commanding officer.

With the second anniversary of the Home Guard's creation one volunteer submitted a series of recollections from 1940 for the *Edinburgh Evening News*. He remembered how on his first night of duty he had walked towards his post on a lovely summer evening and was joined by another man who had served the night before and with whom he subsequently became fast friends. Describing the make-up of his platoon, he said that they were all ex-servicemen, one had served for four years at the Western Front, some had seen service in France, India and Russia, one had been a long-time member of the Royal Marines, and another had spent his youth as a cowboy in Canada. Their officer was a former naval man and had been appointed to command largely because he possessed a gun and ammunition and a tin hat upon which he had had 'LDV' stencilled in chromium lettering.

Describing the first days of duty he remembered how woefully ill-equipped they were with guard duty and patrols being mounted with little or no weaponry. He also recalled how one section had managed to assemble, as its sole armoury, a flintlock pistol, a Mannlicher rifle which was missing its bolt, four revolvers (one of which was broken), a bugle and a Japanese sword. The sword was seen as the 'gem of the collection' and hung for a long time in the guardroom where it became something of a mascot.[14]

The local golf clubs often proved a focal point for LDV/Home Guard units in and around Edinburgh. For the clubs the war came with many sacrifices as incomes were affected, staff left, and many were forced to place obstacles across their treasured fairways and greens to deny them as landing grounds for the enemy. At courses like Bruntsfield Links, Craigentinny, Craigieknowe and Cramond a variety of obstructions ranging from old cars to brick piles were placed on the courses. Some of the courses even went so far as to allow the digging of trenches on their fairways.

All across the city trenches were dug despite the concerns of many residents about the spoiling of the beauty of areas such as Inverleith Park and the Meadows. These trenches seem to have been widely derided by those who realised that an invasion of Scotland was highly unlikely. The trenches also represented a hazard to pedestrians and road users in the blackout and there were a number of incidents of people falling into trench systems and injuring themselves.

The Home Guard was forced, due to their lack of adequate anti-tank weapons, to fall back on their own creativity to fill the gap. One early invention was the flame trap which entailed using a reservoir of oil to flood a section of road. The testing of one of these improvised defences at the hamlet of Hillend went badly wrong when the impressive blaze spread from the road onto the nearby hedge and then to a telegraph pole which carried the main trunk lines to and from Edinburgh. The fire brigade had to be called and thankfully they were able to deal with the blaze without serious damage to the capital's communications network.

It was recorded that the first volunteer in the city was a lawyer who presented himself to an unprepared police officer at a local police station. The recruits came from every aspect of Edinburgh life and included university lecturers, students, civil servants, plumbers, scavengers and others. David Pinkerton Fleming, a judge and volunteer in the 3rd City of Edinburgh Battalion (based at Braid Hills Golf Club) found himself on an early patrol alongside another volunteer whom he had last seen standing in the dock in front of him. Drilling initially with wooden rifles, the men of the LDV maintained their morale with training sessions and impromptu patrols.

A reflection of the enthusiasm and determination of the men of the Edinburgh LDV units was found when the commanding officer of 8th City of Edinburgh Battalion found himself to be too unwell to discharge his duty of command. Lieutenant Colonel Robertson immediately resigned his command but, at his own request, reverted to the rank of private in the battalion which he had commanded.

In Edinburgh the formation of the force was done quite efficiently. This was largely down to the actions of the chairman of the Edinburgh Territorial Army Association. The chairman quickly came to the decision that the force, which would become the 1st City of Edinburgh Battalion, would be organised using the district police boundaries with each district being home to a company. The chairman appointed Lieutenant Colonel D.A. Foulis to command No. 1 Company which would be responsible for patrolling the Cramond to Murrayfield area of the city. As was common, the appointed commander was a man of previous experience as a ranking officer in the previous war. Foulis had been an infantry officer in the trenches, rising to command the 10th Cameronians (Scottish Rifles). During his time in the trenches he had been awarded the DSO.[15] He was also an enthusiastic member of Mortonhall Golf Club.

Foulis acted quickly and placed adverts for men with military experience and the ability to assume command. Less than ten days after Eden's announcement Foulis had a shortlist of potential leadership candidates and he invited five over to his house the next day to discuss points around the formation of the company from the lists of volunteers supplied by the police. One of the early and regular criticisms of the LDV's formation was that it was based on the 'old boy' network. To an extent this was true, but an analysis of Foulis's platoon commanders shows that only one of them was previously known to Foulis and that there were few connections between the five candidates.

Most volunteers put their names in at local police stations, many of which were unprepared and quickly overwhelmed by the surge – a unit of female auxiliary police were brought into the city to cope with the extra administrative work. Others put their names forward at meetings held in local schools and sports clubs (especially golf clubs). Foulis managed, for example, to raise an entire platoon from volunteers at Murrayfield Golf Club. The formation of LDV sections, platoons and companies often reflected the social distinctions of the areas in which they were raised and, as is pointed out by Brian D. Osborne, the 'raising of a company in the affluent western outskirts of Edinburgh' enabled the organisers to arrange things like the establishment of a mobile contingent with volunteers from another golf club, this time the Royal Burgess, agreeing to supply cars and motorcycles.[16]

The early organisation of the LDV was based on the infantry section of ten men and it was initially a disappointment to many of the volunteers that the force was organised on democratic lines with no official ranks although those commanding units assumed suitable rank titles. As many of the volunteers were former soldiers this policy was resented and was quickly altered.

By 4 June Foulis's company was organised with platoon leaders (who were informally ranked as lieutenants) dividing their men into sections based on where they lived (many were friends or at least known to each other) and promoted men to be section leaders on a one-month probationary period. The men, unofficially ranked sergeants, were told by the platoon leaders that their continued status was conditional on them proving that they were effective and had proved that they were neither incompetent nor too strict in their dealings with the men.

In the countryside around Edinburgh the methods were somewhat different as the population, and therefore the volunteers, were more widely dispersed. In East Lothian there had been an appeal for funds to support the raising of the two battalions of LDV. Despite this pecuniary problem there was no shortage of enthusiasm, with 100 men coming forward in the first 24 hours at North Berwick. By the end of the first week there were almost 150 volunteers in North Berwick and a further 100 at Gullane. Further problems were encountered due to the amount of accommodation already taken up by the large number of regular forces stationed locally and the commanding officer of 2nd East Lothian Battalion was forced to appoint sub-commanders by district even though units based in districts were not always the same size.

It quickly became obvious that the best way forward was to organise units along burghs and larger villages. For example, North Berwick became home to two platoons while communities such as Aberlady, Broxburn, Haddington and Macmerry also became homes to units of varying sizes. Once again, the initial formation of the LDV was hampered by the lack of official ranks, systems of command, etc.

By the end of June area commanders in Scotland had been appointed. For the Edinburgh area this was Colonel Hubert Francis Grant-Suttie MC DSO. Colonel Grant-Suttie was in his mid-fifties when he took on the role and had extensive military experience. He had served in the First World War commanding 48th Battery, Royal Field Artillery. At the outbreak of the Second World War he was Assistant Adjutant and Quartermaster General of the territorial 15th (Scottish) Division. He was from a well-known family with extensive local connections socially: his father, Robert, was the youngest child of Sir George Grant-Suttie, 5th Baronet of Balgone, was a barrister and had held the offices of Deputy Lieutenant and Justice of the Peace for East Lothian. Colonel Grant-Suttie was the fourth child and had been educated at Malvern College and the Royal Military Academy, Woolwich. He quickly oversaw the issue of denim uniforms, service caps and the first issues of rifles (drawn from the cadets and from the arrival of a shipment of American Ross rifles) along with five rounds of ammunition per three or four men (for the purposes of practice).[17]

One of the many duties which the LDV set their hands to in the first weeks and months was the construction of strongpoints and defendable areas. For the men of the 1st City of Edinburgh Battalion in the west of the city this entailed many hours filling sandbags with sand collected from Cramond Beach. Because of the large number of duties which the men of the city's LDV battalion found themselves tasked with the city was specifically left out of the temporary pausing of recruitment in July. Indeed, further adverts were placed in the local press asking for more men to come forward.

By July the men of the LDV nationally were becoming somewhat disgruntled with their role and the lack of equipment and began using their connections to petition the government for a more active role in the defence of the country and for greater urgency to be put into equipping the force. Powerful forces in Whitehall agreed and, largely due to Winston Churchill, the decision was made to change the name of the organisation, which had been widely ridiculed widely,[18] to the more positive and dynamic Home Guard.

Although the LDV/Home Guard were organising themselves it was clear to many in authority that a German invasion might succeed in gaining a foothold and thus top secret arrangements were made to create specially selected units of civilians who would be prepared and trained to go underground (quite literally in many cases) during an invasion before gathering intelligence and launching raids on invaders; they were known as auxiliary units. The auxiliaries consisted of two distinct organisations: the most notorious were the patrols which consisted of between four and eight men, known to each other in most cases, who had a good knowledge of the local environment and could move around their localities in the dark. They were trained to mount sabotage raids and even assassinate German officers and British collaborators. The second group consisted of signals and communications sections which were expected to gather intelligence and transmit it to HQ. In the Edinburgh area the signals mother station for the area was at Blackhill. Codenamed Bannock 3, it was concealed in woodland near Smeaton Gardens and was staffed by three men. Most of the men of these sections were employed in some manner which would allow them to move around the countryside without being suspected. The three men of Bannock 3 were typical of this: Alex Niven of Lawhead, James Grieve (the headmaster at East Linton) and Reverend Souter (the minister at Whitekirk).

We have already seen how there were complaints about the provision of air raid shelters in Edinburgh and how the Lord Privy Seal had ordered the matter to be looked into. A year later there were still complaints. A letter to *The Scotsman* on 3 June queried why, after more than eight months of war, there was no shelter in or near to Blackford Hill Park with the nearest public shelter being one which could hold fifty people in Blackford Avenue, a fair distance from the park gates; on weekend afternoons there were hundreds of people in the park and an air raid which hit the park on one of those days would result in many casualties.

Similar complaints came in from other locations in the city. The local authority was keen to reassure the public that they were constructing more shelters as they repeatedly gave updates to the press on the numbers and locations of new shelters. For example, *The Scotsman* of 6 July carried a photograph of the new air raid shelters being built in West Princes Street Gardens. These shelters were being built into the bank below Princes Street and it was hoped that they would be retained after the war for use as shelters from bad weather.

On 17 July there was another in the string of VIP visits to Edinburgh when the Princess Royal undertook a visit of several sites. She arrived at the Scottish Naval and Military Veterans' Residence at Whitefoord House where she inspected an honour guard formed from Royal Scots veterans of the last war. The men were dressed in the red gowns and balmorals of Whitefoord House (which was known as the Scottish Chelsea) and were proud to be inspected by the Princess who was the regimental colonel-in-chief. The inspection was watched by a large crowd who were on the street and from various windows overlooking the site.

Shelters at Princes Street (TS)

Afterwards the Princess inspected some young soldiers of the regiment in a nearby drill hall before undertaking several private engagements where Royal Scots were stationed.

She officially opened the Scottish Rest House for Servicemen at 20 Waterloo Place, of which she would be chief patroness, and was welcomed by the Lord Provost and other dignitaries. The rest house was one of three in the city and already the governors could inform the Princess that they had provided beds for some 2,000 visiting servicemen and over 20,000 meals. It was open 24 hours a day, seven days a week and was staffed by 400 female volunteers and 200 male. The tour which followed the opening ceremony allowed the Princess to talk with several of the officers and staff of the house and she was particularly interested in the four chiropodists who provided their services freely to the house.

After returning to Whitefoord House for lunch with the officers there, the concluding engagement was a visit to the Scottish recruiting headquarters of the Auxiliary Territorial Service (ATS). The Princess was heavily involved with the service and had recently made a broadcast appealing for more volunteers, especially clerks skilled in shorthand typing, to come forward in Edinburgh (and Scotland as a whole). During the course of her visit, during which she spoke to almost all of the staff, she was informed that since her broadcast the numbers of volunteers had increased from 25 to 70 per day. The Princess was also introduced to four new recruits including one who was indeed a skilled shorthand typist.

The day following the visit of the Princess Royal saw Edinburgh suffer its first civilian losses due to enemy bombing. On the evening of 18 July enemy bombers scattered incendiary and explosive bombs over several locations in south-eastern Scotland. One bomb fell on a tenement building at 8 George Street, Leith, killing

Princess Royal opens Scottish Rest Home (TS)

Princess Royal talks with ATS Members (TS)

seven people. Amongst the casualties was Cathie Redpath. Mrs Redpath lived with her husband and two children at Gorgie Street but had gone to visit her 74-year-old mother Cathie Baird at George Street. In the early evening a bomber dropped out of cloud over Leith – there was no air raid warning – and dropped a single bomb before climbing and dropping eight more bombs. The first bomb struck the roof of the tenement and exploded in the common stairwell, collapsing the building. The other bombs resulted in 38 people sustaining injuries of varying severity.

Another bomb fell on 13 George Street killing 15-year-old Jane Rutherford while another exploded just yards from a busy tram. Despite the glass on the tram being blown out and the bomb leaving a large crater in the road the passengers on the tram were miraculously unscathed. There had been no warning, but ARP services quickly went into action, shepherding people, including a number of children who had been playing in the streets, into shelters while at the same time asking for help.

Civilians Killed in raid on Leith, 18 July 1940.

Name	Age
Catherine Redpath	41
Catherine Fallon Baird	74
Jane Bald Rutherford	15
Robert Thomson	25
Lily Duff	23
David Lennie Duff	33
Catherine Helliwell	61
Jane Lyall Wilson[19]	60

With Britain in a perilous situation it was essential that food supplies be maintained. The harvest saw the drafting in of ever larger numbers of volunteers, including women and children. Local schools in Edinburgh and the surrounding area volunteered to supply labour for the gathering of the harvest and to ensure the supply of food during this time of crisis. At Loretto School, Musselburgh, entire classes of boys volunteered, sacrificing their afternoon cricket matches and, in some cases, their summer holidays.

As the Battle of Britain raged some Edinburgh men found themselves fighting for their lives in the skies above southern England. The dangers from the Luftwaffe were not the only ones they faced. Accidents were commonplace, especially as exhaustion and wear-and-tear began to tell. On 6 August, 19-year-old Pilot Officer Henry Britton,

Schoolboys from Loretto School helping with the cabbage harvest (TS)

flying Hurricanes with 17 Squadron from RAF Debden, took off at 10.15 am to carry out what should have been a routine air test, but for unknown reasons his Hurricane crashed at Debden Park shortly after take-off and caught fire killing him. Pilot Officer Britton was the son of Major Albert Britton, Royal Corps of Signals, and his wife Olive.

603 (City of Edinburgh) Squadron was sent south on 27 August. Based at Hornchurch the squadron was in the thick of the action for the rest of the Battle of Britain and ended up as the highest scoring Fighter Command squadron. Although now in the south of England the people of Edinburgh still keenly followed the exploits of 'their' squadron.[20]

Despite its successes the squadron had a rough introduction to the battle losing eight Spitfires in its first three days in action and suffering three pilots killed and two wounded. Its first day in action, 28 August, was particularly difficult as the squadron lost four aircraft in action over Dover against ME109s. Three of the pilots were killed while Flying Officer O.I.S. Ritchie was wounded. One of the pilots killed was 22-year-old Pilot Officer Donald Kennedy MacDonald who was shot down into the sea in his Spitfire (L1046). Pilot Officer MacDonald was the son of James Harold and Isa May MacDonald of Goodtrees, Murrayfield. He was declared missing and his parents and family began an anxious period of waiting until his death was confirmed. MacDonald was a former public-school boy, attending Marlborough, and was obviously a highly intelligent young man. A Cambridge graduate (Peterhouse) who had been a member of the University Air Squadron, he had toured Europe before the war, including periods of study at the Universities of Graz (Austria) and Grenoble (France).[21]

Pilot Officer MacDonald's older brother was also a pilot with 603 Squadron and continued to fly after his brother's loss. Tragically, exactly one month after this (on 28 September) Flight Lieutenant Henry Kennedy MacDonald (28) was shot down and killed in a fight with the ME109s of JG26. 603 Squadron had been in battle over Gillingham at 10.20 am. He had been educated at Cargilfield and Loretto before moving on to Cambridge, qualifying as a Writer to the Signet (a senior solicitor conducting cases in the Court of Session). He had been a member of the squadron for several years and Ken (as he was known to his comrades) had a reputation as a 'keen and skilful pilot' who had shared in the squadron's successes in bringing down German bombers over south-east Scotland. He was 'exceedingly popular both with his fellow officers and the men of the squadron'.[22] He had claimed eight enemy aircraft destroyed (including one at night), and on the day of his death had been 'bounced' by a flight of ME109s, his Spitfire being badly hit. After shaking off his pursuers he made for Hornchurch but his aircraft caught fire. Although he had time to get clear he did not as he was approaching a densely populated area. Instead he remained at the controls to steer his Spitfire away from the area and, having done so, at just 400 feet he climbed from his cockpit onto the port wing and jumped. His parachute did not have time to deploy and he fell to his death. His Spitfire crashed onto the parade ground of Brompton Barracks. Flight Lieutenant MacDonald's body was brought back to Edinburgh for cremation. It seems surprising that he did not receive any formal recognition of his achievements.

The 31st August was one of the squadron's busiest days with one of its pilots, Flying Officer Brian Carbury, scoring five victories (three ME109s and two HE111s) and several other pilots also scored. There were, however, casualties. While on patrol over London shortly before 6.30 pm the squadron tangled with the ME109s of Jagdgeschwader 3 and two Spitfires were shot down. The first was X4271 'N' flown by Pilot Officer G.K. Gilroy, who managed to bail out of his stricken fighter but after landing in Wanstead was mistaken for a German and attacked and injured by a crowd of civilians.

The second loss was X4273 'K', Flying Officer Robin McGregor Waterston, aged 23, the youngest son of James Sime Waterston and Mabel of Haughhead, Ford, Lothian. His father had been president of the Edinburgh Chamber of Commerce and thus father and son were both well known in the city. Flying Officer Waterston had been educated at Edinburgh Academy where he was an enthusiastic aspiring pilot and had obtained a commission in the Auxiliary Air Force gaining his wings in 1937. He had a reputation for courage and boyish enthusiasm and was very disappointed to be on leave when 603 Squadron had gone into action over Edinburgh at the start of the war.

Many Edinburgh men from Coastal Command also lost their lives in action during this period. Mystery surrounds the death of Corporal Douglas Wardlaw Marwick, who was well known in Edinburgh as he had been educated at George Watson's College and was one of the foremost amateur golfers in the area, winning several tournaments. He was a leading member of the Lothian team which took part in the *Evening Dispatch* Trophy Tournament in 1934. Several years before the war he had become a professional and was based at Murrayfield Golf School where he started a scheme of tuition for schoolboys. At the outbreak of the war he had joined the RAF and it was known that he had, despite his category as groundcrew, flown several operations as a volunteer air gunner. On 23 August it was noted that he had lost his life on active service but few details are available and it is not known whether he was killed as a result of enemy action or through accident or illness. He left behind his parents, Joseph and Sarah Marwick, along with a widow, Elizabeth.

On 26 August, Edinburgh was visited by the Duchess of Gloucester. The visit was primarily to accept a cheque from the women of Scotland to the Scottish National Council of the YMCA. The cheque was for £6,145 which the Duchess described as 'a most wonderful effort on everybody's part'. The Lord Provost formally welcomed the Duchess at a banquet (she was an honorary burgess of the city). He praised the work of the YMCA in providing facilities for the many men who had, in many cases, come from thousands of miles away to defend Britain in her hour of need. Speeches then went on to say that the YMCA in Scotland had 90 centres open and 26 mobile canteens. The Duchess then moved on to visit the Red Cross Depot at 5 George Square where she took a great interest in the work as she had been herself an officer in the Red Cross. The Duchess was greeted by Sir Walter Maxwell-Scott, the vice president of the Scottish branch, and Sir David Wallace.

Afterwards the Duchess and her party were accompanied by several RAF officers to an inspection of a detachment of the Women's Auxiliary Air Force at a nearby airfield.

Right: *Duchess of Gloucester inspects Red Cross Depot (TS)*

Below: *Duchess of Gloucester inspects WAAF's (TS)*

This was not a full ceremonial visit but had been requested by the Duchess as she was a commandant of the WAAF. After inspecting the 50-strong detachment the Duchess spoke with many of the women and commented on their smart appearance. Amongst the women present on parade were several with university degrees: an architect, an archaeologist and a talented linguist. Following the parade the Duchess and her party were treated to lunch in the officers' mess.

With the demands of the ARP services for suitable properties, many function rooms and buildings belonging to various organisations were commandeered or rented. Sometimes this caused friction between the renters and those organisations using the buildings. For example, South Queensferry Masonic Lodge was shared by both the local ARP services and the RAF and there were a series of disagreements over whether the ARP or the RAF were responsible for the bills. One for a phone call which amounted to just 10s 5d remained unsettled until August of 1944.

We have already seen how the local authority set up a network of information centres which would be opened in the event of raiding. It was not until the bombing of the Caledonian Distillery bond warehouse in Duff Street on 27 September that the service was fully put into action, and it was agreed there were many problems. At 5.15 am a 500lb bomb, probably aimed at nearby railway lines and yards, hit the warehouse and a fierce fire raged out of control, fed by the large quantities of whisky in storage. People from nearby properties had gathered in the streets, some after miraculous escapes from the blast, and began observing the struggles of the firemen to contain the blaze; in doing so they were probably a considerable hinderance to the emergency services. The fire was so fierce that it was said to be possible to read a newspaper the other side of the city from its light. The returning Luftwaffe pilots reported in their debriefing that the blaze was still visible as they crossed the Danish coast. It soon became clear that the warehouse was a lost cause and the main concern of the brigade became to stop the fire spreading. They were forced to hose down nearby tenement buildings as there were streams of burning whisky flowing down the streets (it was said that the ground still smelled of whisky in warm weather for several years afterwards). Some of the firemen were left stupefied by the fumes due to a lack of breathing apparatus. Despite these efforts several tenements on Duff Street did suffer fire damage but they were evacuated and there were no serious injuries.

On the same night a bomb fell in the grounds of Holyrood Palace but no details were released about this to the public. However, the residents in the nearby tenements at Abbeyhill witnessed the bombing first-hand. They had got into the habit, as had many others in Edinburgh, of holding back-green concerts to raise money for the Spitfire Fund. These concerts consisted of local people gathering and giving performances according to their own individual talents, with a small entrance fee providing a steady flow of income for the fund. One concert had just finished when the bomb exploded and the residents were rocked by the concussive blast. The bomb was obviously a large one, quite possibly a parachute mine, and had probably been aimed at the nearby railway line. A very large crater was left in the Palace grounds and one resident of Abbeyhill saw the opportunity to raise more funds by selling tickets from his upstairs flat to view the crater. This seems to have been a roaring success as it ran for over three days and raised over £300 (at least £16,000 today).[23]

It was essential to keep the ARP and fire services well drilled and throughout the year a series of exercises were held. At the end of September a city-wide exercise was held which featured realistic rehearsals including the extinguishing of a fire at the partly demolished Blackford Hill House and the rescue of trapped survivors from a variety of properties. The drill also involved the first aid workers and the main control room.

As the Battle of Britain entered its final stages, German high command was still contemplating invasion of Britain and the Abwehr was making attempts to

ARP undertaking drills (TS)

gather intelligence. On the morning of 30 September MI5's Regional Security Liaison Officer in Edinburgh, Peter Perfect, received a call from the police headquarters at Banff. The caller informed Perfect that earlier that morning the local police had detained a man and a woman (both foreigners) who they believed to be German spies as a search had revealed that they were in possession of a radio set (complete with Morse key and a number of coding/decoding devices), a Mauser pistol and ammunition, a large quantity of money and suspected forged identity papers. The two had been attempting to board a train at Portgordon when they aroused suspicion and were subsequently detained. Although spy mania was at a high at the time, the discovery of the radio set and pistol seemed to confirm the suspicions of the local police and were enough to persuade Perfect to set off in his car on the five-hour drive to the north.

When he arrived Perfect carried out an initial interrogation during which the woman identified herself as Vera de Cottani Chalbur and claimed that she was working for MI5's B5b counter-subversion division. She also told Perfect that the man who had accompanied her was indeed an Abwehr agent named Karl Drugge and that she had been assigned the mission by the Abwehr to accompany him to London. As well as this the mysterious woman revealed that there was a third member of the party. A man going under the alias of Werner Walti had accompanied them but they had split up shortly after landing in a rubber dinghy after being dropped off at sea by a Heinkel HE115 seaplane in the early hours. She explained how the three had folding bicycles but had been forced to throw them overboard as the dinghy was in danger of being swamped and that after landing they had shared a meal on the beach before separating. A search of the beach revealed the dinghy and the remains of a meal having been cooked while a nearby farmer also informed the authorities that his dog had been disturbed during the early hours. All of this convinced Perfect that not only had he one and possibly two Abwehr agents in custody but also that there was a third on the loose.

An appeal for information was put out to the local railway and police stations and a porter at Buckie station informed the police that a man fitting Walti's description had boarded a train for Aberdeen that morning while staff at Aberdeen were able to confirm that a similar man had later boarded the Edinburgh train. For some reason there was now a breakdown in communication and it took some time for the police in Edinburgh to be informed to be on the lookout for Walti. In fact the police in the capital were not notified until 40 minutes after the train had arrived. Despite this, Edinburgh CID, led by Detective Lieutenant William Merrilees (known as 'Wee Willie') organised a search of the city with enquiries at local hotels and boarding houses while the sidings at Waverley Station were thoroughly searched and the staff questioned.

The search of the station located a sea-salt-stained suitcase at a left luggage office on Platform 19 and a staff member recollected a man fitting Walti's description asking him where he could leave his luggage. Merrilees broke open the suitcase and found that it contained a German wireless set. Aware now that Walti had already arrived in Edinburgh but was planning to return to the station, Merrilees mounted an undercover surveillance operation which involved plain clothes officers as well as volunteers from the WVS (it was less suspicious if the officers were part of a couple). For over three hours the police scanned the crowds passing through the station searching for Walti. Their task was made more difficult by the presence of large numbers of foreign soldiers who were passing through, but at around 9 pm Merrilees spotted a young man of Walti's description approaching the left luggage office and watched as the clearly nervous man asked for his luggage before retreating to wait for it. As he waited, the suspect, who was carrying a briefcase, kept putting one hand in his pocket and Merrilees was concerned that he held a weapon. Bravely approaching Walti, the police officer waved to convince the suspect that he was simply waving at someone behind him. The distracted suspect glanced behind him and Merrilees sprung at him grabbing his arm and pulling his hand from his pocket, which held a Mauser automatic pistol.

Merrilees disarmed the suspected spy and he was bundled into the left luggage office. At this point he managed to draw a flick-knife and attempted to confront the police officers, but he was, none too gently, disarmed and subdued before being transported to police headquarters where he was stripped, searched and photographed. Even though he had been found with the wireless set, pistol and various other incriminating evidence (including a coding disk and a handwritten book which set out radio communication abbreviations, which any competent agent would normally have memorised) Walti continued to proclaim his innocence, claiming to be a Swiss national not German.

This defence was further undermined when a search of his briefcase revealed a box of ammunition for his pistol and over a dozen maps of the eastern half of Britain. Several of these maps were German-made although most were standard Ordnance Survey maps which had been overlaid by the Abwehr with information from aerial reconnaissance flights and a Luftwaffe target grid. The maps were marked with the locations of RAF airfields from Sutherland to East Anglia. Walti's wallet also contained suspicious items including £190, a book of graph paper which had the name of a senior Luftwaffe officer on it, and a blank traveller's ration book.

Subsequent interrogation of the three by the intelligence services confirmed the fact that the two men were indeed Abwehr agents and that their mission had been to spy on RAF airfields in eastern Britain. Walti revealed that his real name was Robert Petter and claimed that he had been ordered to deliver the wireless set to a man at Victoria Station. The two were tried at the Old Bailey in June 1941, both were convicted and were subsequently executed on 6 August 1941.

This left behind a mystery, as the woman who had accompanied them was never formally charged and her real identity remains unknown being variously given as Vera de Cottani Chalbur, Vera Erikson, Vera von Schalbourg and Vera von Stein. The most likely explanation seems to be that she did have some connection with British intelligence (although she was most likely not an official agent) and that she went on to work with the British under yet another identity. Even an account of his life written by William Merrilees gave little to go on, mentioning the third suspect only vaguely and not even stating that this suspect was a woman.

There had been several ongoing problems with the evacuee camps which had been set up to house Edinburgh evacuees. In a probable attempt to pacify and reassure parents, *The Scotsman* ran an article in November on a visit to a camp which had been paid for by the Under Secretary of State for Scotland, Mr Joseph Westwood MP. The Under Secretary was said to be impressed by the successful efforts of the staff in establishing 'a happy family atmosphere' for the large numbers of children who had been transplanted from the city to unfamiliar surroundings in the countryside. The finale of the visit seems to have been carefully rehearsed (and to modern ears seems a little autocratic), with the headmaster asking the children who he was and them all chorusing his name, then following with the question 'what else?' to which the children all answered 'Headmaster', before finally the previous question was repeated and the children all chorused 'Father'. The article concluded that the 'bright and healthy faces of the chorus afforded eloquent confirmation of the claim that the life is agreeing with them'.[24] This was in stark contrast to the realities of life in the two camps. Reports from the headmasters were critical of the lack of facilities while the camps became seas of mud in the winter with the play area in one being referred to as 'the Black Sea'. Repeated appeals by the staff to the Education Committee for improvements went unheeded with the only action being the issue of a supply of clogs for the children. Disease was also a problem through the winter with visits by family members spreading diseases such as measles through the camps.

We have already seen how the women of Edinburgh had rallied behind the war effort but apparently this was not enough. In October the women of Edinburgh, frustrated at their rejection from active service in the Home Guard, took matters into their own hands and formed the Edinburgh Women's Defence Corps. This group quickly proved popular, demonstrating the commitment of Edinburgh women to the war effort along with a determination to be allowed to play a more active role in the war, especially in the event of invasion. Although an unofficial body, the women demonstrated considerable initiative in securing training sites and, in some cases, in forging links with Home Guard units which were more willing to accept their contribution. Some male Home Guard however, remained absolutely opposed to the involvement of women in any active role which might bring them into contact with the enemy.

On Sunday, 10 November, there was a concert at the King's Theatre in aid of the Scottish Services Musical Entertainments Fund. Although there were a number of local acts (such as the cellist Chester Henderson) in the performance the five main performers were Polish professionals who were performing across the country with ENSA. The performers were: bass-baritone Stanislaw Lobaziewicz who sang in both Polish and English; two ballet dancers named Maria Fedro and Pola Nirenska (who gave a display of Polish national dance); two more dancers, Szcepan Baczynski and Jullia Kraszevska, who gave colourful dance duets; while Maria Geist accompanied on the piano.

There were strong links with the Polish army personnel who were stationed in Scotland in what was known as the Polish defence sector and because of this the capital attracted many notable visitors from the occupied countries. In November there were visits from the Polish President, the commander-in-chief and General Sikorsky who accompanied the Prime Minister on an inspection tour. This was followed by a visit from General Ingr, Chief Commander of the Czechoslovakian forces in Great Britain, and Polish General Modelski. The two generals were shown around Edinburgh Castle by Colonel Crew and also toured the Palace of Holyrood and the Royal Mile. During their visit the two praised the Polish troops in Scotland and also the spirit of the people of Edinburgh in welcoming them to their country.

With the large numbers of Polish servicemen based in the Edinburgh area there were constant efforts to integrate these men into the local community. Some men proved popular with the local women, establishing a reputation for being dashing and handsome. Others established a reputation for more cerebral and cultural accomplishments. In November the Royal Scottish Academy Galleries hosted the Polish Photographic Exhibition for a fortnight. The exhibition had been touring the country and had been eagerly anticipated in Edinburgh, but the city almost lost out on the exhibition after it was found that the black and white room of the Academy was not suitable for displaying the exhibits and the only other usable space was the National Gallery (the paintings had been removed for the duration of the war), but this was unauthorised for use during the war. Permission was only secured four days before the opening of the exhibition after an appeal to the Secretary of State for Scotland.

Mid-December saw a performance for the Edinburgh Corporation concert for the Forces at the Usher Hall. The main performer was pianist, Cadet Officer M. Blaszczynski who was studying at Edinburgh Royal Infirmary and was said to be Paderewski's most notable student. The day before the performance the 'Scotsman's Log' in *The Scotsman* related a story of two other musically accomplished Poles. While visiting a local journalist's house the two were talking to the family and the young daughter was asked to play the fiddle for the visitors. Unfortunately the young girl was too shy to perform and instead the violin was passed to the two visitors, both of whom proved to be highly skilled with the instrument.

With considerable numbers of local men being posted missing or captured during the shambolic retreat to Dunkirk, many families in the Edinburgh area were anxiously awaiting news of loved ones through the latter months of the year. In November a remarkable account of a soldier's escape was published in *The Scotsman*. The man in question was Corporal J.A. Martin of 5 Oxford Terrace, Edinburgh. Having been wounded by shrapnel in the back and arm during the retreat, Corporal Martin was unable to be evacuated from the beaches and was taken prisoner, sent to a camp in Germany where the only food available was a lunchtime meal of black bread, cabbage and soup. Escaping the camp by the simple expedient of climbing over the wall, Corporal Martin made for the border after finding some civilian clothing in an abandoned house (taking a huge risk as he could have been shot as a spy if caught out of uniform). Corporal Martin succeeded in reaching France where his knowledge of the language helped him find shelter and he was given a bicycle and several hundred francs for his journey. He managed to bluff his way through several checkpoints before he was arrested under suspicion of being a deserter. After spending three weeks in prison he was released and took a train south. After being briefly arrested again he managed to find his way eventually to Britain. The report seems rather vague and it is assumed that Corporal Martin made his way to Gibraltar before returning to Britain, but there are several inconsistencies. The most glaring is the seeming lack of organisation of the authorities in both Germany and France in failing to detain a man of military age who had no identification papers. Next to this is the claim by the article that Corporal Martin had travelled 13,000 miles to return home (perhaps he boarded a ship bound for Africa first?) but there is no criticism of the account in the newspaper and presumably it was checked by the British authorities upon his return. If the account is correct then it was a remarkable escape and a very determined and courageous effort on the part of Corporal Martin.

Remembrance Day services were, unsurprisingly, very well attended throughout Edinburgh with the congregation at St. Giles' Cathedral (including the Lord Provost, magistrates and town councillors) hearing the Dean of the Thistle, the appropriately named Very Reverend Dr Charles L. Warr, give an address in which he addressed those who had said that the men of the First World War had given their lives in vain. Dr Warr, who had himself fought in the war, stated that had it not been for the sacrifices of the Great War, Britain would not now be able to fight for our liberties as the country would for the last two decades have been 'prostrate in political and economic slavery beneath [Germany's] ruthless jack-boot'.[25] Dr Warr also cast aspersions on some people's perspective of the war claiming that they underestimated the sacrifices that would be necessary and urged those in power to ensure that victory was followed by a united kingdom of God across Europe which did not surrender 'to materialistic forces which will eventually and inevitably encompass its moral and spiritual ruination'.

Beginning on 4 November Edinburgh held its War Weapons Week which was to raise £6,000,000 (equivalent to perhaps £1 billion today) with the slogan of £1,000,000 per day. The campaign proved so popular that over the first two days more than £1,500,000 had been raised per day on average with the sum standing at more the £3,500,000 and this led to the organisers being confident of beating their target and perhaps setting a new record. Competition between communities played an important role and the local press highlighted how Liverpool currently led the way with an average of £14 2s 3d per head of population but that if Edinburgh could raise £6,500,000 then that would mean a new record of £16 per person. By Friday the tally stood at £5,900,000, breaking Liverpool's record, and it was thought that the total would eventually exceed £7,000,000 as new subscriptions were still being promised. The organisers were keen to get even more small individual investors involved and insisted that the scheme could not achieve its highest aims without everyone in the city contributing something no matter how small.

On 6 and 7 November there was a rush to donate at the hut which had been set up on the Mound. Amongst these small donations was one which would surely have encouraged the organisers that small donators were doing their bit. One investor, a widow, admitted that she found it very difficult to save money but still managed to contribute two shillings. She modestly refused to give the collectors her name relenting only as far as to give her initials, A.H.T.

Savings groups set up by firms and local communities were a feature of the week with many being set up during the fundraising period. The first to be formed on 6 November was from the LMS Railway, Slateford. The first on the following day was 'The Silk Shop'. These savings groups made significant contributions to the effort with that of Chalmers & Co. reaching an average of £11 per contributor and by 8 November had raised £170. Amongst the groups formed by local schools, that of South Morningside had achieved a remarkable average of £21 per head.

Numerous events were organised through the week and there was a specially erected stand at the Mound. On 9 November there was a series of speeches on the campaign featuring Mr J.A. Inglis (King's and Lord Treasurer's Remembrancer for

WAAF contingent on parade during War Weapons Week (TS)

Scotland), the Very Reverend Dr James Black, Lady Ruth Balfour and the Rev. Dr. Guthrie. The keynote speaker was to be Mr Ernest Brown (Secretary of State for Scotland).

Two military parades were arranged to take place during the week. The second of these, on 7 November, included detachments from all of the services with the salute being taken by Lieutenant General R.H. Carrington (General Officer C-in-C, Scottish Command). The route took the parade along Princes Street and finished at the Mound. Parading were contingents from the Royal Navy, the Wrens, Army, ATS, RAF, WAAF, Special Constables, Regular and Auxiliary Fire Services, all services from the ARP organisation including wardens and members of the rescue squads, WVS and the Women's Land Army. This last contingent was led by one of the land girls driving a tractor with another bringing up the rear of their party.

On the dais were Lord Provost Steele, the city magistrates and various other dignitaries while large crowds had also assembled. They heard an address by General Carrington in which he said that everyone had a part to play in the campaign as the new weapons purchased would ensure that peace and victory would be secured the sooner. He also praised the RN and RAF for 'guarding this country so magnificently this summer and autumn' but moved to reassure the public that, since Dunkirk, the army had also not been idle and that equipping it would be a vital task if the war was to be won. He concluded by appealing 'on behalf of the Army, and especially on behalf of all Scottish soldiers, for financial help,' adding that 'he knew it would never be said of Edinburgh that she sent her men to do a job without the wherewithal to bring it to a successful conclusion.' The donations hut was reported as being very busy after his speech.[26]

One of the most popular exhibitions at the Mound was a Messerschmitt ME* 109 which, in the words of the local press, bore 'evidence of RAF marksmanship'. Large crowds gathered to inspect this victim of the Battle of Britain and the displays were responsible for encouraging enthusiasm and raising significant sums for the campaign.

---

*   Although the official designation for the early Messerschmitt was Bf, the more familiar ME is used throughout the text.

ME 109 on display at the Mound for War Weapons Week (TS)

Edinburgh's War Weapons Week raised £9,417,000 (as much as £2.5 billion in today terms[27]) with further sums still to be counted. Speaking to a large crowd the Secretary of State for Scotland, Ernest Brown MP, stated that the efforts of the city had been amazing, breaking all expectations; the aim had been to raise £6,000,000. The total raised amounted to an average of over £23 per person resident in the city: they had exceeded the per head sum of every major English city. He praised the work of the city's ARP workers (some of whom had volunteered to work in London to give exhausted ARP workers there a rest) and, perhaps mindful of ongoing criticisms of shelter facilities, told the crowd that the war would not be won by a deep shelter mentality but by ensuring that the forces had the equipment to do their jobs.

Sums raised per head of population during War Weapons Weeks

City	£	s.	d.
Edinburgh	23		
Liverpool	14	2	3
Manchester	9	5	7
Newcastle	9	2	5
Birmingham	7	14	6
Leeds	7	7	8
Bristol	3	10	2

The involvement of local businesses was also impressive:

Companies and organisations contributing to War Weapons Week, November 1940.

Company	Donation (£s)
Scottish insurance companies	1,004,000
Scottish banks in Edinburgh	1,000,000
Scottish Motor Traction	250,000
Bruce, Peebles & Co.	50,000
Edinburgh Savings Bank	50,000
Anonymous	20,000
Shotts Iron Co.	10,000
J & W Stuart Ltd.	10,000
Standard Property Investment Co.	10,000
Thomson & Brown Bros.	10,000
Anonymous	10,000
John & James Tod & Sons	10,000
Kersans Ltd.	10,000
Currie Line Ltd.	10,000
David Stuart Ltd.	10,000
British Ropes, Leith	7,000
Rossleigh Ltd.	5,000
James H. Lamont & Co.	3,000
David Keir & Sons	2,500
Educational Institute of Scotland	2,500
Alder & Mackay	1,000
James White (Contractors)	1,000
John Gibson & Son	1,000
John Inglis & Sons	1,000
Leith Property Investment Building Society	1,000
Edinburgh Licensed Trade Local Veterans Defence Association (Publican Section)	1,000

Other contributions that week from local firms included W.N. Lindsay (£10,000), MacTaggart & Mickel (£5,000), Melrose's (£3,000), Inch Kenneth Kajang Rubber (£2,000), and Kemasul Rubber Estates (£1,000). The local cinemas also got behind the campaign and allowed speakers to talk to cinema-goers about the campaign.

Although these large donations had helped the tally massively it was the donations of small investors which received most praise. Numerous work committees' funds had broken all records for weekly contributions and this had set the example to many within the community. The schools had also played a leading role in the week breaking all records with stories of youngsters saving sixpences to buy Spitfires being common in the city during the week.

Works Committee Contributions to Edinburgh's War Weapons Week

Company	Weekly Average (£)	Total for Week (£)
Edinburgh Corporation Transport Dept.	20	315
Messrs Currie & Co. (Leith)	35	805
M.P. Galloway Ltd. (Leith)	10	223

It took several weeks to calculate the final total. This was £10,234,053, with an average contribution of £25 per head. A major development was the policy, put in place by the chairman Bailie Douglas and supported by a myriad of local businesses, of instituting prize competitions between the savings groups. The committee overseeing the week of fund raising had even gone so far as to obtain the names of firms which had not formed savings groups and the heads of these firms had been 'interviewed'.[28] No doubt they were given stern encouragement and admonished over their failure to rise to the occasion in a patriotic manner. The encouragement seems to have worked as the committee was

Furniture salvaged from Dalmeny House (TS)

able to report that there had been an overall increase of 756 in the number of groups and that by the end of March there were 1,097 savings groups in the city.

For the Earl of Rosebery there was bad news two days before Christmas when a fire broke out at his home, Dalmeny House. The fire badly affected the north-east wing and there were frantic attempts to salvage furniture and fittings.

The year closed with the welcome news of a marked downturn in criminal activity in Edinburgh during 1940. There were 1,213 offences committed during the year and while drunkenness continued to be the main factor this too had declined (possibly as a result of higher prices, limited hours and the blackout). Breach of the peace and disorderly conduct charges (mainly due to drink) had declined substantially with 314 fewer cases during the year. A fall in cases of serious theft seemed to prove incorrect the fear that the blackout would lead to an increase in housebreaking offences. The only disappointment was that the number of juveniles charged with breaking into and damaging houses which had been vacated had gone up.

CHAPTER 3

1941

The year opened with a tragedy at Musselburgh Station when, on New Year's Day, a large goods train engine smashed through the buffers and demolished a bookstall (owned by John Menzies & Co), the stationmaster's office and a porters' room at the station before coming to rest with the nose of the engine, and a pile of rubble, protruding into the street beyond the station. Many of the waggons attached to the engine were derailed and came together in a concertina fashion reaching a height of over 30 feet and smashing the roof of the station causing girders to fall across the platforms (thankfully, without injury).

Porter James Mole had just exited from the porters' room and had spoken to the young woman who was manning the bookstall, Miss Helen Currie Krause (19) (some sources say she was known as Ella). After the crash he immediately ran back to the stall, which had been utterly destroyed, and found the chair which Miss Krause had been sitting on but there was no sign of her. ARP rescue and demolition squads were quickly on the scene and, along with auxiliary and railway workers, worked for five hours clearing wreckage and looking for Miss Krause. Her body was later recovered under debris near the engine. Miss Krause was living with an aunt at 2 South Street as her parents lived in Canada; she had been living in Britain for just over a year. The engine driver and fireman escaped serious injury.

Battered engine after crash at Musselburgh (TS)

In early March the Edinburgh industrial community lost one of its prominent members when Mr William Thomson died suddenly at his home (5 Rothesay Terrace). Mr Thomson had been a prominent Leith shipowner and had been chairman of Messrs William Thomson & Co, owner of the Ben Line. The Ben Line had a 100-year history and had a substantial fleet of vessels (most of approximately 9,000 tons) at the outbreak of war. The regular business of the company was in cargo trade between the Far East and the British east coast. Thomson had also been on boards of the Commercial Bank of Scotland, the North British Rubber Company, the London and Edinburgh Shipping Co (of which he was deputy chairman), the Edinburgh Investment Co, the Life Association of Scotland, and Shotts Iron Co. He clearly led a very active business life as he was also chair of the Leith Shipowners' Society and was the Leith member of the Lloyd's Register of Shipping as well as being a member of the Leith Chamber of Commerce.[1]

On 6 March Sheriff Brown held an inquest into the death of Miss Krause at Edinburgh Sheriff Court. Hearing evidence from station foreman, John Hunter, he was told that Mr Hunter heard the alarm bell ring from Musselburgh signal cabin and was informed that there was a runaway goods train on the branch line. As he replaced the telephone he heard the crash. The stationmaster, Walter Irvine, interviewed the driver immediately after the crash and he told him that the distance signal was off but he could offer no explanation for why he had not seen the Newhailes home signal. He then testified that an inspection of the engine, by himself, had revealed that the brakes were fully on and that the gradient from Newhailes to Musselburgh was very steep.

The train's guard, Alexander Gray, testified that the train was carrying approximately 550 tons and that the first indication he had that anything was wrong was when he felt the train go onto an unfamiliar branch line just past Newhailes signal cabin. He immediately applied the brake in his cabin but testified that the train was sliding down a steep gradient and that shortly after that there was a terrific crash. The signalman at Musselburgh signal cabin, David Little Ramage, said that he had waved a red lamp from his window and blew his whistle as he believed that the train was a runaway. The driver of the train, John Renton Hunter (43) of 170 Main Street, Tweedmouth, testified that the Newhailes distance signal was in the clear position but he did not see the home signal and was not familiar with the Musselburgh branch line. As soon as he felt the train lurch onto the branch line he had applied his brakes but he believed that the weight of the train was too much and he felt the engine begin to skid on the line.

After considering the evidence, Sheriff Brown stated that he could not return a definite verdict as he was unable to determine blame due to the complexity of the case. However, taking into account the evidence of Mr Hunter, he did make a strong recommendation that it was 'the duty of the Railway Company, especially after this occurrence, to make certain … that their safety regulations are obeyed'.[2]

The New Year's Honours List reflected the work that had been undertaken by the Lord Provost of Edinburgh, Henry Steele, who was made a Knight Bachelor. Sir Henry had 'played an indefatigable part in the adaptation' of Edinburgh to the wartime situation, he had played a leading role in the formation and running of the ARP and civil defence schemes for the city, and had also undertaken extensive work

Lord Provost Sir Henry Steele KB
(The Tatler)

to raise funds for the war effort and for charity, especially the Red Cross, the Fighter Aircraft Fund and War Weapons Week.

The blackout continued to contribute to the number of accidents in the city. Early April saw another fatal accident when army dispatch rider Kenneth Chesson of the Royal Corps of Signals crashed his motorcycle into the back of a stationary lorry to the west of Gyle Bridge.

The defences of Edinburgh often proved more of a hazard to the public than they ever would to the enemy in the unlikely event of an invasion. We have already seen how defensive earthworks and trench systems were constructed throughout the city and how they often led to accidents in the blackout. The construction of these defences continued through 1941. The corporation was informed that D Company of 6th Battalion HG required the digging of new trenches at Johnston Terrace, Castle Terrace and King's Stables Road. This went ahead despite the protests of some residents who faced having their gardens dug up at a time when the risk of invasion was decreasing. The construction of pillboxes and blockhouses continued apace and again these often proved to be hazards to the public during blackouts as many seem to have been constructed with little or no regard to nearby traffic conditions.

There was a fatal accident on the morning of 20 June that left four people dead and more than twenty injured which was caused not by any of these things but by a kitten. The accident involved a collision between a crowded bus and a tram in Inchview Terrace on the main road between Edinburgh and Portobello. One of the bus passengers to Edinburgh had boarded and left a basket containing two kittens on a rack near the driver. Unfortunately one of the kittens escaped and jumped onto the face of the driver causing him to swerve and collide violently with the oncoming tram. The collision was so violent that the side of the bus was almost torn off and passengers were left strewn about while many of those on the side of the bus which bore the brunt of the impact were either killed or injured. The tram, which had only a few passengers on board, was also badly damaged although there were no serious injuries and the anti-splinter netting which had been fitted on its windows proved its worth by preventing injuries from shattered glass. The noise of the accident, one of the most serious in Edinburgh's history, was heard across the neighbourhood and many people came out of their houses to render assistance. Two doctors, one of whom had been a passenger on the bus, also helped with the treatment of the injured while ambulances and the ARP services were quickly on the scene and removed the dead and injured. The scene of the accident was investigated and the clean-up, in which locally-based soldiers assisted, took several hours causing delays to the traffic in the area.

Dead and injured from crash on 20 June 1941

Agnes Casey	Fatality
John M. Millar	Fatality
Roy Ritchie (or Keenan)	Fatality
Robert Johnston	Fatality
Jane Wood	Detained at Leith Hospital
James D. Millar	Detained at Edinburgh Royal Infirmary
R. Robertson	Detained at Edinburgh Royal Infirmary
Agnes Nelson	Detained at Edinburgh Royal Infirmary
John Johnston	Detained at Edinburgh Royal Infirmary
J. McKinlay	Detained at Edinburgh Royal Infirmary
Henry Phillips (aged 1)	Detained at Edinburgh Royal Infirmary
Elizabeth Kilbride	Allowed home after treatment at Infirmary
Janet Kilbride (aged 4)	Allowed home after treatment at Infirmary
2nd Lieutenant Baum	Allowed home after treatment at Infirmary
Mrs Scott	Allowed home after treatment at Infirmary
May Telford	Allowed home after treatment at Infirmary
James Sneddon	Allowed home after treatment at Infirmary
Mr Richardson	Allowed home after treatment at Infirmary
George Osborne (conductor)	Allowed home after treatment at Leith Hospital
Robert Graham	Allowed home after treatment at Leith Hospital

Francis Darcy (conductor)	Allowed home after treatment at Leith Hospital
Margaret Smith (or Murray)	Allowed home after treatment at Leith Hospital
Ellen Baxter (or Carrigan)	Allowed home after treatment at Leith Hospital
Susan Plain (or Johnstone)	Allowed home after treatment at Leith Hospital
Irene Patricia Back (or Colman)	Allowed home after treatment at Leith Hospital
Margaret Neill (or Johnstone)	Allowed home after treatment at Leith Hospital
Barbara Johnstone (or Logan)	Allowed home after treatment at Leith Hospital
Margaret Robertson	Allowed home after treatment at Leith Hospital

Although most in Edinburgh remained steadfast supporters of the war effort there were concerns over some of the political groupings who had opposed the war. The solid and worrying support for the Communist Party had continued even though many supporters privately agreed with the war, especially in view of the risk of invasion. The concerns of the authorities were eased in June after the German invasion of Russia. Once again the British Communist Party altered course and the war became a worthwhile cause with many leading British communists making ludicrous calls for the opening of a second front as the German armies made advances against the Soviets.

With most solidly behind the national war effort, the government was determined to further encourage people to become involved and to show them the efforts that were already being made. To this end the Ministry of Information continued to inform the people of Edinburgh of the ongoing war effort. One of the four mobile projection units which it had in Scotland was based in the city and during Edinburgh's Food Week the unit showed sixty-nine public film shows to a variety of groups including clubs, the WVS, works canteens, schools, church organisations, Co-operative Guilds, and Women's Guilds.

By early 1941 the Home Guard was beginning to show signs of becoming a well-trained and efficient force and the increase in available ammunition meant that target practice could be expanded. Ranges at Redford and at Hailes Quarry were used for small arms training as well as mortars and Molotov cocktails. Courses on first aid, map reading, fieldcraft and signalling were all undertaken while local cinemas got in on the act by showing short pieces offering tactical advice on a wide range of military topics including how to attack tanks. At Couper Street in Leith, street-fighting courses were held in which the Home Guards were given a thorough tactical and physical workout. 1941 also saw the introduction of regular large scale, sometimes city-wide, exercises such as Exercise Bruce which was used to test Home Guard response times, tactics and efficiency.

Despite these improvements there were still grumbles from many in the Home Guard that the organisation was being ignored by the military authorities and that greater efforts could be made to ensure that the organisation was made into a more formidable military formation. Many Home Guard units in Edinburgh and throughout south-east Scotland still felt they were being treated unfairly when it came to equipment. On 14 July the Minister for War, Captain Margesson, paid a visit to a school which was being held for 60 zone and area commanders. He admitted that there was little likelihood of the force being given equipment which could deal with heavy armour, but he was keen to reassure them that sufficient equipment to deal with light tanks would shortly be made available. 'The Home Guard feel that they are being called upon to defend their homes,' he said, 'and they must have something to do it with.' The minister concluded by telling the Home Guard that he would not pretend that 'all your troubles will be put right, but we are doing our best to overcome them. The Home Guard is a damn good show.'[3]

Minor crime continued to be a problem and the war led to increased opportunities for petty theft. The docks at Leith were extremely busy and casual labourers had to be taken on to cope with the loading and unloading of ships. In April Edinburgh Court had heard the case of five casual dock labourers who were accused of stealing bottles of whisky from a ship which they were loading. A police officer noticed that the men were drunk and the five were apprehended as they prepared to leave the dock. Bailie Douglas fined each man £2, or 20 days imprisonment if they could not pay.

Others sought to profit by passing themselves off as someone engaged in some glamorous form of war work. James J. Emery, for example, was sent to prison for three months as punishment for ten charges of fraud. Emery had been pretending to be a test pilot in the RAF and had been charged with five counts of passing worthless cheques, four of obtaining lodgings with no intention of paying and one charge of fraudulently obtaining £1 10s from a barmaid in an Edinburgh hotel.

The Luftwaffe's attacks on Clydeside during March and April took some of the pressure off the Edinburgh area although there were incidents of lost or struggling bombers dropping bombs seemingly at random in the area. On the night of 7 April, however, enemy bombers returned to the south-east of Scotland in force. The attack was widespread and no concentration developed. Serious damage was done in Leith when two land mines exploded at around 9.30 pm. The first scored a direct hit on the infants' annexe of David Kilpatrick's School causing severe damage. The school playground housed six air raid shelters and, worryingly, the blast caused three of them to collapse. The second mine fell on a railway embankment beside Largo Place and caused extensive damage to houses, shops and tenement buildings rendering a large number of people temporarily homeless. There were a number of injuries from debris and broken glass and three people were killed. This blast killed Kenneth Anderson (19) and injured his mother, two sisters and his brother. The second fatality highlighted the dangers of those working during raids when air raid messenger Ernest Smith (17) was killed. The final fatality was Janet Young (84) of North Junction Street who died of shock. Once the authorities had assessed the situation it was revealed that 37 people had been seriously injured and almost 100 more required first aid treatment. Twelve houses were demolished and 500 properties required repairs of one degree or another. The ARP, first aid, police and fire services worked tirelessly, while the rescue squads were fully employed in digging out a number of people who had been trapped in the ruins of their houses.

*Damage to David Kilpatrick's
School after raid of 7 April (TS)*

Minor raids, opposed by local RAF squadrons, continued over the course of the next month. Two days after the fatal attack on Leith, 43 Squadron was in action against marauding Junker JU88s which were raiding the south-east of Scotland and were believed to be making for Edinburgh. Amongst the pilots taking part in this action was the Belgian Battle of Britain veteran Pilot Officer Daniel A.R.G. Le Roy du Vivier.[4]

Lessons learned from the Clydebank blitz of April filtered through to Edinburgh. One was the importance of providing an adequate supply of tobacco for the morale of both civilians and ARP workers. It was decided to arrange a supply of 50,000 cigarettes to be stored in the city, and a number of groups and group leaders was formed to take them to stricken areas in the event of heavy attack. Each group was equipped with a van to transport the cigarettes and from which to sell them.

On the night of 6/7 May the Luftwaffe mounted another major attack on Clydeside and this brought further casualties to Edinburgh when a bomber making for Glasgow was caught by the Edinburgh searchlights and damaged by the city's anti-aircraft batteries. The bomber released its bombload on the city below and four exploded at Niddrie Road and Milton Crescent. Three firewatchers who had taken cover beside a wall and shelter in Milton Crescent were killed: William Dineley (37), Leonard Wilde (39) and Joseph Watson (40). Barbara Thomson (86) was killed when debris fell on her bed. The bomber also dropped over 100 incendiaries which fell around the Niddrie Road area but they were quickly extinguished.

At the end of May the news of the death of Sergeant David Alexander Heggie, RAFVR, was broken to his parents at 13 Napier Road. Sergeant Heggie (26) was the eldest son of Maurice and Ada Mary Heggie and had left the family outfitting firm of Heggie & Aitchison Ltd at the height of the Battle of Britain to join the RAF. The local press reported that Heggie had been killed while on active service but failed to give any details. Like many other unfortunate RAF recruits Sergeant Heggie had not lost his life in action against the enemy but had been killed in training. Heggie was based at 54 Operational Training Unit (OTU) at Church Fenton where he was training as a pilot and was night flying in a Boulton Paul Defiant (N1556) when an air raid warning was sounded and the airfield doused its lights. Two aircraft, Sergeant Heggie's Defiant and a Bristol Blenheim (L8377), which were in the circuit at the time were ordered to orbit at separate heights but they collided over Rakes Wood and both crashed killing their pilots. Sergeant Heggie was buried locally at Kirkby Wharfe Churchyard Extension where his parents had the following inscription placed upon his headstone 'BEYOND THE FIGHTING AND THE FRETTING HE HAS GONE HOME.'

The provision of shelter from air raids was still a problem in Edinburgh with those living in tenements particularly vulnerable. During the year Morrison shelters were introduced. Basically these were steel cages which were designed to take the place of a kitchen table and in which people could take shelter during a raid. There were problems with many of the tenement buildings as the floors proved to be in such a poor condition that they could not support the weight of the Morrison shelters.

Total war was an incredibly expensive thing and the people of Britain, keen as they were to contribute to the war effort, would have to make a monumental effort to raise funds. In Edinburgh there were extensive collections for numerous charities and for national funds which provided medical aid, guns, battleships, aircraft and other equipment. It was not only money that was necessary for the war effort, large scale efforts to collect material which could be of use to the war effort were also undertaken. Metal railings were cut down in many locations in Edinburgh to be smelted down, while housewives were urged to donate old pots and pans which, they were told, could be turned into aircraft (in fact they couldn't, but they were useful in other ways).

Sergeant D.A. Heggie, RAFVR (Unknown)

Boulton Paul Defiant similar to that in which Sgt Heggie was killed (PD)

The money raised from salvaged material which was sold to industry was also a contribution to the war effort and Scotland led the way nationally in these efforts. Edinburgh led the way in Scotland with reports that £17 per thousand people had been raised in July. During this month it was estimated that fully a quarter of all household waste in Edinburgh was salvaged for re-use. There were even plans to sell the dust screens from the refuse as fertiliser and it was estimated that this would enable three-quarters of the city's household waste to be salvaged and sold.

There was criticism from some quarters that not every institution in Edinburgh was making its contribution. In September an Edinburgh resident writing only as 'Loyal Citizen' complained to *The Scotsman* saying that local churches were not leading by example in the matter of their railings. He claimed that the churches had larger and thicker railings than most but had not had them removed for the war effort. He also claimed that his own garden railings had been removed and this was a matter of concern for him as his garden had no other protection and, he claimed, the local children destroyed gardens which were unprotected.

Metals, cloth, paper and other items were all collected and the city was festooned with posters urging people to aid the war effort and to save these items. Rags were baled to procure valuable fibre, larger items such as mattresses were burnt to salvage the metal they contained, and old bedding was taken to linoleum works where they were converted into canvas backing. Edinburgh's corporation workers were responsible for much of the collection and processing of the salvageable material. There was far too much work for just the local council workers and extra people were taken on. Many women worked, especially in the lighter roles such as the cleaning of paper but also in heavier work such as the subsequent baling of paper using heavy machinery.

*Campaign posters
in Edinburgh (TS)*

Salvageable household waste (TS)

Tins after being compressed and baled prior to smelting (TS)

Council workers separating salvageable materials (TS)

Mattresses and bedding were also salvaged (TS)

Waste paper was also cleaned and baled (TS)

Rags were baled for fibre (TS)

Women employed as
salvagers (TS)

With the merging of the AFS and the local authority fire brigade to create the National Fire Service (NFS) in August the Edinburgh AFS lost its commandant. Councillor A.H.A. Murray had been widely praised as the man responsible for the effectiveness of the Edinburgh AFS. In August, however, he left the service to take up a role as a fire inspector on the headquarters staff of the Fire Brigades Division within the Scottish Home Department. Through the last week of July the Edinburgh AFS held divisional parades in the city at which Councillor Murray bade goodbye to the men he had represented and served.

The decision of many Edinburgh shops and banks to support the Edinburgh branch of the Red Cross had been a popular one and from 1939, when the collection began, until August 1941, the fund had raised £5,000 which had purchased an ambulance which had been sent to Finland, two ambulances for use in Edinburgh, and had donated £1,000 to the Prisoners of War Fund with the remaining money being held in the fund for future use.

The army depended on a large number of civilian contractors for many things, amongst them building work and forage supplies. One of the leading forage suppliers was John Sloan Larmour (57) and at the start of the year serious allegations were made that he was bribing army officers in quartermaster positions to secure himself contracts.[5] One of the first to be tried was not the ringleader but one of his family. On 25 July, Jean Larmour of Ballycarrickmaddy, Lisburn, was tried at Belfast and found guilty of having bribed a number of army officers to £500. Her counsel pleaded that she was not the ringleader of the scheme and did not realise the seriousness of her offences and asked the bench to show leniency. However, Lord Justice Barington said that he had a duty to the public and deplored the pollution of the army's standards in this manner and sentenced her to six months' imprisonment (without hard labour). Larmour collapsed in the dock and had to be carried away screaming.

In the summer of 1941 Mr Larmour was tried for giving bribes to £1,748 (as much as £400,000 today) to various people, many of them members of the army. The High Court at Edinburgh heard how the bribes had been paid to civilian clerks working for the army or to officers and men working as quartermasters to obtain official War Department contracts, and that the crimes had been taking place for several years extending back to twelve years before the war but that Mr Larmour had not ceased this practice when the country was facing its most serious crisis in 1940. The Advocate-Depute, Mr R. Sherwood Calver, said that 'one would have expected even the unscrupulous contractor to develop, however belatedly, a sense of decency' during wartime and stated that the crimes had amounted to a systematic attempt to corrupt those to whom the bribes were paid and 'to seduce them from their public duty'.[6] As a major contractor Mr Larmour's scheme had not been confined to Scotland but had extended to England and Northern Ireland. A breakdown of the payments showed they had been made in Edinburgh, Belfast, Glasgow, Perth and South Queensferry and that the sums included £449 to a man in Belfast, £215 to an army officer in Edinburgh, £138 to an Edinburgh clerk, and sums from £182 down to £5 to various members of the forces.

Defending Mr Larmour, Mr D.P. Blades appeared shocked by the vehemence of the prosecution's tone and said that if he had known of it in advance he would never have advised his client to plead guilty. He attempted to portray Mr Larmour as both a loyal, patriotic expert and a businessman who had been simply a victim of corruption that, he alleged, was rife within the contracts system of the army. He told how Mr Larmour had enlisted in the Royal Army Service Corps aged just 18 and had served in the army for nine years before being placed on the reserve list. When he left the army he had put his knowledge of the contracts system to good use and had started his own business as a contractor supplying the army with forage, sanitary services and hospital supplies. He had, according to his defence, performed excellent service during this time and had even received a commendation from the War Office for his service (it would seem that Mr Larmour did not serve during the First World War even though he would have been aged 30 at its outbreak – presumably his services as a contractor allowed him to avoid being recalled).

Mr Blades went on to say that the knowledge of the amount of money which a contract had been awarded for was precious to any such businessman and that such 'information was not passed for nothing. That information was not infrequently accompanied by a threat that if the person giving the information did not receive a douceur for having passed the information he would, by giving an adverse report upon the execution of a contract' have that contractor removed from the list of approved contractors and so would severely affect their future business. Thus Mr Blades alleged that the practice of army officers and civilian clerks seeking bribes for confidential information was widespread and even a tacitly accepted part of the business. In an attempt to portray his client as the innocent victim, Mr Blades stated that in all cases army personnel had approached his client rather than his client corrupting innocent army officers. He said that although his client admitted that in the last fourteen years he had gained contracts worth £25,000 from the illegal obtaining of information, this was from a total of contracts worth £700,000.

Mr Blades informed the court that Mr Larmour's continued work was of the utmost national importance and that nobody could take over the business if his client was found guilty and imprisoned. He informed the bench that Mr Larmour had extensive agricultural interests in Northern Ireland, he owned substantial farmland at Ballycarrickmaddy, Magheragall, Lisburn, and that the Ministry of Agriculture in Ireland had 'been using all their powers in order to get Mr Larmour back to Ireland to attend to those interests'.[7]

In summing up Mr Blades said that Mr Larmour was 'more the victim of circumstances ... than anything in the nature of a seducer' and argued that the matter of the illegally obtained contracts could surely be settled by the imposition of a fine rather than any custodial sentence as this would allow Mr Larmour to 'carry on the public work which is of the utmost importance at the present time'.[8]

Mr Calver responded that the matter of Mr Larmour's work being of national importance was irrelevant; he had been informed by the Army Council that whatever the decision of the bench, Mr Larmour 'would never have the opportunity in the future of discharging contracts of this kind'.[9]

Thanks to the thoroughness of the police investigation into Mr Larmour the case had several sequels which rumbled on for the next year. Two months after Mr Larmour had been imprisoned, fifteen people, including army officers, appeared privately in Edinburgh's Sheriff's Court charged with contravening the Prevention of Corruption Act in connection with bribes paid by Mr Larmour. Some were accused under the Official Secrets Act. This was because much of the information that had been passed to Mr Lamrour involved details not only about army contracts but also details of camp locations and movements as well as coastal defences.

On 22 October a civil servant working in Scottish Command, Robert Addison (51), was sentenced to prison for nine months. Addison had admitted his guilt in breaching the Official Secrets Act by passing information to Larmour for money over a period of twenty years. Addison had been a civil servant for 27 years and had previously been of good character but evidence found in the office of Mr Larmour left it in no doubt that Mr Addison had been supplying information to him from 1920 to 1940 and that much had been secret and concerned information on army camps and pending contracts. In mitigation his counsel said that the main thread through all of the evidence against his client and others was that they had been used as pawns 'by a master mind, the master mind being the Army contractor, Larmour'.[10] He also stated that in committing these offences his client had lost his gratuity, pension rights and had brought disgrace upon his family. He added, rather unrealistically, that Mr Addison had not realised the seriousness of what he had done as he believed at the time that the information was not vital.

On the same day Private Vincent O'Connor (28) was sent to prison for six months after he admitted accepting bribes (over £11) from Mr Larmour to remove tenders for army contracts from mail which he was dutybound to collect from the Post Office; he was acting as a mail orderly and messenger, so Mr Larmour could open them and read them before they were delivered to Army HQ. The court heard how Private O'Connor had served in the Black Watch between 1931 and 1938 and had been recalled at the start of the war. The Sheriff said that although he had to take the matter seriously, he realised that O'Connor was the tool of others in the matter and had got himself 'mixed up in an ugly and very dirty business'.[11]

Three days later another related case was heard. This case highlighted how once one man had become involved, a spider's web of illicit actions could be established through word of mouth as one man involved a friend in the deceit. The trial was that of a War Office clerk, William John Ross (39), who admitted accepting payments amounting to over £138 from Larmour in exchange for information regarding army tenders and work done at army camps. Again letters had been found in the possession of Larmour which confirmed the accused's complicity. Ross's defence explained how his client had become involved with Larmour when he had been introduced by a friend who was already accepting money from him (this was one of the men previously sentenced). On this first occasion Larmour took the two men to lunch at a hotel and at the end of the lunch slipped a 10 shilling note into Ross's hand. Ross asked his friend why he had done this and was told that Larmour often gave the clerks money for a drink. In the course of his duties and in subsequent meetings with Larmour, Ross realised that Larmour had access to information regarding contracts and camps which even he did not know. By the time he had begun relaying information to Larmour he explained that his client had already accepted quite a lot of money and that he 'felt under an obligation'.[12] In this case the Sheriff seems to have taken a hard line and he sentenced Ross to fifteen months imprisonment.

On the 28th three more cases were heard in relation to the Larmour case. Two clerks who had in the past been employed by the RASC, John Ferrie (41) and Edward Morris (47), admitted contravention of the Official Secrets Act and the Prevention of Corruption Act and were sentenced to two years' imprisonment each. Ferrie was a married man with four children and had given Larmour information about tenders, contracts, camps and movement of troops and had been paid over £182 as, he told the court, he had been badly in need of money following a spell of unemployment during the war. Ferrie had been at first involved by an associate who was already involved. Morris, who was at the time working for the NAAFI, had admitted accepting over £126 between 1938 and 1940. This had been in exchange for communicating to Larmour the details of troop movements, lists of contractors applying for tenders, and copies of letters from Scottish Command. He also admitted that he had failed to send tenders out to some firms and had suggested to Larmour what bids might be successful. Morris had served in the Army for 21 years and had retired as a warrant officer in 1935. His solicitor said in mitigation that his client had spent much of the money on drink, that Larmour had always been free with his money (even when not receiving information), that since his employment in the NAAFI at the start of the war he had been unable to provide any useful information and that the breaches of the Official Secrets Act had been committed before the war began.

The third case was that of Lieutenant Joseph William Partridge, Royal Artillery, who appeared before the court in uniform and wearing a medal ribbon from the First World War. Partridge also admitted contravention of the Prevention of Corruption Act. Partridge (45) had joined the RASC in 1937 as a corporal after service in the army of 23 years (he was transferred to the Royal Artillery and commissioned in May 1941) and between 1937 and 1938 had received just over £85 from Larmour for giving him information, obtaining army contracts and for ensuring that contracts for the army only went to Larmour. Sheriff Principal Brown felt some pity for Partridge, who had applied for the transfer to the Royal Artillery as he was worried about his previous contact with Larmour; he also took into account his previous service and said that he was treating the case as 'only fairly bad and not very bad' and sentenced him to nine months' imprisonment.

The case was an incredibly serious one with the country still struggling to bring in necessary supplies, and with the army on the defensive it is no surprise that the plea of being a victim would not find much sympathy, either in society or the establishment. With the defendant having pleaded guilty to the bribery charges and with the strong suspicions that, perhaps, the matter was even more serious than the trial had allowed for, Lord Stevenson imposed a sentence of three years penal servitude on Mr Larmour.

In December the case had spread its tendrils to London and a Lieutenant Gerald Patrick Walsh, RASC, was summonsed before West London Police Court accused of having accepted bribes amounting to £3 from Edinburgh-based Mr Larmour when he was a corporal in the RASC in 1938. At this time Walsh (33) had been employed as a clerk at Kensington Barracks where he had access to information on army forage supplies. When Larmour's property in Edinburgh was searched the police found 140 letters from Walsh which made it obvious that he had been receiving money from Larmour since 1930. It was a familiar tale, with the young soldier accepting payments and then feeling he was in Larmour's power and unable to resist further demands. In 1933 Walsh had an attack of conscience and went to the police where he made a full confession. Hearing of this (the sources do not say how) Larmour called Walsh before him and 'threatened him with direct penalties' whereupon Walsh was intimidated and tore up the confession in front of Larmour. Mr Larmour later apparently pasted the confession together, as it was found during the police search. Walsh pleaded guilty and admitted that in all he had accepted bribes of £40-£50 but that since the outbreak of war when he was commissioned he had refused to accept any further bribes from Larmour.[13]

Given the stringencies of the rationing system it is no surprise that there were criminal elements who sought to exploit the system either to profit from the resale of rationed items or simply to obtain extras for themselves and their families. The first case of someone fraudulently using ration books reported lost took place in December. The allegation was that between 1 April and 29 May 1940 a Mrs Violet Smith (also known as Potter or Johnston) of 9 Hay Avenue had stated to the authorities that two ration books from her household had been lost. She had been given replacements and then gone to her grocer on two or three occasions per week (using different ration books) to obtain rationed items. The grocer had become suspicious and reported the matter. Upon investigation the two books supposedly lost were discovered and the names on them had been altered to Mrs Smith's married and maiden names. The court heard testimony from a handwriting expert who stated that the writing was Mrs Smith's and she was found guilty and sentenced to one month's imprisonment.

Milk was a valuable commodity and in the same month a Robina Ella Scott (also known as Chapman) of 9 Orwell Place admitted having obtained by fraudulent applications some 683 pints of free milk between 1 April and 25 October. Her defence argued that Scott's household income was only £3 3s per week (compared to an average of £5 3s 8½d) and that she had four children (aged between 1 and 5).

The sheriff, however, said that cases like this were becoming all too common and he could no show leniency; he sentenced Scott to three week's imprisonment.

Local men who had been awarded medals were often named in the press. Sometimes accounts were told, often drawn from the official gazette, but increasingly just the bare bones of the award were mentioned, along with perhaps some personal details. In October *The Scotsman* carried the announcement of the award of the DFM to RAF navigator Sergeant David Bowie. Sergeant Bowie was born in 1914 in Musselburgh but had moved to Devon at some point and worked as a clerk before he enlisted in the RAF in 1935. He was awarded his DFM for his service while flying Bristol Beaufighters with 252 Squadron of Coastal Command. No other details were given.[14]

War Weapons Weeks were extremely effective ways for the government to raise funds for the war effort and were good for morale. Edinburgh had prided itself on its success in these drives and this continued to the end of 1941 with the city's Warship Week which took place in December. The organisation which went into these campaigns was impressive with donations being collected by street groups, industrial groups, private donations and other means. The announcement of the Warships Week found enthusiasm amongst all sections of Edinburgh society, which was unsurprising given the presence of a major naval base. Before the campaign had even got underway many of Edinburgh and Leith's institutions had already pledged funds: Standard Property Investment Co, Edinburgh University, The Royal College of Surgeons, Edinburgh Merchant Company, Edinburgh Royal Infirmary, the Astley-Ainslie Institute, the Church of Scotland Trust, the Highland and Agricultural Society of Scotland, George Heriot's Trust, the Widows Fund of the Society of Writers to the Signet, the Edinburgh Chartered Accountants' Annuity Fund, the Police-Aided Scheme for Destitute Children, the Royal Bank of Scotland Widows' Fund, the Grand Lodge of Scotland, and the Royal Incorporation of Architects in Scotland.

In Leith a target of £1,000,000 had been set and a week before the campaign got underway the Lord Provost could announce that he had received promises of £600,000. Many industrial concerns of Leith were involved: James Currie & Co. (shipowners), George Gibson & Co, A.F. Henry & MacGregor, Kersans Ltd, Leith Salvage and Towage Co, Henry Robb & Co, C. Salvesen & Co, William Thomson & Co (Ben Line Steamers Ltd.), J. Tod & Sons, D.J. Thomson & Co, William Crawford & Sons, Leith Provident Co-operative Society, MacDonald & Muir, Scottish Co-operative Wholesale Society, James Bertram & Son, Garland & Roger, Park Dobson & Co, London & Edinburgh Shipping, William Fergus Harris & Son, British Ropes, and Scott-Lyon Ltd.

Edinburgh school children were already playing a part in the war savings effort, but it was felt that the Warships Week would catch their imaginations. It was decided to promote a prize essay competition based on the theme. Lord Provost Darling stated that the prizes would be savings certificates and that although the competition meant a little more work for the city's teachers he remained confident that they would throw themselves fully behind it.

While the War Weapons fund was being tallied, the Red Cross penny-a-week fund was continuing to collect money throughout the city. During the week £457 was raised and it was reported that over the last 49 weeks the fund had raised £17,089. The East Lothian branch of the Red Cross was able to provide a grant of £500 to the work of the Red Cross overseas; it pointed out that it was unable to increase this grant as they had also agreed to take on responsibility for servicemen from the area who had been taken prisoner and not yet adopted by other charities.

In December it was announced that from 5 January 1942 many non-vital rubber items would only be manufactured under licence. Anticipating a shortage there was a rush to buy hot water bottles and queues developed at shops in the city. One shop owner on George Street reported that some customers were attempting to buy several bottles even though there was at present an adequate supply. He said that one customer had attempted to purchase twelve bottles but he had limited customers to just two, although he said that if someone could prove they were buying on behalf of, for example, a nursing home, he would relax this. A shop owner from Princes Street warned that people were panic buying assuming that supplies would be limited but warned that if the 'demand for hot-water bottles continues, stocks may be exhausted by another year. Only those people who really need a bottle should buy one.'[15]

Local golfers were also worried about the restrictions on rubber, facing a scarcity of new balls. Sellers were rationing players to just two per customer and many a young Edinburgh boy took a break from collecting shrapnel and other wartime mementoes to go hunting for lost golf balls to be resold to desperate sportsmen. Other threatened rubber items were tennis balls, Wellington boots, galoshes, and rubber overshoes.

Of course the rubber manufacturing industry in Edinburgh had replaced orders for golf and tennis balls with far more profitable orders for materials vital to the war effort, and the North British Rubber Company continued to turn a healthy profit with its wartime activities.

CHAPTER 4

1942

As the New Year opened, the aftershocks of the Larmour scandal again hit the headlines when yet another civilian clerk employed by the RASC was tried for accepting bribes (this time £7) from Larmour in respect of contracts to supply the army. Described as 'an innocent dupe who had become embroiled in the mesh of a nefarious scheme', George C. Munro seems to have been as much a victim as a criminal. The court heard how he had been involved in only a minor way and that he had been 'rather led into it by his superiors' and that it 'would be fair to say that accused had been both tricked and terrorised'.[1] Acknowledging these facts the court sentenced Munro to a fine of £20.

The Merchant Navy was doing a fine job in exceptionally hazardous conditions and suffering appalling casualties, but the lack of glamour in this service was irksome to some. In January the Sheriff's Court at Edinburgh heard a case of a man who had been accused of masquerading as a lieutenant in the RNVR. It was said that Francis Hugh Morrison, a radio operator in the Merchant Navy, had been challenged by the police in an Edinburgh hotel when seen wearing the insignia of an RNVR lieutenant on his Merchant Navy uniform. When charged, Morrison, of Burntisland Place, admitted that he had bought the insignia and had fastened them onto his uniform. It was acknowledged that there had been nothing sinister behind this; it rather appeared to have been simple vanity on the part of Morrison. Taking this into account the sheriff ordered Morrison to pay a fine of £5.

For many Edinburgh youths who were just too young to join up, the war could provide a background of excitement and adventure and many joined various associations set up by the armed forces. The Air Training Corps (ATC) had proved particularly popular since its creation in 1941 and by January 1942 there were 15,000 members in Scotland. This was undoubtedly partly because of the glamour of the Battle of Britain pilots. Many of the youngsters in Edinburgh had of course witnessed British fighter aircraft pursuing enemy bombers above their heads.

It had been obvious for some time that the campaign being conducted by RAF Bomber Command was failing to seriously impact the enemy and was being fought at an extremely high cost in the lives of British and Allied aircrew. As a result of the Butt Report which highlighted the inaccuracy and waste of the campaign, the commanding officer, Air Marshal Sir Richard Pierse, was removed in early January. The campaign was temporarily restricted and there was much debate over the future of the force and the entire bombing campaign of the RAF.

These restrictions resulted in a fairly quiet winter for the command although several raids were still made against German cities when conditions were ideal.

The main focus of the command during the winter months was the port cities of northern Germany and France. Many of the sorties flown during this period involved minelaying in the waters off these ports and in areas used by Axis shipping. One of the primary targets was the port of Brest and on the night of 3/4 January the command sent fourteen Wellingtons and four Stirlings to bomb it, while ten Hampdens were dispatched to lay mines in waters off the port and in the Frisians. Even these relatively simple operations could be very dangerous and on this night the command lost two aircraft. Hampden I (AT123) of 106 Squadron took off from RAF Coningsby shortly before 5 pm to lay mines off the Frisians but nothing more was heard from Pilot Officer D.A. Howard DFM and his crew and the aircraft was posted missing. One of the wireless operator/air gunners in the four-man crew was Flight Sergeant Kenneth McKenzie DFM who was a native of Leith. McKenzie was aged 20 and had served with 106 Squadron for some time receiving the DFM on 18 July 1941 (the same time as his pilot). He left behind his parents Kenneth and Susan, and a brother, Lance Corporal John McKenzie, and, with his crew, is commemorated on the Runnymede Memorial to the Missing. The parents were left with an anxious wait as all they could be told at first was that their son was missing after operations and it was not until July that they were informed that he could now be presumed dead.[2]

On 30 January there was a disaster when an Edinburgh-Glasgow express train collided with a stationary coal train at Cowlairs. The accident was down to a signalling error compounded by the blackout conditions and resulted in the express train hitting the back of the stationary train. Fourteen people lost their lives and twenty-five were injured. The driver of the freight train was an Edinburgh man, Charles Robertson of Ardmillan Terrace. Robertson was pinned underneath a coal truck and had serious injuries, including a partially severed leg. A 23-year-old Edinburgh doctor who had been a passenger on the express, assisted by two medical students and a Polish doctor, amputated Mr Robertson's leg using only a pen-knife and a pair of scissors so that the he could be taken to hospital; unfortunately Mr Robertson died in hospital.

An Edinburgh airman, Aircraftman 2nd Class George Thomas of the 945th Balloon Squadron, was on his way back to his unit after leave and was seriously injured in the crash. His wife rushed to his side in Glasgow but Thomas lost his life on 1 February; *The Sunday Post* published a photograph of him in their account of the accident. Thomas (40) lived at 4 Murdoch Crescent and had three children. The youngest, George Winston (he was born on Churchill's birthday) was aged thirteen months; his second child, Nancy, was 12, and his eldest son, William, was aged 19 and in the RAF. Aircraftman Thomas had seen William off back to his unit just two hours before he boarded the ill-fated train.

Aircraftman George Thomas and his son, George Winston (TS)

Just over a month after the death of Flight Sergeant McKenzie DFM, the minelaying campaign against the Frisians claimed another Edinburgh victim. On 7 February Bomber Command launched a daylight raid using 32 Hampdens but it was detected. German fighters were vectored into the area and three of the bombers were shot down. One was Hampden I (AE306) of 50 Squadron, piloted by Flight Sergeant R.N. Smith. It had taken off from Skellingthorpe just after noon and was shot down into the sea off Terschelling by an ME 109 flown by Oberfeldewebel Detlef Luth; all four crew were killed.[3]

The validity of the campaign was now under serious question for the second time in the war (the first being after the early daylight bombing debacles of 1939 and 1940) and powerful voices argued for the command to be reduced in size and restricted to a tactical role. Others argued that the best way to defeat Germany was by bombing its cities into submission and that Bomber Command should therefore be built up to a force of 4,000 aircraft (mostly being the new four-engined heavy bombers which had recently come into service). Sir Charles Portal, in a wildly optimistic claim to Churchill, argued that if this force was in place Germany would collapse within six months. Churchill was a supporter of strategic bombing but was not taken in by this optimism. He told Portal there was no way the stretched economy could be shifted to provide such a force but that he would continue to back the force at its current size, expanding when possible. On 22 February Air Chief Marshal Sir Arthur Harris was appointed commander of Bomber Command with orders to implement the newly fashioned area bombing campaign. Harris knew he had to establish successes almost instantly and initiated a series of audacious operations. On the night of 8/9 March he launched one of his first major area raids on Essen. The city was always a difficult target to hit due to the thick industrial haze which surrounded it, along with fearsome defences. On this night the command dispatched 211 bombers (115 Wellingtons, 37 Hampdens, 27 Stirlings, 22 Manchesters, and 10 Halifaxes) but results were poor with most bombs falling on the southern outskirts of the city and the main target, the Krupp factory, not being hit; eight aircraft failed to return. Amongst the aircraft lost was Manchester I (R5779, OL-G) of 83 Squadron. The bomber had taken off from Scampton shortly before 2 am but nothing further was heard and it transpired that it had been shot down in flames by a night-fighter and crashed at Drenthe killing five of the seven-man crew. The second pilot (at the time inexperienced pilots flew operations as second pilot to gain experience) was an Edinburgh man, Sergeant James Thomson Heggie Mowat. Mowat was just 18, the son of Thomas and Georgina Mowat of Gilmore Place.[4]

The Ben Line of Leith had already suffered losses and on 5 March the company suffered another. Around 11 pm the SS *Benmohr* was steaming 210 miles from Freetown with a cargo of silver bullion, pig iron and rubber bound for Freetown when it was torpedoed by U-505. The ship sank but the entire crew of 56 were rescued by an RAF Sunderland flying boat.

The army was in action in several theatres including against the Japanese in Burma. This 'Forgotten Army' was not, in fact, forgotten, certainly not by the friends and family of those who were serving in this gruelling theatre of war. Amongst the many Edinburgh men serving here was 24-year-old 2nd Lieutenant Thomas Blane Moodie, 2nd Anti-Tank Regiment, Royal Artillery. Before the war Moodie had been training as an accountant with the Edinburgh firm of Maxton, Graham & Sime. He had just passed his final examination and was embarking on his apprenticeship. In 1940 he gave up this promising career and enlisted in the RA as a gunner but was commissioned in 1941 and posted to Burma. By March 1942 Moodie was serving on attachment to the 6th Anti-Tank Battery of the Royal Indian Artillery. On 24 March he was killed in action during the fighting at Toungoo.[5] His body was never recovered and he is commemorated on the Rangoon Memorial.

As has been previously mentioned, many of the defences which were constructed at vulnerable points in the city had interfered with the safe flow of traffic. By 1942 the situation was so problematic that Edinburgh police undertook a survey of accident blackspots in the city and focused particularly on those near to newly constructed pillboxes. They quickly established that many were indeed causing problems and had contributed to 155 accidents which had injured 55 people. The defences outside Redford Barracks acquired notoriety due to a fatal accident, while that on the corner of Princes Street and Lothian Road had witnessed over forty accidents with nearly a score of injuries. Many of the pillboxes had been positioned in such a way that they created blind and tight bends on what were already busy roads and were especially hazardous in blackout conditions.

In February the Commandant in Scotland (the Duke of Hamilton AFC) and the officer responsible for the Edinburgh and South East Scotland area (Wing Commander J.L Chalmers MC) launched a week-long campaign to boost recruitment to the ATC. This was open to any boy aged 15½ to 18 who was not already associated with another youth movement. The Edinburgh and South East Scotland area had twenty-four squadrons and four independent flights with the Edinburgh squadrons (under the command of Squadron Leader A.H. Bruce). The youths of Edinburgh had been enthusiastic: 21 per cent aged 15-17 were already members. There were 1,500 members in Edinburgh and many former members had gone on to join the RAF or Fleet Air Arm and were making reputations for themselves.

The ATC week was to begin with a church parade at St. Giles' Cathedral (Roman Catholic members attended a service at Randolph Place Chapel and Episcopalian members at St. Mary's Cathedral) followed by a route march through the city culminating in the salute being taken at the Mound by Lord Provost William Y. Darling. Key to the recruitment drive would be the invitation to the parents of interested youths to examine the training that their sons would receive in the ATS. This included drill, aircraft recognition and (an emphasis was placed on this) instruction by RAF and civilian experts in a variety of technical trades. Wing Commander Chalmers was at pains to point out that without the time voluntarily given by the civilian instructors the work of the ATC would be impossible and he reserved especial praise for the 200 or so volunteer instructors.

The residents of the Parkhead and Sighthill districts had long been complaining about the lack of facilities, especially public transport, in parts of their area. Having got nowhere, in February it was decided to hold a meeting to establish interest in setting up a ratepayers' association to place pressure on the Town Council to listen to their grievances. The meeting was held at Murrayburn School where the school hall was filled to overflowing. Representing the council were Baillie Margaret Geddes and Councillor Hamilton Gray. Their speeches were followed by a lively question and answer session which brought both criticisms and suggestions by the residents. A popular suggestion was that the buses in the city be converted to run on gas as had been done in many other towns across Britain. The proposal to form a ratepayers' association was unanimously approved.

The local and national press ran many stories informing people of the awards made to members of the forces for their gallantry. During February one article highlighted the courage of a young Edinburgh airman serving as a wireless operator/air gunner with 144 Squadron who had been awarded the DFM. Sergeant Lewis Powrie (21) had flown with 144 Squadron for some time. Flying Handley Page Hampden bombers as part of Bomber Command, Powrie had operated against some of the most heavily defended targets in Germany including operations to Bremen, Frankfurt, Kiel, Mannheim and Wilhelmshaven. In November 1941 he had written home to his mother at her 5 Arboretum Road home describing a low-level attack which he had been a part of. He described how they had attacked a large and well defended German convoy off the Frisian Isles, sinking the largest ship. He graphically described the attack. The weather had been so poor that the crew had to fly at 50 feet, just so that they could see the surface of the sea, and had flown over the convoy before turning to attack. The pilot had exclaimed to the navigator/bomb aimer, 'Pick the second so-and-so: it's the biggest.' They dropped their bombs onto the ship from just 30 feet and saw a direct hit. Powrie said, 'It was a grand show, and I wouldn't have missed it for anything.'[6]

At around this time, Edinburgh Sheriff's Court was concluding the trials which had become commonly known as the Larmour series. At the beginning of February a case was heard which resulted in a rare acquittal. The accused was another member

of the RASC, Sergeant Arthur Emrys Owen, who was accused of taking bribes from Larmour in exchange for information on government tenders while he was employed as a chief clerk at Leith Fort. Opening for the prosecution was a detective constable who testified that when Larmour had been arrested, Owen's name had been found in his ledgers of payments and that when arrested Owen had said, 'Thank goodness: I want to get it over.'

Larmour's nephew testified that his uncle had told him to pay several RASC clerks off the books and that he knew Owen and that his uncle had visited Owen at his house. Under cross-examination by Owen's solicitor, Miss M.M. Logan, Larmour junior admitted that he had never heard Owen giving his uncle information or accepting bribes from his uncle.

Sergeant Powrie described an attack on an enemy convoy he took part in (EEN)

The next witness was Edward Morris, one of those who had already been imprisoned for his part in the corruption scandal, who testified that Larmour had given him £1 to treat Owen to drinks as he suspected that Owen had realised that he (Morris) was in the pay of Larmour. Morris said that he didn't think Owen knew anything and that he had never seen Owen with Larmour.

Finally, Larmour himself was called as a witness but, unsurprisingly, he proved to be a hostile witness who determinedly resisted the judiciary. He testified that he had met Owen in various bars but did not know him well and had no idea how he was employed. When asked if he had visited Owen at his house in Leith he said that he did not remember and when pressed refused to either confirm or deny it. He then claimed that many of the names in his books were made up as he did not keep particularly accurate records and he made up entries to make up the money as it appeared in his accounts. Warned by the sheriff of further punishment if he continued to prevaricate, Larmour simply said that the experiences he had gone through had been traumatic and that he could not remember details anymore. He was then asked whether or not he had paid out thousands of pounds to various army clerks in the last year or two but he answered that he had not paid 'out thousands of pounds'. Larmour continued to obfuscate and prevaricate through the remainder of his testimony, repeatedly claiming that he could not remember. Even though there were no witnesses for the defence, the sheriff said that although 'the case reeked with suspicion' there was no evidence to support the charge of taking bribes to the amount claimed, that Larmour's evidence was 'worthless' and that there was no corroboration of much of the evidence that had been given; he had no choice but to direct the jury to reach a not guilty verdict and acquit Owen.[7]

Two days later another clerk employed by the RASC, James John Green, was brought before the Sheriff's Court. Charged with accepting bribes of £17 10s Green pleaded not guilty and the prosecution called witnesses. This evidence was weakened by the fact that, in view of Larmour's unreliability as a witness, his diary had been declared as inadmissible and therefore the Procurator Fiscal reduced the amount in question to £8. Despite Green's protestations of innocence and claims that he had nothing do with contracts or tenders, letters discovered in the possession of Larmour were signed by Green and involved matters such as the strength of certain army units and items regarding the supply of hay, oats, straw and wood to army camps. One letter was particularly incriminating and was signed, 'Trusting this is what you want – J.G.' Larmour's nephew again gave evidence, saying that his uncle had instructed him to pay £1 to Green but that, at the time, he believed this was because Green had helped his uncle to clear up some late payments. Cross-examined by Miss Logan, he admitted that some army contracts were paid on time but others lapsed and became late and that he did not know if Green was showing favour to his uncle. However, he also testified that he was aware that his uncle wanted to obtain information of tenders and contracts as such information was valuable when bidding for future contracts.

Larmour was called and again was uncooperative, claiming that he could not remember facts and even going so far as to say that when he had previously pleaded guilty at the High Court to paying Green he had done so 'foolishly'. He said that the many entries next to Green's name in his books were guesswork and that he could not remember details. When shown a letter from Green to him on which it was claimed he had also written a response, and asked if the writing was indeed his own, he attempted to prevaricate and was cautioned by the sheriff: 'Be careful, Mr Larmour.' At this he reluctantly admitted that the writing 'was very like "his own scribble"'.[8] Green was then called to the stand and declared that he was employed in stores but that he could not have given information on the strength of army units and had merely done his job in ensuring that overdue bills were paid to Mr Larmour. Under examination he admitted that he had once accepted £2 from Mr Larmour but that he had been told that this was simply a small gift from Larmour for the work which he had performed in ensuring the contracts were paid up. The jury decided by six votes to one to convict Green and he was sentenced to one month in prison.

The following day another RASC soldier found himself before the sheriff. Warrant Officer Thomas Laing was accused of accepting bribes to the value of £7 for supplying information to Larmour. Larmour's nephew testified that on the instruction of his uncle he had, on three separate occasions, paid Laing money to the total amount of £7. With the evidence against him Laing had little choice but to plead guilty and he was sentenced to three months in prison.

In late February there was yet another case. This one involved Lieutenant Charles Arthur William Flood, RASC, who stood accused of accepting bribes amounting to £205 from John Sloan Larmour and of a payment at the start of the war (when Flood was a warrant officer) of over £12 by Larmour on behalf of Flood to a firm of contractors to remove the lieutenant's furniture from Edinburgh to near Chester. Lieutenant Flood was stationed at Leith Fort and it was alleged that he had consulted with Larmour over the possible location of new gun sites. During the period the charges referred to (September 1939 to November 1940) the army was frantically building up its coastal defences in anticipation of a Nazi invasion. Valuable contracts were available and Flood, as a quartermaster, held considerable sway when the awards of such contracts were decided at a local level. In addition to this the numbers of soldiers, sailors and airmen in the Edinburgh area meant that new camps had been constructed, and there were contracts available for providing forage and other supplies. Although Flood denied the charges a former secretary in Larmour's office confirmed that although she did not know Flood personally she could confirm that someone of that name telephoned Larmour on a regular basis and that a cheque she was shown for over £12 was signed for the purpose of moving Flood's furniture to England. Mr Larmour's nephew (John Sloan Larmour junior), a driver in the RASC who had been brought over from Ireland to work for his uncle in 1937, confirmed that he had pored over a map with Flood in order to establish sites for new gun positions at Leith Fort and that the cheque for over £12 was indeed to fund the removal of Lieutenant Flood's furniture. Under questioning Larmour refused to either confirm or deny the payments made to Flood and said that he was uncertain over the matter of fourteen monthly entries in his books for payments of £10 apiece to someone called Flood. Mr Larmour then, somewhat unconvincingly, said that he believed that he may have spent the money referred to on drink. Appearing on behalf of Lieutenant Flood, his commanding officer testified that his 'conduct and work were exemplary. "He was the best quartermaster I had in my area".'[9] Taking this into account and the fact that with Larmour refusing to confirm the payments except for one of £15 which had earlier been confirmed, the Procurator Fiscal agreed to reduce the amounts concerned in the charges to £15 plus the fee of the removal of furniture although the question of the missing £190 would also be investigated later.[10]

A trial in March involved a recently promoted army officer. Showing the scope of Larmour's activities the charges were heard in Liverpool and dated back to 1928. Lieutenant Walter Boyd Paul (39) had in 1929 been a sergeant chief clerk with the 55th West Lancashire Territorial Division and thus had access to information regarding the prices of camp provisions and details of future tender opportunities. When Larmour was arrested there were thirty-nine letters from Paul found in his possession. Two of the letters related to the charges of accepting bribes of £5 for information supplied. Paul pleaded guilty and admitted that in the course of his acquaintance with Larmour he had accepted payments totalling approximately £30. Lieutenant Paul brought forward several witnesses to testify to his previous good character. He had enlisted in the army aged 17 and had worked his way thought the ranks before being commissioned in 1939. During his service he had been awarded the MBE for his service in Palestine and Northern Ireland. When he was arrested in August 1941 he had been a temporary captain but had been reduced in rank to lieutenant and suffered the loss of pay. Except for his interaction with Larmour he had been an exemplary soldier and officer and his representative argued that conviction would risk him losing his commission altogether; he therefore urged the magistrate to place Lieutenant Paul on probation. While the magistrate recognised Paul's good qualities he said that he could not overlook the seriousness of the matter even if the information provided would have been of no 'use to an enemy' and he had no choice but to impose a sentence of one month's imprisonment.[11] Paul's counsel then informed the magistrate of their intention to appeal against the sentence and asked for bail in the amount of £10 for his client, which was granted.

In June another commissioned officer in the RASC was tried for accepting bribes and revealing information to Larmour. The trial at Edinburgh High Court again revealed the huge web that had been spun by Larmour, one of the witnesses claiming that it was 'common knowledge that contract clerks always get a back-hander from the contractor'. The accused, Lieutenant Horace Browning, had been a private soldier who had enlisted in 1925 before rising through the ranks and being commissioned. Accused of accepting bribes worth £128 12s 7d in the period August 1937 to March 1940 and of passing classified documents to Larmour regarding army camps, contracts and tenders, Browning pleaded not guilty to all charges. His defence again played on the defendant's fine record of service, claiming that his service had been 'in every respect perfect' other than his involvement with Larmour when an NCO.[12] The judge was also told that Browning was a married man of 40 with three young sons and that his family would suffer if he was sentenced unduly harshly. Since the beginning of the war Browning had been on active service and had been wounded during the siege of Tobruk in 1941 before being evacuated back to the UK to face the charges brought against him. Lord Justice Clerk said that Browning had betrayed his 'public duty under circumstances which I am bound to regard as of serious gravity…

In imposing sentence… I must also have regard to the sentences already imposed on others concerned in similar offences.' He sentenced Browning to 2½ years in prison.[13]

Monday, 20 April, was a spring holiday and people in Edinburgh ignored the governments stay-at-home appeal. Many public houses in the centre of the city did not open, largely due to publicans' fears that their limited stocks would not be enough to cope with a holiday rush. This caused much resentment and even the president of the Edinburgh Licensed Trade Association said that the publicans should realise they were 'servants of the public' and that it was a breach not to open for the licensed hours (12-3 and 5-10 pm). He added that while spirits were in short supply, beer was not and shutting would only damage trade in the future. One publican who had opened, interviewed by a reporter from *The Scotsman*, confirmed this view saying, 'Spirits are scarce but we are well off for beer.'[14]

For some people in Edinburgh if they had their way the closure of the public houses would become permanent. A united temperance demonstration held at Carrubber's Close Mission passed a resolution expressing to the government 'the necessity for taking immediate action to stop the waste of valuable grain and sugar in the manufacture of beer' and also asked the government to curtail the availability of intoxicating liquor as it represented a threat to young people. They argued that production of beer was still at pre-war levels and that 600,000 tons of barley and sugar, equivalent to six weeks' ration for the whole of Britain, were used every year for beer making. This was a minority view and it is not surprising that the letter sent to the government was ignored.

Despite the support of the railway companies and the Scottish Motor Traction Company for the stay-at-home appeal, large numbers queued for buses in the city. At St. Andrew Square the queues included hikers wearing backpacks, golfers with their clubs and anglers with their fishing rods. Waverley and Princes Street Stations were also very busy with popular destinations including Glasgow and Fife.

As the Home Guard became more proficient and received better equipment, the Home Guardsmen took over an ever-increasing roster of roles. In April the Lord Provost appealed for men, especially those who had served in the artillery during the last war, to volunteer for the newly forming Home Guard anti-aircraft batteries which were being placed in and around the city. The recruiting offices at Easter Road and 15 Melville Street reported encouraging numbers of men coming forward to volunteer.

We have already seen how many of the women of Edinburgh wished to play a more active role in the defence of the country and, inspired by women elsewhere in Britain, were keen to become more involved in a manner similar to that of the Home Guard. Edinburgh women had taken matters into their own hands and set up the Edinburgh Women's Home Defence Corps in 1940 and by February 1942 there were 110 members. At this time this was the only such corps which had been created in Scotland. By mid-February the corps was going from strength to strength and in a recent miniature rifle shooting competition the corps had beaten an Edinburgh Home Guard unit by 880 points to 804. The average age of the members of the corps was 25 and they drew their ranks from all sections of Edinburgh society.

The War Office remained steadfastly opposed to women as combatants, but the members of the corps were undaunted. The corps was forbidden access to official uniforms and the women had to create their own which consisted of blue trousers and jumpers (with white collar) and blue berets. Officers were marked by their wearing of ties and jackets. Their attitude was summed up by Captain Alice Lumsden who said that despite government opposition 'we are determined to be ready to defend our country in the event of invasion, and are now training hard in guerrilla methods'. Because the War Office forbade women to carry firearms the women of the corps had armed themselves with sheath knives and had obtained training in the use of knives from local army instructors. They had also managed to secure training in the use of the bren gun and other automatic weapons and were confident that in the event of emergency they would be fully capable of using these weapons. They also set up their own miniature rifle club at which members could practice marksmanship. The commanding officer of the corps, Major Elizabeth H. Thompson, said that while the Edinburgh Women's Home Defence Corps did not 'want to usurp the duties of any other organisation ... we are convinced that, for the proper defence of our homes, women should be trained as well as our menfolk.' She said that in the event of an invasion 'we may be asked to assist the Home Guard. When that day comes we'll be ready.'[15]

In February the Home Guard held another large-scale exercise. Codenamed 'Peggy' it pitted the 3rd Battalion (City of Edinburgh) and the Midlothian Battalion (along with reinforcements) against the 52nd Reconnaissance Corps who were ordered to penetrate defences in the Hillend and Penicuik areas. There was still resentment between the Home Guard and the regular army and the Home Guard were not happy when it was decided that 52nd Corps had won. Other exercises held at this time included 'Badger' which was designed to test the defences of Leith Docks. Demonstrating the commitment of the Home Guards, the exercise was declared a complete success despite the appalling weather and heavy snow.

The Home Guard had progressed from the early makeshift days and now had uniforms and was well-equipped with weapons. Efficiency had also improved with patrols and other duties now being undertaken with full military rigour and discipline. However, the previously mentioned writer in the *Edinburgh Evening News* maintained that the 'comradeship, the good spirit, is there, and discipline is enforced in the best of ways – that of friendliness'. He described a typical scene in a guard-room in 1942 after a patrol: there might be two men playing cribbage (one a former naval man, the other a Seaforth Highlander), a couple of the younger lads reading, one spinning a yarn from his youth (the former cowboy) and the corporal keeping an eye on the kettle while others engaged in good natured argument. At the end of the room, meanwhile, was a university lecturer marking and correcting papers. Clearly this was a happy unit and one in which the comradeship of men from differing backgrounds was a defining part of the experience of Home Guard service. He went on to relate two particular experiences, the first of which was when a duke on an inspection tour called in on the unit only to be denied entry by the duty sentry as he had never heard of him. The second incident occurred on a patrol during an air raid alert when the Home Guards stopped 'a pompous Army colonel' who did not have his identity card with him and was therefore taken to the guard-room until he could be identified. This process took over an hour and apparently the colonel was rather insulting towards the Home Guard. When a soldier from the same regiment was also taken to the guard-room to await identification, upon being told of the affair with his colonel, he asked the Home Guards if they couldn't keep the officer for good the next time.

The writer told an anecdote involving an Edinburgh Home Guard who was a rather indistinct speaker. After being sent to inspect a house which was showing lights during the blackout he knocked on the door to admonish the occupant. This turned out to be an elderly lady who, when confronted by this fully-armed man with rifle and bayonet and being unable to understand him, she believed the invasion had occurred and fainted.

The writer said that Edinburgh Home Guard units had attained a high level of military proficiency, but told another anecdote in which his corporal was caught by an umpire in a training exercise on his own enjoying a smoke. Asked what he was doing the corporal thought on his feet and answered that he was a casualty and that as he was dead 'he can surely dae as he likes'.

He commented on how many former members of his unit had visited and told how useful their training had been after they had been called up. One youngster said that the English Home Guard took it all very seriously while the Scots version, while taking it seriously, 'thank goodness, we get fun out of it too'.[16]

The Lord Provost was, at the time, busy organising the forthcoming Edinburgh Allies Week which was scheduled to run from 2-9 May. The week-long campaign would raise funds and provide information on twenty-seven of the allied nations and their wartime contributions and sufferings. It was to open with a 'Monster Rally in the Usher Hall' addressed by Anthony Eden and the Scottish Secretary. A particular emphasis of the week was to be the 'unity of purpose among the 27 allies, and the need for a greater will to sacrifice'.[17] There would be lectures, films, rallies and parades with bands, both military and civil, including a visit from the Netherlands Military Band. There would be a women's demonstration at the Central Hall, Tollcross, featuring women from all twenty-seven nations in national costume. Speakers were to include Madame Maisky, wife of the Russian ambassador, and Mrs Winant, wife of the American ambassador. Other plans included a youth meeting organised by the Student's Representative Council, held at Pollock Hall.

Coal had been rationed in January and it was clear that there was a thriving black market in the commodity throughout Scotland. An Edinburgh meeting of the Co-operative Coal Trade Association discussed the matter in May. The chairman reported that the black-market problem in the coal distributive trade was growing and that many customers were offering large bribes to distributors to bypass the regulations. He called for more active enforcement of the law and demanded that not only the merchants should be prosecuted but their employees and customers too. One member decried the decline in the number of miners in Scotland (down from 140,000 to just 80,000) and said that the government should release 20,000 miners from the army as this would be more beneficial than employing 50,000 clerks to enforce rationing regulations.

The coal ration proved to be one which was long-lasting and divisive showing some of the cracks which lay below the surface of a nation supposedly at one fighting a total war. Many agreed with the rationing system, comparing it to the situation in the First World War, and finding the complaints which were being put forward to be distasteful and unpatriotic. One letter writer in June argued that the system had worked in the previous war and that a 'war for survival is now in progress, and it seems out of place' to 'hurl abuse at the Government for introducing a rationing scheme for fuel and light'. He argued that the fairest way to apply the scheme was to assess premises by the cubic feet of rooms and, while acknowledging that many would find the ration a shock initially, it would be better to economise now than to 'suffer hardships later on'.[18]

In August there were two letters to *The Scotsmen* which demonstrated this. The first, signing himself as 'CARBON', blamed both the government for not foreseeing the difficulties and the miners for not acting in a patriotic manner befitting the sacrifices that others were making for the war effort. He said that although many people sympathised with the miners they were not 'playing the game' and that instead of making a greater effort, output per man had actually dropped. The writer urged the Ministry of Fuel to tackle the problems of productivity more energetically. The second correspondent displayed a dismaying lack of concern for those less fortunate than himself despite his occupation as a clergyman. Signing himself as 'PETRIFIED CLERIC' he said that he was the sole (compulsory) occupier of a fourteen-room house of which nine rooms were regularly used. He said, 'a 4-roomed Corporation house could be built in my dining room. Together, with the drawingroom [*sic*], a 6-roomed bungalow would be possible. A two-storied house of good dimensions could be erected in my hall.' He bemoaned that his house, according to the fuel allowances, was only entitled to 170 units, 'Yet the 4-roomed house is allowed 120 units, the 6-roomed bungalow is 150 units.' He went on to claim that the year before, he and his wife, restricting themselves severely, had used 499 units but that in future they would have to find a way to make a further economy of sixty per cent, something which he described as 'an utter impossibility'.[19] Clearly such an attitude, while possibly borne out of genuine concern, came across as arrogant, failing to take into account the hardships being experienced by those who were not fortunate enough to find themselves in a secure and safe profession with a large and comfortable dwelling.

Despite the popularity of the Holidays at Home movement there were still many Edinburgh residents who ignored official advice and decided to travel further afield on the holiday over the first weekend of July. Long queues were present at railways stations and bus stands. Most of the travellers were not merely day-trippers but were going away for the entire weekend. The most popular destinations were Fife and locations in the Borders, with many travellers having failed to book in advance and simply going 'on-spec'. At Waverley Station the queues were reported as being fifty yards long and at Princes Street Station they stretched along the platforms, through the station and out of the main entrance.

The announcement that sweets would be rationed from 26 July brought consternation to Edinburgh's children, but the announcement that the ration would be just two ounces per week led to dismay amongst the city's confectioners. They claimed it would lead to a drastic drop in sales and income, that the scheme was uneconomic as it would result in a waste of paper bags and would increase the workloads of staff, and that instead of a weight ration it would have been better have set the ration at 6d per person. Sweet manufacturers, on the other hand, claimed that the ration was to be expected and it had come as no surprise to them given the rationing on sugar. The government proceeded carefully ensuring that at the end of the first month of sweet rationing there would be a surplus supply of sweets so that the ration could be adjusted according to demand and public reaction to the ration. The trade reported that they could reasonably expect 10-20 per cent of the population to forgo their sweet ration altogether but this could not be guaranteed. There had clearly been a problem before the ration as one confectioner said that it would at least 'stop the activities of "shop crawlers," who spent their time collecting all the sweets they could get while others had to go without'.[20]

As rationing and the effects of the Battle of the Atlantic continued to restrict food supplies, the people of the Edinburgh area turned to the frugal staples of Scottish cuisine to fill out their diets. Stovies made with corned beef (or any offcuts if these were available) always remained a firm favourite with the flavour being enhanced by the addition of the ubiquitous OXO cube. Potted haugh or heed (made from the lower leg or head of a sheep) was not always so welcome but was nourishing and ensured that the most was made out of any available protein. Soup was made from the meat boiled from a sheep's head with a broken marrow bone added. Tripe continued to make its contribution to many an Edinburgh diet, as did haggis and other offal dishes such as boiled cow's udder. Spam fritters were almost ever-present and fish cakes provided some variety (although they contained noticeably more potato than before the war). Families who kept livestock had more options available to them. Every possible piece of a slaughtered pig would be used: the blood to make black pudding and the head to make brawn. Hens not only provided meat but, more importantly, a steady supply of eggs, to eat or be sold or bartered to neighbours and friends.

Some areas set up communal feeding centres in schools and churches where families could get a nourishing meal. Most of these were set up under the scheme known as British Restaurants. The idea originated in the need to provide cheap nourishing food to those who had been bombed out during the Luftwaffe's campaign against Britain. Building on the experiences of the National Kitchens of World War One and the setting up of emergency feeding centres, they were originally called Community Feeding Centres but were renamed on the instruction of Winston Churchill who preferred the patriotic boost of the new name. Organised by the Ministry of Food the British Restaurants were run by the local authorities or volunteers on a non-profit basis and aimed to supply (off-ration) meals for a maximum of 9d per serving (approximately £1 today). As the scheme developed, cafés, schools and other buildings were taken over, and mobile canteens and a delivery service (called the Cash and Carry Restaurant) was organised in some areas.[21]

For children the shortage of sweets resulted in a growing popularity for such items as liquorice root and Ovaltine or Horlicks tablets, while those who had managed to grow rhubarb might have got used to the delicacy of a stick of rhubarb dipped into a bag of (rarely available and precious) sugar.

With the entire population being mobilised for war, Edinburgh women found themselves with opportunities which would otherwise have been denied to them. The Ministry of Labour and National Service ran a war work for women display and information centre at 14-16 Shandwick Place. The display was opened with some ceremony by the Lord Provost, Lord Wark and Mr M.S. McCorquedale MP (Parliamentary Secretary to the Ministry of Labour) and events included a display by young women from the Ramsay Technical College who were completing their engineering training. Women who were already engaged in war work in the Midlands were also to be present to answer questions on living and working conditions in that area (which many of the volunteers would be sent to) while a photographic exhibition would highlight the varieties of war work which could be undertaken. Films by the Ministry of Information were shown every Tuesday and Wednesday and there were weekly talks given. The ATS, Land Army, NAAFI and various nursing organisations were also heavily involved, as were private companies.

The actions of RAF Bomber Command in bombing German towns and cities had found widespread support and enthusiasm amongst the vast majority of the Edinburgh public. At the end of June the command launched its third and final thousand-bomber raid. The impact of these massive raids had captured the public imagination and the showing of a newsreel including live shots taken from bombers during the raid at the New and New Victoria cinemas attracted large audiences and loud praise. The newsreel also featured footage of a low-level raid by RAF Boston aircraft on a French target. The newsreel was widely advertised in the local press which reported that the footage of what it described as a 'thunderbolt' raid was well filmed and exciting.

While German raiders were less active, small numbers of hit-and-run raiders were still an occasional problem. On the night of 6 August radar detected three such raiders approaching the coast from the south-east before turning inland over Dunbar. Shortly after 11 pm one of them passed low over Edinburgh and dropped four bombs over the Craigentinny area. One (believed to be 500 kg) hit a tenement at 35 Loaning Road and blew off the gable end of the building. It destroyed the ground floor flat and seriously injured Elizabeth Veitch and her 2-year-old daughter while another daughter, Betty (13), was buried in the rubble. Rescue squads worked frantically for hours to locate and extricate the young girl but when they reached her she was dead. The caretaker at Craigentinny House, Robert Wright (66), was also killed when a bomb destroyed his quarters. Another hit and seriously damaged a tenement at 29 Loaning Road and another at 1 Loaning Crescent while the final two bombs hit and wrecked the eastern wing of Craigentinny House. There were many people left temporarily homeless and the emergency rest centre system once more swung into action with 345 people being cared for at St. Christopher's Church Hall and St. Ninian's Rest Centre.

The dangerous business of training pilots claimed another Edinburgh life in August when 20-year-old Sergeant Robert Ian Darg Forsyth of 21 Stenhouse Gardens lost his life. Forsyth was a member of 57 OTU and on 16 August he took off from RAF Hawarden in Wales in Spitfire IIa (P7549) in company with another Spitfire. The two collided and Sergeant Forsyth's aircraft crashed and he was killed. Before the war Forsyth held an office of the Inspector of Taxes in Galashiels. He left behind his father, Joseph Festus Darg Forsyth, and his stepmother, Marion.[22]

In September the press carried the story of an Edinburgh officer in the Royal Army Medical Corps who had taken a leading part in the dramatic rescue of a young boy who was injured and lying in a coastal minefield. Captain W.T. Paterson was stationed in Lincolnshire and he and a major in the Royal Artillery commandeered a mechanical digger, tied a ladder to its scoop and then had the driver take it to the edge of the minefield before using the scoop to lift both officers over the minefield. Both officers then crawled along the ladder and managed to reach a concrete platform in the middle of the minefield. Another officer then passed another ladder down from the top of the crane. The RA major then lay down and supported the ladder on his chest so that Captain Paterson could crawl along it towards the boy. However, the ladder was too short and Captain Paterson was forced to crawl through the minefield to reach the boy. He then carried him back across the two ladders and the mechanical digger recovered both officers and the boy.

Following complaints in Edinburgh that customers of the greyhound track at Stenhouse were unfairly using the tram system, the authorities in the city acted in September. Many of the punters were coming out of the track and instead of going to the nearest tram stop were instead boarding a tram bound the other way to the nearby terminus and then remaining on the tram so that those who were queuing at the terminus were unable to get seats or sometimes even forced to wait for the next tram. Following the end of the meeting of 12 September, however, there were several police officers at the terminus who ensured that all passengers disembarked and were made to join the end of the queues. In minutes the queues were fifty yards long and four or five deep. Furthermore, a tram inspector saw to it that there was sufficient room on each tram to pick up passengers further on its journey. There was also criticism of the fact that there was a queue of more than fifty taxis parked not far from the track to take bookmakers and punters to the city.

As it became clear that Hitler's Nazis were responsible for the deaths of an untold number of Jews, members of the large Jewish community in Edinburgh became ever more involved in raising money to support the war effort. In late October, Jewish Freemasons of the Solomon Lodge presented the city with a mobile canteen intended for the use of civil defence workers. The presentation took place at the Mound and attracted a large crowd of dignitaries including the Lord Provost and his wife, various councillors, Rabbi Dr Daiches, Viscount Traprain (Grand Master Mason of Scotland). Dr Daiches blessed the canteen and Viscount Traprain then paid tribute to the Jewish brethren and friends for their generosity in supplying the funds. Accepting the gift the Lord Provost thanked the Jewish community before hinting at some of the problems which had afflicted the community in Edinburgh saying that 'there were many unwise and unreflecting people who tried to break the unbroken links of the community' but that the 'times were too grim for men and women to accentuate their differences'.[23]

On 23 November the Leith-based Ben Line lost another vessel to enemy action when the armed merchant SS *Ben Lomond* was torpedoed by an enemy U-Boat 750 miles off the Amazon while en route from Cape Town to Suriname and New York. Hit by two torpedoes the ship sank within two minutes and there was only one survivor, Chinese Second Steward Poon Lim. After drifting for several hours, he came across a life raft and managed to haul himself aboard. He then spent the next fifty days living off the supplies on the raft, drinking rainwater and catching seabirds and fish for food. At one stage he managed to catch a shark and drank its blood to quench his thirst. On 5 April, after 133 days adrift, Poon Lim was finally rescued by the crew of a Brazilian fishing boat. This remarkable survivor was able to walk when landed ashore and the British consul arranged for his return to Britain. Upon arrival in Britain he immediately volunteered for further merchant service.[24]

In October and November there was an outbreak of smallpox in Edinburgh. At the end of the first week of November there were eight cases, all of which could be traced back to two medical establishments. At this stage all of the cases were male and included three medical students (two Poles and a Briton), an 18-year old and a 16-year old boy. By late November there were over twenty cases and there had been four deaths. The authorities' hopes that they had the outbreak under control were dashed on 21 November when a 17-year-old woman from Merchiston fell ill after a journey on a train to Balerno. Most worryingly she had had no known contact with other cases and Doctor W.G. Clark from the Ministry of Health advised everyone who had journeyed on the train to get vaccinated.

We have already seen how dangerous training for the role of aircrew could be in wartime Britain with many Edinburgh men losing their lives before they could even reach operational squadrons, but for some the training period was even more

Poon Lim adrift in his raft (PD)

dangerous as they were rushed into action before they had even completed their training period. Some members of 10 Operational Training Unit (OTU) found themselves sent on operational detachment to St. Eval where they were on loan to Coastal Command to fly dangerous anti-submarine patrols to help thwart the U-Boat menace. The crews were a mixture of experienced crews who had flown tours and were on instructional duties and inexperienced novices. Losses to crews and aircraft from this detachment were heavy with fifty-three Whitley bombers lost between August 1942 and July 1943.[25] On 29 October the detachment had two Whitleys fail to return from anti-submarine patrols. There were twelve men aboard the two aircraft: one came down into the sea and five of the crew were subsequently picked up, all aboard the other were killed. A 19-year old Edinburgh man, Sergeant George Cameron MacKenzie, died in the first crash. He appears to have been flying as navigator (or possibly second pilot) and suffered a compound fracture to one of his legs when his aircraft came down and that, combined with the effects of exposure, resulted in the young airman losing his life. It would appear that MacKenzie was either buried at sea or failed to make it into the crew's dinghy as he has no known grave and is commemorated on the Runnymede Memorial to the missing. He left behind his parents, Finlay and Isabella MacKenzie.

The fuel situation in the country was becoming ever more serious and the authorities in Edinburgh and Glasgow announced that bus and tram routes would be curtailed. From 8 November bus and tram runs would finish between 10 and 10.30 pm on weekdays and Saturdays and at 9.30 pm on a Sunday. Censuses of passengers were taken to assess which were the most vital bus routes. The corporation tried to put a positive slant on the news by announcing 'Stay-at-Home Evenings'.

With the public being constantly urged to save waste paper, the police and the city authorities decided to crack down on litterers and those who placed paper in their bins. Policemen were detailed to be on the lookout for people throwing away paper including bus tickets and cigarette cartons and by mid-November a dozen people had been fined 5s apiece with no excuses being accepted by the courts. Meanwhile the authorities were refusing to empty bins which they found to contain paper until the person responsible had removed the paper.

CHAPTER 5

1943

The New Year passed relatively quietly in Edinburgh with far fewer people out and about than in peacetime. The blackout, the shortages of food and drink and the grimness of a fourth wartime New Year all combined to keep people indoors although there were some younger people who went first-footing in the early hours. The police reported making only twenty-four arrests, mainly for drunk and disorderly behaviour (one man was arrested for being drunk in charge of a horse drawn lorry). On New Year's day, football matches attracted large crowds as did the city's cinemas and theatres. There were few restaurants open but those that were reported brisk business despite the food shortages. One of the most popular events held in the city was the annual Powderhall New Year Handicap race.

One of the effects of wartime scavenging and production demands was that there was a chronic shortage of toys available for young children. A new year meeting of the council recognised the generous contributions of toys which were being made by the civil defence services. The men and women of the casualty services, rescue services and the report centres had crafted or bought 700 new toys which were distributed to local nurseries while Edinburgh timber merchants had handed over scrap wood. Other businesses had donated scraps of cloth and wire and these materials had been fashioned into dolls and animal toys by women in the civil defence services.

The new year brought a rash of fatal accidents in Leith. The first occurred at Commercial Street near Sandport Street late on 31 December when merchant seaman Daniel Morrison (66) of 14 Hope Terrace was struck by a tram. He died the next day in hospital. Two pedestrians were killed while crossing the road in the blackout. The first was Adam Wilson (69) of 4A Elbe Street, Leith, who was found in the road at Tolbooth Wynd opposite Sugarhouse Close shortly before 3.30 am. He had been struck by a vehicle and suffered fatal head and leg injuries. The second occurred at Leith Docks when Robert Proudfoot (50) of 56 West Bowling Green Street fell into the water and drowned while he was going about his duties as a firewatcher.

Throughout January preparations were being made for Edinburgh's part in the national book drive which was to use unwanted or old books either for salvage or for distribution to the forces. Mr N.G. Wilson, the city's Inspector of Cleansing, was in charge of the effort and had enlisted the chief librarian's help in organising a committee which would ensure that valuable or rare books would not be lost. Mr Wilson had set the city the target of 1,000,000 books over the fortnight, starting from 31 January.

Even though it was midwinter, the 'Dig for Victory' campaign continued apace with gardeners, allotment holders, and pig and chicken clubs all being exhorted to ever greater efforts. At Portobello a meeting was addressed by the secretary of the Scottish Gardens and Allotments Committee, Mr George F. Porthouse, who said that 'More people are growing vegetables in Scotland than ever before' and that the number of allotments had increased fourfold since the war began with over 80,000 allotments now being tended in Scotland. More than ever people were growing vegetables in their own gardens and this was to be praised, but Mr Porthouse warned that the next winter and the spring of 1944 would, he thought, be the most testing period yet faced, and so plans had to be put in place immediately and the growing of winter and storage crops had to be greatly increased. As vegetable supplies from England would not be so easily obtainable it was essential that Scotland increase her own production and 'make a supreme effort to attain self sufficiency'. Mr Porthouse said 'the kitchen plot would assume still greater importance.'[1]

Despite suspicions over the officially reported accuracy of the bombing efforts of RAF Bomber Command, there was continuing support for the bombing of Germany's cities. Many Edinburgh men found themselves in the forefront of the campaign. Towards the end of 1942 its commander, Sir Arthur Harris, had begun formulating new tactics and experimenting with new equipment and by 1943 he was ready to launch his main offensive beginning with an extended campaign against the industrial heartland of the Ruhr. First, however, he had to feel his way to this objective and to fulfil an order to raid the towns which were bases for the German U-Boat fleets. The new year opened with Harris throwing his bombers against the city of Essen and its enormous Krupps engineering works, to test the new Oboe blind marking equipment which, it was hoped, would dramatically increase bombing accuracy. From 9-14 January, Bomber Command targeted the city on successive nights with small forces of bombers ordered to drop bombs on the Pathfinder markers dropped by Mosquitos. On the final raid of this series the command dispatched 69 aircraft (3 Mosquitos and 66 Lancasters). The planned Oboe trial went wrong on this night with two of the Mosquitos having to abort their sorties due to technical problems while the third dropped its markers which failed to ignite above the cloud base. Despite this it would appear that the small force of bombers did indeed bomb accurately but four Lancasters were lost in the raid. One of the bombers which failed to return was Lancaster I (R5690, ZN-T) of 106 Squadron. After taking off from Syerston nothing further was heard from the bomber and it transpired that it had been shot down by a night-fighter over Holland and all of the crew were killed. The flight engineer was a 22-year old Edinburgh man, Sergeant Alexander Dunbar.[2]

At 28 Mansionhouse Road Mrs Katherine Mary Barratt, wife of Chaplain 4th Class the Reverend Harold Norman Barratt, Royal Army Chaplains Department, received the telegram that every family dreaded. It informed her that her husband had succumbed to wounds he had suffered while on active service in North Africa. Reverend Barratt was 34 years of age and had graduated from the University of Leeds in 1935 before becoming a deacon at York in 1937 and shortly afterwards a curate at Acomb. His widow was an Edinburgh woman and the couple had three young children. The Reverend Barratt was buried at Tabarka Ras Rajel War Cemetery in Tunisia and after the war his widow had the following inscription placed upon his headstone: 'FOREVER AN INSPIRATION TO THOSE WHO LOVE HIM DEARLY. KATHARINE, MICHAEL, NORMA, MARY.'

Days after Bomber Command's offensive against the Ruhr, the command attacked Stuttgart with 314 aircraft (152 Lancasters, 109 Halifaxes and 53 Stirlings). It was important that locations outside the Ruhr also be attacked so that the Germans could not concentrate their defences. For 405 (RCAF) Squadron it was a bad night with four Halifax bombers failing to return to their base at Topcliffe. Halifax II (W7803, LQ-B) crashed at La Malmaison in France killing all eight men aboard. The navigator in the crew was Pilot Officer William Watson Kirkpatrick, RAFVR. Kirkpatrick (29) was a married Edinburgh man and was one of four RAF men in this crew. His widow Mary had a moving inscription placed on his headstone in La Malmaison Communal Cemetery: 'HIS MEMORY, TO US A TREASURE; HIS LOSS, A LIFETIME'S REGRET. MARY.'[3] The raid was not a success as the main force was late and bombing was not concentrated.

As the Bomber Command main offensive got underway the list of targets grew. Amongst them were several in Italy. Most of the crews looked forward to these raids with less fear than they did targets in Germany as it was felt that Italian defences were far weaker. However, the distance involved was sobering as was the fact that the bomber stream had to fly over occupied France to reach the target and this exposed crews to the risk of night-fighter attack. Despite being referred to as 'an ice-cream operation' (the ground crews even painted an ice-cream cone instead of the traditional bomb on aircraft which returned from an operation to Italy) a great many aircrew were to lose their lives on such raids. On 13/14 April the target was La Spezia. 103 Squadron at Elsham Wolds contributed several Lancaster bombers to the effort with two failing to return. One of these was a Lancaster I (W4318, pm-G) piloted by Flight Lieutenant E.C. Lee-Brown. After taking off at 8.20 pm the crew began the long journey to Italy but while over Le Mans the aircraft crashed with the loss of all seven crew. Amongst them was flight engineer Sergeant George Watson Houliston. The 31-year old married man was from Edinburgh where he left his parents and his widow Mary.[4]

By early 1943 the Home Guard was a well-trained and reasonably efficient force which could boast adequate, if not spectacular, equipment with which to do its job. The 1940 era of muzzle loading rifles and shotguns had long since gone, replaced by the service Lee-Enfield rifle and sub-machine guns. Many of the Thompson sub-machine guns were being replaced with the cheaper Sten gun. Home Guard units in Edinburgh and the surrounding area were being equipped with field guns and other anti-tank equipment as the regular army received newer equipment. Vast quantities of ammunition were now available to the force, a far cry from the early days, but the storage was proving a problem. There was consternation and no small degree of anger when it was discovered that the headquarters of 8th Battalion at 1 Grosvenor Gardens had 200,000 rounds of small arms ammunition and 4,500 grenades in storage. This was a residential block and the danger to life which would have been caused in the event of a fire were unimaginable. Worse was to come when the ammunition was inspected by the Royal Army Ordnance Corps and pronounced dangerous due to the poor condition in which it had been kept. Not only was this dangerous but it was also a waste of valuable wartime ordnance and it is surprising that there do not seem to have been any legal ramifications resulting from the case.

As the threat of invasion receded the Home Guard battalions of Edinburgh struggled at times to maintain the interest of their members. In many of the battalions this was at least partially accomplished by the organisation of a healthy and active social scene. This did not meet with the approval of every Home Guard, with some seeing the shift as being a move away from the original martial intent of the organisation. One Edinburgh Home Guard commented that if Hitler (or for that matter any German) had seen the battalion magazine they would have come away with the impression that the Home Guard was primarily concerned with 'suppers, concerts, and whist drives'. They would have also heard of the 'large dance, battalion darts and football leagues, billiard matches, and a non-military film show'.[5] However, the social events helped to cement unit cohesion and to ensure morale was maintained, which was especially important after service became compulsory for some men, and many of the events in the social calendar were also organised to raise funds for wartime causes.

The warden service also had to cope with plummeting morale and public indifference. The situation became so severe that Lord Rosebery, in his capacity as Regional Civil Defence Commissioner, was despairing of maintaining interest in the service. Some of the staff were even being used to construct toys, always in short supply in wartime Britain.

We have already seen how the construction of pillboxes in Edinburgh had resulted in a rash of accidents and how the police had launched their own inquiries into the matter. Yet, with the threat of invasion, or even raiding, becoming ever more remote still the military authorities refused to have defences removed.

The large numbers of Polish forces present in the Edinburgh area generally got along well with the local population. However, at the start of the year there was some disquiet over the circulation of a leaflet amongst officers in the Polish Army. The leaflet, entitled 'Walka', contained violent attacks and diatribes against Russians, Czechs and Jews and was of serious concern to the Polish and British authorities. It was believed that the pamphlet was published in Edinburgh and distributed from hand to hand but enquiries drew a blank and the authorities were left perplexed as to those behind it.

Newspapers still kept people informed of the activities of the RAF and a tragically fatal raid on London on 20 January was interesting for the people of Edinburgh. In the aftermath, Spitfires were scrambled from Biggin Hill and intercepted the enemy formations as they tried to make their escape. Leading the Spitfires of the Biggin Hill Wing was 23-year old Edinburgh-born Wing Commander Richard Maxwell 'Dickie' Milne, DFC and Bar. Milne, who was on his fourth operational tour, shot down two of the German aircraft bringing his score of victories to thirteen. Talking to a reporter from the *Daily Mirror*, Milne related how he 'caught up with five of them going south, just over Pevensey. I gave one a two and a half seconds burst. He caught fire, rolled over, and went into the sea. No. 2 went straight in – smack! – after a brief blast from my guns.'[6] Milne's first victory was a Focke-Wulf FW190 and his second a Messerschmitt ME109. The aftermath of the raid was widely reported as bombs fell on a school killing at least 34 people (including 30 children) and trapping many others in the rubble. On 14 March, Dickie Milne, while still leading his wing, was shot down into the sea by Focke-Wulf 190s (after he had shot down a Messerschmitt ME109). He was captured by the Germans, spending the rest of the war in a PoW camp. At the time of his capture Milne had shot down at least fifteen German aircraft with several others possibly destroyed or damaged.[7]

On 13 May the Leith-based Ben Line lost another ship when the 6,434-ton SS *Benvrackie* was sunk by a U-Boat. *Benvrackie* had been a part of convoy OB-312 but it had been dispersed and *Benvrackie* was hunted by U-105 for thirty-four hours. She was carrying a mixed cargo which included silver and an aircraft (a Tiger Moth) on a route London-Loch Ewe-Capetown-Beira, and had also picked up twenty-five survivors from the SS *Lassell*. Shortly before 8 am, some 700 miles from Freetown, the ship was hit by two torpedoes and sank within six minutes. Thirteen crew from the *Benvrackie* were lost along with fifteen of the survivors from the *Lassell*. The remaining fifty-five survivors took to the boats and were questioned by the Germans before being set adrift. After thirteen days in the lifeboats the survivors were picked up by the hospital ship HMHS *Oxfordshire*.

With the success of the previous year's Warship Week, Edinburgh had high hopes for its Wings for Victory Week. Interest had already been widely expressed, especially for the city's 'own' 603 Squadron. At the inaugural meeting held at the City Chambers the Lord Provost was able to inform the committee that by the end of the first day some £4,150,000 had been pledged towards the initial target figure of

Wing Commander Richard Maxwell 'Dickie' Milne in the cockpit of his spitfire (PD)

£10,000,000. A network of street, school and industry groups had been created and, given Edinburgh's previous success in fundraising for the war effort, it was hoped that the target figure would be exceeded. The chairman of the Scottish Savings Committee, Lord Alness, informed the committee that up until April the capital had contributed £62,430,571 to the war effort (as much as £10 billion today). This was 15 per cent of the total donation from Scotland as a whole and represented an average donation of 16s 9d per week per head of Edinburgh's population against an average Scottish contribution of 9s 8¼d. The campaign was proving to be exceptionally popular, and with the recent publicity for the campaign to bomb German cities it was expected that the target might be exceeded. The Lord Provost commented that Edinburgh had a fine reputation when it came to fund-raising. £3,000,000 of the £4,150,000 promised had already been paid by the end of the first day.

Some contributions on first day of Wings for Victory Week 1943.

Donator	Amount donated
Scottish Co-op Wholesale Society	£197,500
Fund for Widows of the Members of the Faculty of Advocates of Scotland	£102,450
Edinburgh Royal Infirmary	£50,000
Royal Bank of Scotland (for clients)	£71,500
Brown Bros	£25,000
'Anonymous'	£25,000
John Menzies & Co	£25,000
Co-op Permanent Building Society	£20,000
'A Brewery Firm'	£20,000
William Younger & Co	£20,000
McDonald & Muir Ltd, Leith	£20,000
Commercial Bank of Scotland (for clients)	£18,000
Royal Insurance Co. Ltd.	£15,000
British Linen Bank (for clients)	£11,200
Halifax Building Society	£10,000
Huddersfield Building Society	£10,000
'The People of Gorgie'	£150
'Children of Sighthill'	£7 4s

The inauguration of the campaign included the releasing of a carrier pigeon by Lord Provost Darling. The pigeon bore a message to the Chancellor of the Exchequer announcing the beginning of Edinburgh's campaign and informing him of the target which had been set. With the efforts of RAF Bomber Command finding such favour with the general public it was no surprise that one of the most popular events was the exhibition of one of the Lancaster bombers, which attracted large crowds to Bruntsfield Links.

The street groups proved to be a particular success. There were 182 street groups in Edinburgh with 2,300 collectors. Since August 1941 the street groups had raised £1,150,000 for a variety of campaigns. In the period from September 1942 until April 1943 the school groups had raised £61,707. Local industry had also thrown itself into the fundraising efforts and by April 1943 there were 1,422 industrial groups covering every major industrial concern in the city.

On 21 May it was announced that the total so far reached was £9,550,000 and that, somewhat surprisingly, was still short of the target. A feature of the campaign to date was the eagerness of Edinburgh legal firms to make donations. The efforts of industrial groups was also praised, with many firms setting their own targets and reaching or exceeding them. The confectionery firm of W & M Duncan, for example, had originally set a target of £200 but had easily reached this and, with three days to go, had increased it to £2,000. The directors of the firm agreed to donate an extra £10,000 on top of the amount reached. The bakery firm of Smith's of Hawkhill had also exceeded their target of £3,000 and hoped to reach £4,500. To raise funds the firm had opened

Lord Provost releasing pigeon (TS)

Crowds at exhibition of Lancaster bomber on Bruntsfield Links (TS)

a shop selling their wares and this had already raised £1,000 from small savers. Their competitors, Martin's Bakery Ltd, had exceeded their own target of £5,000. The Scottish Motor Traction Company had also set a target of £5,000, with the directors encouraging contributions by offering prizes to their workers and offering to double the amount raised. J & J Todd & Sons had raised £1,785 which exceeded their initial target of £1,000. The George Watson College had set itself a target of £3,000 but had exceeded this and, by 21 May had raised £3,945; they had decided to raise their target to £5,000 to purchase their 'own' Spitfire. To spur this effort on a concert was held featuring the RAMC Medicos and the Signals Serenaders. On the same day the Lady Provost visited the Edinburgh Stock Exchange and was told that this body had raised £26,400.

The public and local businesses duly reacted to the news of the shortfall and by close of business on 22 May the total raised stood at £12,050,000 of which Leith had contributed £1,050,000. This meant that Edinburgh had set a new Scottish record and that the average contribution per head of population was £28 14s 3d. Small savers had made a huge contribution of over £1,000,000 which equated to over 50 shillings per head; it was hoped that, with one day remaining in the campaign, this total would exceed the £1,125,000 raised by small savers during the previous Edinburgh Warships Week. There were several individuals and groups who managed far larger donations, including that of £12,000 by 'Four Edinburgh Ladies' and one of £10,000 by two clients of the Royal Bank. Amongst the companies to contribute were Pearl Assurance, which donated £109,000 (as much as £20,000,000 today).

Industrial firms' contributions to Wings for Victory Week on 21 May 1943

Contributor	Contribution (£)
Cable & Wireless	100,000
Power Securities Corporation and Balfour, Beatty & Co	50,000
Howard & Wyndham	20,000
William Crawford & Sons, Leith	20,000
David Stuart Ltd	20,000
Scottish Power	10,000
William Murray & Co	10,000
Drybrough & Co	10,000
A.B. Fleming & Co	10,000

Final day's company contributions to Edinburgh Wings for Victory Week 1943

Company	Contribution
Edinburgh Savings Bank	£150,000
Scottish Amicable Life Assurance	£20,000
W & J Burness	£15,000
John L. Ford (per Wallace & Guthrie)	£12,000
Royal Exchange Assurance	£10,000
Alliance Assurance, County Fire Office Ltd, National Boiler & General Insurance	£10,000

Fund Raising for the war effort in Edinburgh

Campaign	Scottish total (£)	Edinburgh total (£)	Edinburgh average donation per head per week
War Weapons Week 1940	50,028,675	10,234,053	£25
Warship Week 1941	57,754,446	15,482,032	£35 19s 3½d
Wings for Victory Week 1943		12,050,000	£28 14s 3d

With the total tallied, Edinburgh could once again reflect on a mammoth voluntary financial contribution to the war effort and there were congratulatory messages sent to the city from the RAF, the Chancellor and from 603 Squadron. Edinburgh's effort was just one part of a national campaign across Scotland which had aimed at reaching £60,000,000 and Edinburgh had made a very significant contribution to this. As a result of this one of the RAF's heroes visited the city on 9 June. Squadron Leader R.A.B. Learoyd VC visited the headquarters of the Scottish Savings Committee which was based in Edinburgh at York Buildings. After a tour of the headquarters Learoyd signed a large photo of himself which was being used in a number of Wings Week campaigns across Scotland and followed this with lunch with the committee members and city dignitaries.

The problems facing the local authorities over the education of the city's youngsters continued throughout the year. One was that there was insufficient time for teacher training. Staggered summer holidays and the numbers of teachers supervising pupils who were helping to gather in the harvest further reduced the available time for the training. Despite this, courses for teachers were set up at both the Moray House Training College and the College of Art for Edinburgh. These courses focused on youth leadership, citizenship, mental testing, handicrafts during wartime, and

Squadron Leader Learoyd VC inspecting chart of Wings for Victory progress (TS)

infant teaching. The ongoing shortage of teachers was also a problem and, looking to the future, the council agreed to approach the government to ascertain the viability of early release of student teachers from the services after the war had ended.

With the general resentment of the blackout regulations and the receding threat of enemy bombing, although it was still present, there was a rather alarming slackness in the blackout in Edinburgh during May and Councillor Tom Stevenson raised the matter with the Civil Defence Committee saying that there was a growing carelessness in both mornings and nights. Although blackout times were printed every day in local and national newspapers the committee was concerned that many people seemed to have only the vaguest idea of the hours of blackout. The chief constable addressed the committee and told them that the enforcement of blackout regulations would be a priority.

Throughout the war the communities of Edinburgh took part in annual book drives where old books could be handed in. The books were sorted and either pulped, sent to the forces, or used to resupply libraries which had been damaged by enemy action. The drives were always popular and attracted large numbers of donations. It was announced in June that the drive held in February had seen 1,384,925 books handed in. 1,268,405 (91.6 per cent) of these were pulped, 62,428 (4.5 per cent) were handed over to the forces, and the remaining 53,192 (3.8 per cent) were set aside for donation to libraries. The chief librarian was able to report that 56,052 of those destined for the forces had already been dispatched (39,427 by the Libraries Department and 16,625 by the WVS). One set of 250 volumes had reached a unit of the First Army in North Africa. The remaining service books were, in the meantime, being stored at the Central Library.

With the government urging people not to travel unless it was absolutely necessary, the holidays-at-home movement had proved a great success and remained popular throughout the war. The opening of Edinburgh's holidays at home period happened on 31 May with the first in a series of dances. This dance, at which the Royal Scots Dance Band provided the music, broke all previous records when it attracted 3,376 people. The Lord Provost addressed the gathered dancers at Princes Street Gardens, praising the efforts of those who had put together a lengthy and varied programme of events which would appeal to everyone. Of course, the holidays at home scheme also raised funds for Edinburgh Corporation as money was made from many of the events and from the rental of three grounds in the city (Meadowbank, Saughton Sports Stadium and Pilton).

The second week featured a boxing tournament on Leith Links in aid of a collection for the 603 Squadron Benevolent Fund. A sheepdog trial was held to raise funds for the Lady Provost's Comfort Fund and the Edinburgh branch of the Red Cross.

Other notable events were football competitions at Leith Links, Craigmillar and Saughton Park, swimming galas, cycle tours and historical tours of the city. The tours of the city proved to be popular and it was commented that many of those who had attended them had been reintroduced to beauty spots and sites of historic interest in the city. One event which encouraged solidarity in the workplace was the holding of an inter-works sports meeting on 31 July at New Meadowbank in aid of Leith Hospital. Sports included athletics, cycling, five-a-side football, tug-of-war, musical competitions and others and admission was 6d. Local service personnel got involved in the scheme with a women's inter-service sports contest, also at New Meadowbank.

Two events taking place in August aimed to raise funds for the Dunfermline Service Women's Hostel and the Broxburn War Comforts Fund. A garden fete was held at Admiralty House in North Queensferry with the permission of Admiral Sir Wilbraham T.R. Ford and Lady Ford and featured, for the admission price of 1s (or 6d for service personnel and children), dancing, a funfair, games, a naval band, side shows, stalls and a tea. At the Craw's Nest at Broxburn a horse-jumping competition was held (sponsored by the British Linen Bank) with first prize of £5 and two further prizes.

The holidays at home period for 1943 included a very popular programme of dancing displays held in the East Princes Street Gardens. There were fifteen dances held from 2 July until the final performance on 20 August. A number of dances were also held at West Princes Street Gardens which were participatory and consisted of modern dancing. One of these, on 16 July, was recorded by the BBC. At East Princes Street the dances were displays of Scottish country and Highland dancing. Bailie Duncan said it was felt that, despite the 'almost overwhelming' popularity of the modern dances, some people would prefer to watch the older and more traditional

Right: Holidays at Home Events (TS)

Below: Holidays at Home Sports Meeting (TS)

CORPORATION OF EDINBURGH.

HOLIDAYS AT HOME.

INTER-WORKS SPORTS MEETING
(Under S.A.A.A. and N.C.U. Laws),
IN AID OF
LEITH HOSPITAL,
AT
NEW MEADOWBANK, EDINBURGH,
ON
SATURDAY, 31st JULY 1943,
At 2.45 p.m.
ATHLETICS, CYCLING, TUG-OF-WAR,
FIVE-A-SIDE FOOTBALL, CHAMPION-
SHIP EVENTS, MUSIC.

To be Opened at 2.30 by
The Right Hon. Sir WILLIAM Y. DARLING,
C.B.E., M.C., Lord Provost.

Admission 6d.   Trams 4, 5, 15, 20, 21, 22, and 26.
Buses 3, 5, 15, and 16.

IN AID OF DUNFERMLINE SERVICE WOMEN'S
HOSTEL.

GARDEN FETE

(By kind permission of
Admiral Sir WILBRAHAM T. R. FORD, K.C.B.,
and Lady FORD).

In Grounds of ADMIRALTY HOUSE, ROSYTH
(Train to North Queensferry
or Bus to South Queensferry and Ferry.)

SATURDAY, 7th AUGUST 1943,

To be Opened at 3 p.m. by Admiral FORD.
Admission, 1s; Members of H.M. Forces and Children, 6d.

Side Shows, Stalls, Games, Dancing, Teas, Naval Band.
ALL THE FUN OF THE FAIR!

IN AID OF BROXBURN WAR COMFORTS
FUND and EDINBURGH ROYAL INFIRMARY,
At the CRAW'S NEST, STATION ROAD, BROXBURN,
On WEDNESDAY, 18th AUGUST 1943, at 5.30 p.m.,
£50 OPEN PONY TROT.

On SATURDAY, 21st August,
GRAND OPEN HORSE JUMPING CONTEST.
1st Prize .... Cup and £5
2nd Prize .... Cup and £2
3rd Prize .... Cup and £1
Handy Hunter Trials and Pairs Jumping Contests.
Sheep Dog (Working) Exhibition by Mr D. Murray,
Peebles, Working 1 and 4 Dogs.
Entries to G. A. SHIEL, J.P., BRITISH LINEN
BANK, BROXBURN.

dance forms and the gardens were a most fitting setting.[8] Duncan thanked the audience for coming and confirmed that large audiences had watched every show and that the performers seemed to have enjoyed themselves almost as much as the audience.

Over 200,000 people had attended dances at Princes Street Gardens; an increase of 60,000 from the previous year. Other open-air dances held at Leith Links and Portobello had attracted 20,000 each. The many concerts which were locally organised and held in various city parks had attracted 63,000 people while the five zoo days held by Edinburgh Zoo had attracted a further 30,000. The Provost was amazed to learn that during the course of the holidays at home period, 174,000 bottles of milk had been consumed at events in the city. He thanked the many staff and volunteers who had made the programme such a success and said that for next year he was keen to see the open-air theatre performances extended and that he believed that some aspects of the holidays at home scheme might be retained in peacetime as they were entertaining and provided a welcome boost to so many worthy charities and organisations.

For those looking for more high-brow entertainment, St. Giles' Cathedral hosted an organ recital performed by Mr John Holton (whose organ band played at the Palais de Danse in Fountainbridge). The recital, which was the third that Mr Holton had performed in the cathedral, featured music from Bach, Mozart and Mendelsohn along with a composition of his own which he had written in commemoration of his infant daughter who had recently died.

With rationing impacting every household, the make do and mend campaigns found widespread support amongst Edinburgh women and many petitioned for new thrifty ideas from women's organisations. The WVS and several other organisations agreed to put together a 'Mend for Victory' exhibition. It was scheduled to begin in Edinburgh's Martin Hall, New College, running from 3 to 10 September before moving on to other Scottish cities. The exhibition had three main aims: to encourage interest in the make do and mend campaign, to encourage women to take advantage of educational classes on the subject, and to 'promote "make do and mend" work parties, children's clothing exchanges, and advice centres'.[9] Mrs Scott of the WVS added that there were additional objectives: the economising of fuel, the economising of food, and 'household jobbery'. The exhibition would feature talks and lectures, parades of mannequins wearing dresses made without the expenditure of a single clothing coupon, quizzes (hosted by the Lady Provost), demonstrations and exhibits. Among the exhibits were a saucepan made from a tin can, various items which had been repaired, a brush fashioned from clippings from a horse's tail, a dried heather switch (something which would not have appeared out of the ordinary to many a Scottish housewife), and a patchwork pinafore.

Workplace tensions, held largely in abeyance during the first years of the war, began once more to become a problem. With coal productivity falling the government was determined to get more miners into the pits and throughout the year there were a number of surface workers in the mines who found themselves directed by the National Service Officer to undertake underground work. While many accepted this there were a significant number who resented it, seeing it as an affront to their demarcation rights. In June two Lothian surface workers refused to do underground work to which they had been assigned under the Defence Regulations. They pleaded guilty to the charges and Sheriff MacDonald sentenced them to one months' imprisonment. This sentence was viewed by many as being unnecessarily harsh: others who had committed far worse offences had been fined and not sent to prison. The men were supported by the Mid and East Lothian Miners' Association and by early August almost 1,500 Lothian miners had come out on sympathetic strike. The action was focused at the Newcraighall and Woolmet collieries owned by the Niddrie and Benhar Coal Company. Alexander C. Cameron, the Secretary of the Mid and East Lothian Miners' Association, after consultation with miners, came to an agreement with them. The men agreed to go back to work so long as Mr Cameron was given permission by the Secretary of State for Scotland to visit the two men in prison and persuade them to undertake the work to which they had been assigned.

By this stage in the war, although people were still aware of the risk of gas attack, it had become much more unlikely and a general complacency had crept in. Although most still carried their masks with them (indeed it was an offence not to) many did not take advantage of the warden service offer to inspect the masks to ensure that they were still in good repair. This was necessary as with time the rubber fittings could and often did perish rendering the mask ineffective. Throughout July warden posts across the city were open to anyone for mask inspections but by the end of the month it was reported that only 20,000 people had taken advantage of this. The posts agreed to remain open for a further two days and encouraged people that 'this is a duty which should not be overlooked'.[10]

With so many goods being stored in warehouses, the area around Salamander Street in Leith was one in which fire could rapidly spread. On the night of 30 July a fire broke out in a two-storey warehouse. The fire caused local alarm, but the fire services were well drilled and by the time the NFS arrived on-scene the local works firemen were already tackling the blaze. Several lines of hose were deployed by the NFS and the blaze was completely extinguished within an hour and a half.

The creation of the NFS in 1941 had brought about a far more professional approach to both fire-fighting and fire prevention. By the summer of 1943 there were static water tanks scattered throughout the Edinburgh area but this was only the most easily recognisable feature of the growing professionalism. One of the greatest developments was the far higher levels of training which were now commonplace in the service. Training centres had been set up throughout Scotland and men who reached the rank of Leading Fireman (the equivalent of an NCO in the army) could be sent to a school which would assess their skills and competence before they could proceed to become officers in the service.

Many of these developments were hidden from the ordinary man in the street and thus the service began a press campaign to impress on the public just how the service was developing. Early in the year a new training school centre was opened in Edinburgh and in the summer the press were invited to look around. It accommodated classes of twenty-four Leading Firemen in a course which lasted three weeks. Candidates attended lectures and took part in practical training using the latest fire-fighting and rescue equipment and techniques. These included scaling tall buildings using hook ladders, rescues with wheeled equipment, and pipe laying techniques. The reporters were informed that in Edinburgh and south-east Scotland men of the NFS could lay 1,000 feet of six-inch steel pipe in under thirteen minutes. They had developed their own specialist piece of equipment to aid them in this, named the 'south-eastern tongs'.

Lectures were varied and sometimes quite complex, from the causes of fire spreading and techniques in fire prevention to administrative duties. Firemen were trained in the theory behind the automated sprinkler systems that were used in many industrial buildings, along with a course in building construction so that they could assess the dangers of a fire when on the ground. Practical classroom activities included sessions on some of the chemical reactions that firemen might encounter. One of these experiments demonstrated how coal gas was not flammable by itself but that when it was mixed with air it became explosively flammable.

The press visiting the centre were told that there were now millions of gallons of water, from indestructible sites, available at a few minutes notice, but that much of the NFS's time was being wasted on maintaining the static water tanks as people in some areas of Edinburgh seemed to think that it was fine to throw rubbish into them. They were told by the commanding officer, Commander W.B. Muir, that in one Edinburgh static tank 336 milk bottles had been recovered (and this at a time when glass was in short supply).

Amongst the war news the local press still found time to celebrate the happier occurrences of life. At the end of July there was a wartime wedding in the North British Hotel when Miss Elsie May Darling married Lieutenant G.A. Craig of the RAMC. The bride was the daughter of the late Dr Alfred Darling of Tinto, Corbiehill Place, Edinburgh, while the groom came from Belfast. Miss Darling had followed her father into the medical profession and after working for two years as district sister for Niddrie had gone on to a post as senior gynaecological tutor at Belfast Infirmary. Amongst the guests were Surgeon Lieutenant G.A. Bell (the best man), Major Hamilton Wylie (who gave away the bride), Sir William and Lady McKechnie, along with several local doctors and the matron of the Elsie Inglis Hospital.

Fund raising continued apace throughout the year with 23-28 August seeing a French Welfare Funds Week. This consisted of a wide variety of events opening with a mannequin display held at the North British Hotel organised by nine leading Edinburgh firms. The 176 tickets, priced at half a guinea apiece, sold out quickly. One of the most anticipated events of the fund week was the concert which was to be held at the Usher Hall featuring French and Scottish performers along with an address by the Hon. Harold Nicholson MP. Other events included whist drives, a flag day (featuring girls in French and Scottish national dress), fruit and vegetable shows, a concert by a French military band at Princes Street Gardens, a French-themed cinema performance at the Caley, and a week-long funfair at Rossleigh's Showroom on Shandwick Place. Over seventy Edinburgh shops had agreed to put in place window displays in celebration of the occasion.

While most of Bomber Command's campaign consisted of the bombing of city targets, it did, when ordered, undertake precision attacks and one such attack was

French Welfare Fund Week
Advertisement (TS)

French Welfare Funds' Week

(Under War Charities Act, 1940)

From 23rd to 28th August

under the patronage of

THE RT. HON. SIR WILLIAM Y. DARLING

C.B.E., M.C.

Lord Provost of Edinburgh and Lady Darling

★ **WEDNESDAY, 25th AUGUST**
3.30 p.m. to 5.15 p.m.
MANNEQUIN PARADE and DRESS SHOW
at the North British Station Hotel
In the Chair : LADY HADDINGTON

★ **THURSDAY, 26th AUGUST**
4.30 p.m.   RECEPTION by the BRITISH COUNCIL
in the NORTH BRITISH STATION HOTEL
7 p.m.   WHIST DRIVE at the
SCOTTISH-FRENCH HOUSE, 28 Regent Terrace
Tickets (including tea) 3/6

★ **FRIDAY, 27th AUGUST**
USHER HALL, 7.30 p.m. to 10 p.m.
GRAND CONCERT by French and Scottish Artists
TALK on FRANCE by The Hon. HAROLD NICOLSON, M.P.
Chairman : LORD BESSBOROUGH G.C.M.G., P.C.
GENERAL MONCLAR, Commander of the French Foreign Legion, as Guest
Tickets, 3/6, 2/6, and 1/- obtainable at Methven & Simpson, Ltd.
Paterson, Sons & Co., Ltd.   Rae, MacIntosh & Co., Ltd.

★ **SATURDAY, 28th AUGUST**
FLAG DAY
FRENCH GIRLS in NATIONAL COSTUME
will help with the Collecting.

★ **FRIDAY AND SATURDAY**
27th and 28th AUGUST
FRENCH MILITARY BAND will march from
28 Regent Terrace to Princes Street Gardens
where they will give a Concert on
FRIDAY, 27th AUGUST, 2.30 p.m. to 4.30 p.m.
SATURDAY, 28th AUGUST, 4.30 p.m. to 6 p.m.

★ **SUNDAY, 29th AUGUST**
CINEMA PERFORMANCE at
the CALEY PICTURE HOUSE
"FIN DU JOUR" and "ACTUALITIES"
Popular Prices

★ **ALL-WEEK FUN FAIR**
Rossleigh's Showrooms, 16 Shandwick Place
10 a.m. to 8 p.m.
Hoopla ; Skeeball ; Aunt Sally, etc.
Entrance Fee, 3d.

The cost of this advertisement has been defrayed by
R. W. FORSYTH, Ltd., Princes Street, Edinburgh

ordered for the night of 17/18 August. It had been established that the Baltic island of Peenemunde was the site of Nazi rocket weapon development and posed a risk to the British Isles. Bomber Command sent 596 aircraft: 324 Lancasters, 218 Halifaxes and 54 Stirlings, with a force of Mosquitoes for a diversionary attack on Berlin. Forty aircraft were lost but this was thought to be acceptable given the importance of the target. Wickenby-based 12 Squadron lost just the one aircraft: Lancaster III (DV168, PH-F) flown by Squadron Leader F.B. Slade DSO, a Glaswegian. The Lancaster was shot down by a night-fighter and all seven crewmen were killed when it crashed into the sea off Denmark. The wireless operator was another Edinburgh man. Pilot Officer John Francis Bell MacIntyre was aged just 21 and is commemorated, along with the rest of the crew, on the Runnymede Memorial.

On 15/16 September the command mounted two raids against precision targets. 369 aircraft (209 Halifaxes, 120 Stirlings, 40 Lancasters, and 5 American B-17s) were tasked with bombing the Dunlop rubber factory at Montluçon in central France. The raid was unusual not only in the fact that it was against a single factory but it was flown in moonlight conditions (bombers were generally stood down during full-moon periods) and involved control by an appointed master bomber (in this case Wing Commander D.F.E.C. Deane). The raid was reported by returning crews to have been successful. Only three aircraft were lost from the force. Amongst them were two Halifaxes, one of which was a 427 RCAF Squadron Halifax V (DK253, ZL-M) piloted by Sergeant A. Chibanoff, RCAF. After taking off from Leeming at 8.30 pm nothing more was heard but it is clear that the aircraft reached the target. In the early hours of 16 September the people of the Harmondsworth heard an aircraft passing low overhead. It was ZL-M and reported by observers to be experiencing control difficulties. It appears that the Halifax may have had a hang up of some of its bombs as there were reports of bombs being jettisoned but these remain unconfirmed. It is also possible that the stricken bomber was attempting to land at what was then London Airport (now Heathrow). At 2.50 am the Halifax crashed at high speed near the River Colne, bouncing 25 feet back into the air, disintegrating as it went. The engines travelled for a quarter of a mile after the impact while the fuselage disintegrated and exploded on Middle Moor. All seven of the crew were killed instantly. The bomb aimer was Flying Officer Kendall Bell Begbie, RCAF. Aged 26, Begbie had come from Riverside, Ontario, to take part in the war effort. His parents were from Edinburgh and like many Scots had emigrated to Canada to secure a better future. Begbie was a married man and still had family in Edinburgh, as a notice in *The Scotsman* showed. It was placed by Begbie's uncle. The Canadian's body was taken to Edinburgh (Warriston) Crematorium and over 300 people attended a service for the crew held at the crash site.[11]

Since the famous attack on the Ruhr dams, 617 Squadron had been largely inactive, practising until further operations were mounted. In September its new commanding officer was ordered to mount an attack on the Dortmund-Ems Canal with the new 12,000 lb *Tallboy* bomb which had been developed by Barnes Wallis. On 15/16 September the squadron dispatched eight aircraft but when they reached the target area they found it was shrouded in mist and defended by light flak batteries;

Flying Officer Begbie (seated on left) and crew (Unknown)

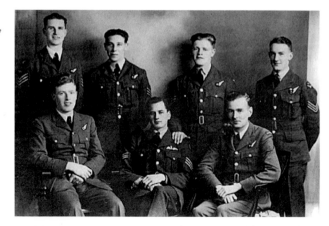

Flying Officer Rodger, 2nd from front behind his pilot, Photographed at Scampton in the days after Dam Busters Raid (PD)

only three aircraft returned to Coningsby. One of the Lancasters which was lost, shot down by light flak, was that of Flight Lieutenant H.S. Wilson (JA898, KC-X). Wilson's navigator was Edinburgh-born Flying Officer James Alexander Rodger. A 32-year-old married man, Rodger left behind his widow, Muriel, in Edinburgh, where they lived at 56 Cowan Road.[12] The crew had been trained for the dambusters raid but had missed out as one of the crew was ill on the night of the operation.

A meeting of the council in September saw concerns over the state of the Transport Department raised by several councillors, including the chairman of the Public Utilities Committee. There was a chronic shortage of labour in the department: the chairman outlined how 35 per cent of the staff had been lost to the services and that, while 960 conductresses had been trained, some 360 had been released and sent to other areas by the National Service Order. As a result, the department found itself short of 126 conductresses. This had a serious knock-on effect on fares being taken and it was increasingly commonplace for travellers, especially on short journeys, to not be charged by a conductress. Although uncollected fare boxes had been set up these depended upon the honesty of travellers. There seem to have been problems in using the manpower which was available and there were complaints that men who had been released from the services and returned to employment within the department were not being employed suitably. These matters had resulted in a loss of morale while there was also animosity in how the department collected clothing coupons on a yearly basis from its employees but issued them with a new suit only once every three years. Councillor Trainer said that, as he understood it, 'there was a great deal of discontent' in the department and 'that Councillors should take greater interest in the welfare of the employees'. Trainer also 'pleaded' with the council to allow service personnel to be given reduced fares on council run services.[13]

Some councillors seem to have sided with those who resented the ongoing blackout regulations. In September Councillor Sutherland argued for experiments to be made to modify the lighting scheme in the centre of Edinburgh. He admitted that the greatest stumbling block would be securing the agreement of the Ministry of Home Security but that they should be persuaded of the need for modifications and that, after that, they could quickly proceed with various experiments. Sutherland concluded by saying that if they pushed this through, the council 'would certainly earn and deserve the appreciation of the people'. Resistance to the proposal was considerable, led by Bailie Johnson-Gilbert. The general feeling was that no action should be taken by the council without recourse to the service authorities. Acting without this, argued Bailie Johnson-Gilbert, would 'risk jeopardising the lives of the citizens'. Treasurer Falconer joined in by saying that any increase in lighting would require an increase in the coal supply and that, due to the shortage of labour in the mining industry and the low coal stocks in the country as a whole, the 'proposal would not help the war effort in any way'.[14] A vote to move the entire question back to committee to be reconsidered was taken and won by 32 votes to 16.

Lack of a sense of purpose in the Home Guard continued to be a problem. With the enforced service in the Home Guard, levels of absenteeism were increasing in some areas and the authorities were determined to crack down on this. Many of the Home Guards were now being used to man anti-aircraft defences around the city and such service sometimes proved unpopular. In September two Home Guards were tried for repeated absenteeism. David Paterson Barrie (a carter from 1 Dean Street) pleaded guilty to absenting himself from parades for a period of five months. The sheriff heard how this amounted to Mr Barrie missing some forty parades that were his duty to attend and had no hesitation in fining Barrie £5. The second case involved sugar warehouseman Thomas Jinks of 22 Bothwell Street. Mr Jinks had been absent from his duties with a Home Guard anti-aircraft unit for a period of over two months and also had a previous conviction for a similar offence; he was thus fined £10.

The fighting in Italy continued unabated and the vicious combat resulted in horrific casualties. Many Edinburgh men, particularly in the Scots Guards, suffered casualties and for Edinburgh families with loved ones in this theatre it was a particularly tense time. By the end of October the early rapid advances had faltered and the Allies found themselves facing the mighty defences of the Gustav Line. At 64 Home Street, widower Mr Richard Tweedie received a telegram informing him that his youngest son David had died of wounds on 21 October. Guardsman David Tweedie of the 2nd Battalion Scots Guards was 33 and is buried at Minturno War Cemetery.

Bomber Command had been ordered by Sir Arthur Harris to prepare for its next major campaign, against the German capital, Berlin. In the build-up to this the pressure had to be maintained on other German city targets and there was a series of heavy raids throughout September, October and November. Three of these were on Berlin, with others on Munich, Hannover and Stuttgart amongst others. The crews of 8th Group (Pathfinders) led the way to these targets and their duties, aside from bombing, were to drop marker and illumination flares to guide the main force to the target area. Theirs was an incredibly dangerous job as they were often amongst the first over the target and they had to fly a longer operational tour than those of the main force (45 operations compared to 30).

Flying the reliable Avro Lancaster, 97 Squadron, based at Bourn, had joined the Pathfinders in April. Amongst its most reliable crews over that summer was that of Flight Lieutenant Duncan McNaught Moodie DFM, RCAF. Moodie was born in 1916 in Shanghai but his boyhood home had been Edinburgh and his parents still lived in the city. After education at Edinburgh Academy[15] he had gone on to a career at the Leith shipowners C. Salvesen & Co for five years, followed by a move to the firm of Hadden & Co, shipbrokers, Batavia. He joined the RCAF in 1941 and by 1942 was a pilot officer. Volunteering for Pathfinder duty Moodie quickly established a reliable reputation on the squadron including one very 'dicey' operation to Hamburg on the night of 27/28 July (the firestorm raid) when his aircraft was coned by searchlights before being attacked by a night-fighter. Having evaded these attacks the bombs were dropped on target and the navigator, Flight Sergeant J.T. Bundle DFM, plotted a new course back to base. On the night of 2/3 August the crew were again attacking Hamburg when heavy icing made control of the Lancaster difficult. Moodie, however, struggled on and successfully bombed the target before returning home.

Shortly after 5.30 pm on 18 October, Moodie and his crew set out on a raid to Hannover. This was the fourth time they had been sent to this target (they had been forced to abort one operation due to an oxygen failure). On this night they were part of a force of 360 Lancasters. The sky over the target was cloudy and the Pathfinders were unable to mark the target resulting in the raid being scattered with most bombs falling in open country to the north of the city. Eighteen Lancasters failed to return including Lancaster III (JB220, OF-O) of 97 Squadron; the pilot was Flight Lieutenant Moodie. Moodie and his crew had crashed near Nienburg on the bank of the River Weser at Erichshagen. Six of the seven-man crew had been killed with the only survivor being the bomb aimer Flight Sergeant H.W.N. Clausen DFM. A postscript to the loss of this crew was that, after the first operation to Hamburg, Moodie had been recommended for the DFC while his navigator and his bomb aimer had been recommended for the DFM. These awards were subsequently promulgated in November. Moodie's citation stated that he was the 'captain of a most reliable and capable crew'.[16] Flight Lieutenant Moodie and those who were killed were buried at Becklingen War Cemetery.[17]

We have clearly seen evidence of the huge sacrifice made by Edinburgh men and women serving in the forces, and their families. It was, however, not only news of those who were killed which pulled at the heartstrings of the people of the city. Many men and women suffered severe injuries in their service with modern warfare being exceptionally horrendous. At the end of October five Scottish servicemen who had been blinded were repatriated from the PoW camps and brought back to their homeland via St. Dunstan's (where they had been having treatment and rehabilitation) and detrained at Princes Street Station. One was from Edinburgh, one from Portobello and one from Leith and there were crowds of relatives and onlookers to welcome them back home. The sergeant-major who had escorted them back 'described them as the cheeriest party he had ever handled'. Driver John Rodgers of the Royal Armoured Corps was the first to leave the train and he instantly recognised the voices of his many relatives and friends who had gathered to welcome him (he lived at 6 Bridge Street, Portobello). Private Robert Smith of the Royal Scots was also welcomed by relatives although his wife had a few anxious moments after, in her enthusiasm, she had rushed past the carriage which bore her husband, but the two were soon reunited and were in each other's arms. They had been married only ten days before he had been deployed to France in 1940. He had been taken prisoner at St. Valery in 1940 after losing an eye and afterwards the other eye had been affected by his injuries. For some time he had been completely blind but the attention and care of Dr Charters meant that by the time he returned home he had limited sight in one eye.

For Corporal W.S. Deuchars, Gordon Highlanders, it was an especially poignant moment as he was introduced to his 3½-year-old daughter, Elaine, who had never seen him before; sadly Deuchars would never see his daughter. He had been due for leave after Elaine's birth but this had been cancelled and he had been sent to France instead. His older daughter Catherine (5½) was also there to welcome home her father and said she had forgotten what he was like. Deuchars had also been severely wounded in the fighting at St. Valery in 1940, being blinded and having lost an arm. His wife had initially been told that he was missing. However, around a year after this an underground source in France managed to smuggle information to her that her husband was in fact a PoW. After informing the War Office, contact was made. While in the camp, Deuchars was assisted by other prisoners who wrote home for him and then St. Dunstan's sent him a typewriter (presumably a braille one) which he was learning to use with one hand. His wife said how glad she was to see her husband looking so happy and well despite his injuries and experiences.

One of the men, Private J. Legge of the Seaforth Highlanders, had no family to greet him. His father had predeceased him and his mother was unable to make the long journey down from their home in Urquhart, but the 'gentle spoken lad' had plenty of friends there eager to welcome him home. Legge told reporters how while in camp Germans had told him they feared British raids, but that they would far rather the British won rather than have Russia invade Germany. During his time in captivity he had studied physiology with Dr Charters and anatomy under Captain Dr E.V. Barling, with a view to becoming a masseur.

There were of course many tears at the station, although they were mainly from friends and relatives and not from the five injured men and, after the lengthy initial greetings had been made the men and their families were escorted to the Royal British Hotel where the management had volunteered to welcome them with a meal. All five declared themselves delighted with their treatment and reception after coming back to Britain. One said, 'We are all right, and nobody needs to worry about us.'[18] All of the men were keen to express their admiration for the man that they called 'their hero', Major Dr David Livingstone Charters. He was a Glaswegian surgeon who had been taken prisoner and refused repatriation so that he could remain behind to work with blinded servicemen in the PoW camps (Captain Barling had also refused repatriation for the same reason).

On 23 December the draw was made for the annual Powderhall New Year Spring Handicap. There were 142 runners who had been accepted out of an initial entry of 226 and there would be eighteen heats. The event had attracted an impressive line-up, with runners from the north-east of England (including the previous winner, Nelson Taylor from Blyth) and London and Wales. Other notable runners included Liverpool footballer J.H. Mitchell (who had won in 1936) and the three Gall brothers from Dundee.

One of the more unusual meetings to take place in Edinburgh over the Christmas period was that of the Society for Recording Abnormal Happenings. The meeting, at 30 Heriot Row, discussed how over the course of the war people had become more open to the idea of the supernatural and that there was now a general acceptance that there were happenings outside the material plane. The meeting discussed three cases which had come to their attention during the year. The first involved an apparition accompanied by unexplained noises in the house of an Edinburgh businessman who

Private Robert Smith after being repatriated in October 1943 (Sunday Post)

had previously been a sceptic until he witnessed the apparition several times in his bedroom. The second case occurred in the south of England but was reported to the society by an Edinburgh woman: the ghost of a nun who appeared punctually in the grounds of a school at 6.15 pm on New Year's Eve. She had been waited for and had duly appeared on several occasions, once talking with the headmaster. The third case was at a large house in its own grounds in Musselburgh. The society had been invited to investigate by the owner, a well-known businessman, after he, his wife and various guests had heard abnormal sounds in several parts of the house. The society discovered that the property had a long history of abnormal occurrences and sounds going back before the time of the current tenancy.

One of the most popular films of the year (released in November) was *Millions Like Us*, the story of a family in wartime Britain focusing largely on a young woman sent to work in an aircraft factory who falls in love with a Scottish bomber crewman who is killed shortly after their marriage. The film had begun life as nothing more than a Ministry of Information short propaganda film but the writers had found such a rich seam of stories about women in factories that they had rewritten it as a full-length film. The character of the young Scottish airman (played by Gordon Jackson) found particular favour with the audience in Edinburgh. *The Sunday Post* described it as 'THE picture of 1943. I'll go further and say I have never seen a more convincing study of British middle-class life.'[19]

As preparations for a fifth wartime Christmas continued apace in Edinburgh households it became increasingly obvious that the tide of the war had changed. On Christmas Eve the people of Edinburgh read of the appointment of General Eisenhower as Supreme Allied Commander of the British-US-Allied invasion forces, and were reassured that the Battle of Ortona (a small Italian port town) was going well with the Canadians making advances against the German forces holding the town. One local columnist, a carpenter by trade, wrote how he had got up on Christmas morning while it was still dark, eaten a breakfast complete with black pudding, and listened to some music on the wireless. He then set out into the city, which was very quiet at that hour with very few people on the streets, although he did encounter a lone piper. The writer then took a coach to Colinton where the church bells were tolling for the Christmas morning service, although there were still very few people abroad. His journey then took him through Balerno (past the extensive paper mills) and he took the time to walk up to the site where a Luftwaffe bomber had crashed in the spring. He then returned to Edinburgh via the farms of Slateford. Walking through Gorgie the writer decided to visit Dalry House, to find that the ground floor was now being used as a British Restaurant (named 'Fare Ye Weel'). After partaking of a cup of coffee and chocolate biscuit he set out once more into the city where he took a bus to Princes Street. Noticing the fashions of those around him the writer reflected on how wartime had brought about a change in dress in Edinburgh, with young women dressed in colourful trousers and wearing scarves on their heads as opposed to the pre-war preference for hats. Many of the young men on the street (and probably a fair number of women too although this goes unremarked) were in uniform. Out of curiosity, the author followed one group of Polish soldiers into a rest house in Waterloo Place where he found men and women from various services, including 'a black man in uniform', at a long bar. There they were able to purchase a Christmas lunch of soup, turkey, and Christmas pudding for just a shilling. Before they left each received a gift of a warm article of clothing, while in another room they could relax after their meal and listen to music, converse and write home. Returning home, the carpenter enjoyed his own Christmas repast of 'a good fowle', fruit pudding and sauce, and 'other comforts'. Then he did a couple of hours work in his workshop before settling down to read *A Connecticut Yankee in King Arthur's Court* and then retiring to bed.[20]

On Boxing Day *The Scotsman* informed readers of further progress in the war across the globe. There was further positive news of the Battle of Ortona, alongside an account of the successful engagement by MTBs of a German cruiser off the coast of Yugoslavia. The newspaper also carried an account of the 'GREAT FORCE ASSEMBLED' for the invasion of Europe, saying that the US forces that were still arriving were receiving their final advanced training at amphibious warfare schools in Scotland. Readers were, rather optimistically, assured that the Americans were preparing for landings within ninety days and it was believed in 'Military circles in Washington' that orders had been issued to the RAF and the USAAF to 'complete the wiping out of Berlin before invasion starts'. There were reports of the pre-invasion bombing campaign already underway with over 2,000 aircraft attacking targets in Calais and the Pas de Calais areas. The public were warned of heavy casualties in the near future but were also told that of 1,300 US bombers sent out on Christmas Eve not one was lost. Sidebar stories informed the Edinburgh public of progress on the Russian Front with reports of ten German divisions being routed and large territorial gains being made. There were reports of hundreds of tanks and armoured vehicles being destroyed and advances of twenty-five miles in places. The largest headline was reserved for news of the Boxing Day sinking of the *Scharnhorst* during an ambush off northern Norway. The battleship was lured out by a British convoy bound for Russia (the Germans were increasingly desperate to stop this supply line and the Allies actions against U-Boats had been increasingly effective), only to be engaged by a combined force of British cruisers, destroyers and the battleship *Duke of York*.[21] To the people of Edinburgh this Christmas must have seemed the best, in terms of war news, since the war began.

For the Edinburgh men in RAF Bomber Command the news of the destruction of Berlin must have been somewhat bemusing as, since 23 August, the command had already launched ten major attacks on the German capital in what became known as the Battle of Berlin, during which they had suffered dreadful losses. A total of 332 heavy bombers had either failed to return or had crashed on landing (not including many which had failed to return from supplementary activities). For those in Edinburgh with loved ones in the campaign, the Christmas period must have been shot through with anxiety as they listened to radio reports of the raids and accompanying heavy losses.

Amongst the events planned for the New Year was an Edinburgh Royal Choral Union performance of *The Messiah* at the Usher Hall. By 29 December the performance had sold out. The Usher Hall was also to host an evening concert on

CONCERTS AND RECITALS

LUNCH-HOUR CONCERTS,

NATIONAL GALLERY OF SCOTLAND,
THE MOUND,
TO-DAY (WEDNESDAY), 1-2.15 p.m.
DAISY BADGER
AND
HILDA STEPHENSON.
JAMES REID, BARITONE.
Programme includes Works for Two Pianofortes by
Somervell, Milhaud, Harry Hodge, Saint-Saëns, &c. Songs
by Gibbs, Stanford, Parry, Hughes, &c.
Tickets, 1/-, at the Door.

THE EDINBURGH ROYAL CHORAL UNION.

USHER HALL,
NEW YEAR'S DAY,
"THE MESSIAH."
COMPLETELY SOLD OUT.
At 7 O'CLOCK.
EVENING CONCERT.
ISOBEL BAILLIE, SOPRANO.
MARGARET McARTHUR, CONTRALTO.
HEDDLE NASH, TENOR.
BOOTH HITCHIN, BASS.
NORMAN LONG, Entertainer—
A Smile, a Song, and a Piano.
Accompanist: S. WEBSTER, Mus.Bac., F.R.C.O.
Only Remaining Tickets for Evening Concert:
Unreserved, 2s and 1s.
Methven Simpson, Ltd., 83 Princes Street.

THE EDINBURGH CONCERT SOCIETY, LTD.

THE SCOTTISH ORCHESTRA.

SEVENTH CONCERT,
USHER HALL,
FRIDAY, 7th JANUARY,
AT 6.45 P.M.
Leader: REGINALD WHITEHOUSE.
Conductor: WARWICK BRAITHWAITE.
SOLO PIANOFORTE,
LAMOND.
Overture: "Leonora" No. 3 .... Beethoven.
CONCERTO No. 5, in E flat (The
"Emperor") for Pianoforte and
Orchestra .... BEETHOVEN.
SYMPHONY IN D MAJOR. "THE CLOCK" HAYDN.
Fantasia on a Theme by Tallis ...... Vaughan Williams.
Overture: "Die Meistersinger" .... Wagner.
Tickets:
Grand Tier, 7/6, 6/-; Area, 5/-, 3/6, 3/-; Res.,
Organ Gallery, 2/6; Upper Tier, 2/-, Unreserved.
BOOKING AGENTS:—
PATERSON'S, 27 GEORGE STREET.

THEATRES

KING'S.
Box Office, 10-8.
'Phone, 51027.
Daily at 2 and 6.30 until 8th Jan., thereafter
Mats. Tues., Wed., Thurs., and Sat., at 2
HOWARD & WYNDHAM, LTD.
PRESENT THEIR 37TH ANNUAL PANTOMIME,
"GOLDILOCKS
AND THE THREE BEARS."
ADELE DIXON.   JACKIE HUNTER.
MARY NAYLOR, JACK HAYES, MARY HONER,
GEO. AND JACK   THE DOLINOFFS
D'ORMONDE   AND RAYA SISTERS.
Orchestra Stalls, 8/- and 6/-; Grand Circle, 8/- and 6/-;
Upper Circle and Pit Stalls, 4/-, Sold Out Jan. 1.
Telephone Seats must be claimed by 12 Noon the
day before the date of Performance.

EMPIRE THEATRE.
ONCE NIGHTLY, EVENINGS, 7 p.m.
MATINEES at 2 p.m. on 29th December,
and 1st, 3rd, 4th, 5th, 8th, 12th, and 15th January.
"THE STUDENT PRINCE,"
With All-Star Cast of 50 Artists, including
BRUCE TRENT as Prince Karl Franz.
MARION GORDON as Kathie.
CYRIL JAMES as Lutz.
HARRY BRINDLE as Dr Engel.
Box Office Open 10 to 9.   BOOK NOW.

THEATRES (Continued)

ROYAL LYCEUM.
Box Office, 10-8.
'Phone, 24166-7.
Evenings at 7. Matinees at 2.
Prior to London Production.
ARTHUR RISCOE
IN
"JILL, DARLING."
With Hollywood's Famous Radio Star,
BARBARA BLAIR.
ROSEMARY RIGGS.   TERENCE DELANEY.
MATINEES Dec. 29, 30; Jan. 1, 4, 5, 6, 8.
Thereafter WEDNESDAY, THURSDAY, and SATURDAY.
Prices, 9/-, 7/-, 4/6, 3/6, 2/-, 1/6.
Sold Out Evening Jan. 1st.
Telephoned Seats must be claimed by 12 Noon the
day before the date of Performance.
The Scotsman says: 'Gay, gorgeously dressed,
enormously amusing, and uncommonly happy, carefree
comedy.'

MONSEIGNEUR NEWS THEATRE,
Princes Street. 11 a.m. to 10 p.m.
News, Musical, Sport, Travel, Disney.
Price of Admission, 1/9; Children, 1/-.

PICTURE HOUSES

REGAL (LOTHIAN ROAD.)
Open 12.20.
HUMPHREY BOGART,   BETTE DAVIS,
EDDIE CANTOR,   IDA LUPINO,
ERROL FLYNN,   ANN SHERIDAN,
JOHN GARFIELD,   JOAN LESLIE,
DENNIS MORGAN,   OLIVIA DE HAVILLAND,
ALEXIS SMITH.   DINAH SHORE,
In the Greatest of all Musical Classics,
"THANK YOUR LUCKY STARS."
Showing approx. 12.55, 3.17, 5.39, 8.01.

THE RUTLAND.   ST ANDREW SQ.
TO-DAY.
DEANNA DURBIN,
JOSEPH COTTEN,
IN
"HERS TO HOLD" (U.)
Rutland at app.:—1.10, 3.35, 6.5, 8.35 p.m.
St Andrew Square—1.25, 3.50, 6.20, 8.45.
Also Full Supporting Programme
of News, Interest, and Comedy Films.

NEW VICTORIA.   THE NEW.
1.15 to 10.5.   12.15 to 10.5.
'Phone, 438051.   'Phone, 251711.
TO-DAY.
ERIC PORTMAN, PATRICIA ROC,
IN
"MILLIONS LIKE US" (U.)
Showing New Vic.—1.45, 4.0, 6.10, 8.25.
Showing The New—1.10, 3.35, 5.0, 8.25.

THE PLAYHOUSE,
LEITH STREET. Continuous from 12 Noon.
RETAINED FOR THIS WEEK ONLY.
BETTY GRABLE,
GEORGE MONTGOMERY, CESAR ROMERO,
IN
"CONEY ISLAND" (U.)
A Grand Musical Entertainment
(in Technicolor.)
At 12.5, 2.55, 5.45, 8.35.
Also JOHN ABBOTT, MARY McLEOD, in
"SECRET MOTIVE" (A.)

DOMINION.   CHURCHILL.
TO-DAY, JOAN CRAWFORD, FRED
McMURRAY in, "ABOVE SUSPICION" (A.)
Showing at 2.58, 5.57, 8.56.
THURSDAY, FRIDAY, SATURDAY.
GRAND NEW YEAR PROGRAMME.
ANN MILLER and WILLIAM WRIGHT
IN
"REVEILLE WITH BEVERLEY" (U.)
Showing at 5.9, 6.6, 9.3.
And REX HARRISON, VIVIEN LEIGH in
"STORM IN A TEACUP" (A.)

POOLE'S SYNOD HALL,
CASTLE TER. Prices, 2/3, 1/9, and 1/-.
TO-DAY—Open 1 p.m.; Com. 1.15.
JAMES CAGNEY, PAT O'BRIEN,
and OLIVIA DE HAVILLAND, in
"THE IRISH IN US."
A Real Holiday Tonic.
Fast Moving in Thrills and Laughs!
At 1.15, 3.40, 6.10, and 8.40.

Christmas entertainment in Edinburgh (TS)

New Year's Day. This was to feature four singers (a soprano, contralto, tenor and bass) along with entertainer Norman Long in his show *A Smile, a Song, and a Piano*. Tickets were reportedly selling fast although there were still some left priced at 1s and 2s.

The cinemas were also popular over Christmas, with offerings that included *Thank Your Lucky Stars* and *Millions Like Us*, as were Edinburgh's many theatres. The Empire was showing a production of *The Student Prince* featuring an 'all-star cast'. The King's was hosting its 37th annual pantomime and was always popular. This year it was *Goldilocks and the Three Bears*; the New Year's Day performance was already sold out while tickets for the other daily performances were priced between four and eight shillings. The Theatre Royal was hosting *Dick Whittington*. The Royal Lyceum was hosting a performance of *Jill Darling* starring Arthur Riscoe and the American actress and radio star Barbara Blair. Reviews described it as an 'enormously amusing, and uncommonly happy, carefree comedy'.

CHAPTER 6

1944

For the tired men of RAF Bomber Command the New Year opened with the announcement of yet another large raid on Berlin. This was the third such raid in five days and heavy losses had already been suffered. At least two Edinburgh men lost their lives on this raid. The first was Sergeant Alexander Ross, a 21-year-old wireless operator flying Lancasters with 61 Squadron. His crew had taken off from Skellingthorpe at midnight on 1 January, one of sixteen bombers which were lost during the outward flight to Berlin. Lancaster III (LM377, QR-F) came crashing down near Büren after being shot down by a German night-fighter killing the crew of seven.[1] The son of James and Elizabeth Ross, Sergeant Ross was a married man and left behind his young widow Isabella. His parents had the following inscription placed upon his headstone in Hannover War Cemetery: 'IN LOVING REMEMBRANCE OF OUR ONLY SON. MAY HIS SACRIFICE NOT BE IN VAIN.'

The second Edinburgh man to lose his life on this raid was an experienced bomber pilot. Flying Officer Robert Leo Mooney DFM was aged 23 but had already flown a tour with 106 Squadron in 1941 (and was awarded the DFM on 23 December 1941) before returning to the fray with the Pathfinders of 97 Squadron at Bourn. On 16/17 December he had flown a mission to Berlin and on return the crew (like all on that night) encountered very poor weather conditions. Running low on fuel and with conditions making a landing risky, Mooney took the decision to abandon the aircraft after engaging the automatic pilot steering the aircraft out to sea. The crew were originally posted missing but all turned up safely and it was confirmed that their aircraft (S-Sugar on this occasion) had crashed into the sea. On 2 January the crew once again found themselves bound for Berlin. Lancaster III (JA960, OF-E) flown by F/O Mooney had taken off at 1 am and successfully bombed before turning for home. Near Aachen the bomber was hit by flak and crashed killing all seven crew. Flying Officer Mooney DFM was another married man who left behind a young widow at their home in Leith.[2]

Flying Officer Robert Leo Mooney DFM (Unknown)

Despite the fact that any invasion or raiding of Edinburgh was now almost beyond consideration, the military authorities continued to be reluctant to allow the removal of any defences in the city and, indeed, at the beginning of the year the military was attempting to obtain permission to construct further defensive fortifications throughout the city.

Once again Edinburgh proved its commitment to the war effort and its generosity by raising £8,500,000 in just three days during 'Salute the Soldier' week. The city had set itself the target of £10,000,000 and was well on the way with people giving very generously. Leith had already exceeded its target and had raised £750,000 in the first three days. A key feature of the week was a large military parade through the city watched by tens of thousands of spectators. The parade, described as 'one of the most spectacular Edinburgh has seen for some time',[3] included representatives from all the military services and the ARP, civil defence and the cadets. Of great interest to the crowds were the tanks, anti-aircraft guns and the mules carrying special jungle equipment. The parade, which included a dozen bands, ended in Princes Street where the salute was taken by the Lord Provost and the GOC Scottish Command, accompanied by music from the band of the King's Own Scottish Borderers.

With the arrival of US military personnel in 1943 the docks at Leith had taken on an even greater importance as Liberty ships carrying supplies and equipment for the US Army began to appear in ever greater numbers. To assist in the unloading and distribution of equipment a large detachment of mainly coloured troops from labour units of the US Army were posted to Leith. Although there were some tensions, most of the workers at Leith got along well with the coloured soldiers whose main duties were the unpacking and assembly of Jeeps and tanks (which were assembled at a nearby disused bus station). In the build-up to D-Day the American units began to withdraw to the south of England and there was some consternation locally over the destruction of surplus stores. The wastage was unthinkable for a wartime population which had put up with six years of rationing and shortages. At least one Leith dockworker used his friendship with some of the coloured soldiers to his advantage. Amongst the items being destroyed were a large number of wooden packing crates which had been used to ship jeeps to Britain. The dockworker arranged for some of the soldiers to deliver two of the crates so that he could use the timber to construct a shed, rabbit hutch and a greenhouse.[4]

Although we now see 1944 as a year of victories for the Allies, for many Edinburgh residents it was simply another year of stress and worry. We have already seen how there were many Edinburgh men risking their lives in nightly aerial operations over Germany. For those with relatives and friends in the Army the invasions of Sicily, followed by Italy, resulted in an increase in concern.

The fighting in Italy proved to be some of the most bloody of the war with the 8th Army becoming bogged down in a brutal slog against tenacious German defenders. It had been thought that the Germans would simply abandon their erstwhile allies but Hitler had anticipated both the collapse of Mussolini's Italy and the Allied invasion and had ordered the German army to prepare a series of strong defensive lines constructed using Italy's geographical features. Weather conditions were often appalling and the latter part of the campaign saw scenes more reminiscent of Passchendaele than those we associate with the Second World War. Worse, the soldiers in Italy now believed themselves to be largely forgotten in what they saw as an extremely bloody sideshow with little relevance to the outcome of the war. Between January and May the Battle of Monte Cassino raged for 123 days seeing four assaults on the heavily defended German lines to open up a path to Rome. Although the Allies were ultimately successful the battle resulted in 55,000 Allied casualties. Many of the British casualties were men who had served in the bitter fighting in the desert before the invasions of Sicily and Italy.

One man with Edinburgh connections to lose his life in the fighting at Cassino was Captain Robert Robertson Brackenridge. He was one of the 177 former students at Edinburgh Academy who lost their lives during the war. Captain Brackenridge had been an apprentice surveyor before joining the Royal Signals in November 1939 and then going on to serve in the Royal Artillery in Britain, the Western Desert and Italy. It was while serving with the 75th Heavy Regiment that the 26-year-old was wounded on 22 May; he died eight days later. Captain Brackenridge's family lived in southern England at Wimbledon Common but it seems that they had previously lived in Edinburgh as he had relatives who had also attended Edinburgh Academy.

Another Edinburgh Academy graduate to lose his life during the fighting in Italy was Captain Alan Archibald Cowan. Cowan was a good scholar and after leaving Edinburgh Academy he went on to Rugby and Edinburgh University. Cowan was commissioned in the Royal Artillery in 1938 and saw active service during the fall of France and the Dunkirk evacuation. Afterwards he was promoted to captain and because of his special training as a forward observer was posted to 625 Air Observation Post Squadron RAF in 1942. A year later he was transferred to 657 Air Observation Post Squadron as a flight commander and sent to the Middle East. Flying in the Taylorcraft Auster light observation aircraft he flew many missions in the desert before following the 8th Army to Sicily and Italy. Captain Cowan subsequently died of wounds received in action on 17 June.[5] This was a fortnight after the fall of Rome and during this period there was heavy fighting to the north of the city.

It was increasingly obvious that a second front would be opened at some point in 1944. This brought further anxiety for Edinburgh folk as the newspapers prepared people for the probability of heavy casualties.

The day before D-Day was one of considerable excitement in Edinburgh. The news was that Rome had fallen to Allied forces. The people of Edinburgh rejoiced at the fall of the first capital city of one of Britain's enemies and many took it as a sign that the recent heavy losses in the Italian campaign had been worthwhile.

There was also another VIP visitor to the city: Mary, Princess Royal and Countess of Harewood. In the morning the Princess Royal visited Queen Street Gardens to inspect a parade of the Girls' Training Corps and Girl Guides of Mary Erskine School before being entertained to lunch by the Edinburgh Merchant Company. In the afternoon she attended a commemoration service at St. Giles' Cathedral in honour of the 250th anniversary of the founding of the Company of Merchants of the City of Edinburgh and of the Mary Erskine School for Girls.[6] The corporation was represented by the Lord Provost and a number of councillors while the University, the Royal College of Surgeons, Faculty of Advocates and the Faculty of Actuaries were all represented. Other guests included Lord and Lady Rosebery, the Chancellor of the Duchy of Lancaster, Sir Thomas Holland and Sir Gilbert Archer, while the Very Reverend Charles L. Warr (Dean of the Thistle and the Chapel Royal) officiated.

Taylorcraft Auster similar to that flown by Captain Cowan (PD)

The dean looked back on the history of girls' education in Edinburgh before stating that the future would bring 'formidable and complex' problems, but that whatever developments lay ahead they must never forget that Christian principles must be the bedrock of education. He concluded by instructing the girls of the school who were present to 'set before themselves gracious and lovely ideals of womanhood and to preserve their personal honour at whatever cost'.[7] Following the service the Princess Royal was entertained to tea and a reception at the City Chambers. The Princess Royal then moved on to 21 Charlotte Square where she chaired the annual general meeting of the Scottish Branch of the Duchess of Northumberland's Comfort Fund for the ATS (the Princess was vice-patron of the ATS). The meeting heard that over the course of the previous year some 17,000 woollen garments and over 15,000 other items had been distributed and that this had allowed many ATS quarters and billets to be improved and made more homely. Representatives from the Scottish Command and Anti-Aircraft Command stated that these contributions made a big difference to ATS members and greatly aided in maintaining morale. It was then revealed that the expansion of the force had resulted in some financial difficulties and that there was a small deficit for the first time but it was hoped that further funding would be obtained in the next year. Concluding the meeting the Princess Royal told the gathering that she had been most impressed with the improvements which she had seen in ATS billets during her current tour of Scotland.

Many Edinburgh men found themselves taking part in the fighting on D-Day and there were many casualties. For several months Bomber Command had switched away from its area bombing campaign of German cities and had instead embarked on

*Princess Royal
inspecting Girl Guides
from the Mary Erskine
School (TS)*

what was known as 'The Transportation Plan'. This focused attacks on transport hubs to limit the Germans' ability to react to any invasion. On the night of the invasion the command flew a series of complicated diversionary missions while other bombers concentrated on hitting coastal batteries. Halifax III (LW638, MP-W) of 76 Squadron took off from Holme-on-Spalding-Moor at 2.30 am on the morning of 6 June tasked with bombing a coastal battery at Mont Fleury; it never returned. The Halifax had been shot down in the region of Ver-sur-Mer and Graye-sur-Mer. The seven-man crew were all killed. The rear gunner was 20-year-old Edinburgh man Sergeant Thomas Andrew McRobbie.[8]

The use of paratroopers and glider-borne troops to capture key strategic objectives ahead of the main landings was an innovative but highly dangerous ploy. For the paratroopers of 5th Parachute Brigade their journey to war took place aboard the Stirling bombers of 190 and 620 Squadrons. The latter dispatched twenty-three of its Stirlings beginning at 11.30 pm on 5 June. The aircraft had to fly at a level which exposed them to anti-aircraft fire (which was described as 'moderate' in intensity) and three of the aircraft from 620 Squadron failed to return while four more had been damaged. Upon inspection after returning it was found that twenty-seven of the Stirlings from the two squadrons were rendered unserviceable due to battle damage (the ground-crews worked feverishly throughout the day to get the aircraft ready to take part in further operations later that day). One of the three Stirlings to be shot down was that of Pilot Officer A.H. Barton. One of the gunners was Sergeant John Gillies Smith (23) of Edinburgh. Six men of the crew were killed when the Stirling was hit by flak and crashed just south of Grangues. Tragically, the Stirling had not yet dropped its complement of paratroopers and nineteen of the paratroopers were also killed.[9]

For the men of 12th Battalion (10th Green Howards), The Parachute Regiment, D-Day began with their scattered drop into France shortly before 1 am. The battalion was tasked with capturing the strategically vital village of Le Bas de Ranville (Ranville therefore became the first place to be liberated) before pushing on to relieve the glider forces which had been tasked with capturing the bridges over the River Orne and the Caen Canal. The 12th Battalion successfully captured the village, held off two counter-attacks and withstood heavy bombardments before they were relieved and could push on to help at the bridges. The battalion's casualties included 19-year-old Edinburgh man Private Thomas Anderson Skellett. Like many of his comrades who were killed in the D-Day fighting, Skellett is buried at Ranville War Cemetery where his parents, Thomas Henry and Anne, had the following inscription placed on his headstone: 'IN SACRED MEMORY OF OUR DEAR SON TOMMY. LOVED AND REMEMBERED ALWAYS.'

Sub-Lieutenant Julian Roney, RNVR, lost his life manning a landing craft on D-Day. He was the 24-year-old son of Arthur and Dorothy Roney and was married to Marjory who lived in Edinburgh. On D-Day, Roney was the commanding officer of Landing Craft Tank (Assault) 2191 as part of the 100th LCT(A) (HE) Flotilla. He and his crew were tasked with the delivery to Queen Red Sector of Sword Beach of several Centaur tanks of the 5th Independent Battery, Royal Marine Armoured Support Group. Due to the sea conditions the LCTs were running ten minutes late and by the time they reached the beaches the first assault waves were under heavy fire and suffering severe casualties. LCT(A) 2191 beached at the far easternmost flank of Queen Red Sector and after the tanks had been unloaded the craft came under heavy and accurate fire from a mobile 88mm gun. The landing craft stood little chance: it was hit by shells several times, was turned around by the impact of the shells and caught fire. The second shell hit the bridge where Sub-Lieutenant Roney, another officer and a signalman were stationed. The hit was devastating and killed both officers instantly.[10] Other hits resulted in the deaths of several more crewmen with others severely injured. For his actions in leading his crew on D-Day Sub-Lieutenant Julian Roney was mentioned in dispatches.

Although the worst carnage was at Omaha Beach, the British and Canadian forces landing on Sword, Gold and Juno also faced stiff opposition and there were heavy casualties in places. Amongst these was 21-year-old Marine Sydney Norman Brownlee Taylor. He was one of the crew of a Landing Craft Assault of the 525th LCA Flotilla. The flotilla was based aboard the SS *Empire Spearhead* on D-Day and was responsible for landing the 231st Infantry Brigade, 50th (Northumbrian) Division on Gold Beach. The Royal Marines had to draft in large numbers of men to plug gaps in the landing

LCT(A) 2012 of 100th Flotilla: LCT(A) 2191 was identical (Unknown)

craft flotillas which would be so vital on D-Day and there were 500 RM officers and 12,500 marines manning the craft. Each LCA had a four-man crew and could carry forty soldiers. The LCA flotillas making for Gold Beach had a difficult task which included a journey of ninety minutes in high seas and difficult tidal conditions. The Germans had seeded the approaches to the beach with 2,500 obstacles, including mines, and nests of German machine guns maintained a heavy fire on the approaching LCAs causing many casualties. The men packed onto landing craft were particularly vulnerable and those crewmen of LCAs assaulting Gold Beach were particularly at risk as the tide had come in quicker than expected and many of the beach obstacles had not been removed and many LCAs were damaged or destroyed as a result. Added to these risks was the poor sea conditions which made the armoured support late and heavy fire from fortified beachfront houses and a 75mm gun. The crews of the LCAs suffered a large number of casualties; amongst them was Marine Taylor.

For some young Edinburgh women, more prosaic matters were occupying their minds. There were complaints in the local press that they were paying 3s 6d or 4s to enter the city's dance halls but were not guaranteed a dance as many of the men simply sat around drinking during the dances. They argued for a change to the Glasgow method of operating dance halls which saw every second dance being a ladies' choice. Many were, of course, already undertaking vital war work but there was an ongoing campaign to encourage young women to enter domestic work in hospitals and convalescent homes. The campaign featured adverts in the local press emphasising the fact that this was a priority job and that the work was vital in ensuring the recovery of wounded servicemen.

Advert for women domestic workers to help nurse and care for the wounded (Sunday Post)

While the fighting went on in Normandy the airmen of Coastal Command continued in their task of protecting sea routes and attacking German shipping. On 17 July a Consolidated PBY Catalina of 210 Squadron took off from its base at Sullom Voe in Shetland tasked with patrolling over the North Sea to cover the British Fleet as it made its way homeward after the unsuccessful Operation Mascot (which was an attempt to sink the *Tirpitz*). The pilot was 24-year-old Flying Officer John Cruickshank, a former bank clerk in Edinburgh. The crew spotted Type VIIC U-boat U361 and Cruickshank put the Catalina into a diving attack despite heavy return fire. This first attack was unsuccessful as the Catalina's depth charge failed to drop. Aware now that the element of surprise had been lost, Cruickshank took the immediate decision to make a second attack, despite the risks. Shouting to his crew, 'Everybody ready? In we go again,' they dived into the now accurate and heavy fire. During this second attack the Catalina was hit repeatedly with explosive and incendiary shells and the navigator/air bomber Flying Officer John Charles Dickson was wounded. Despite this Cruickshank managed to drop the depth charges himself straddling U361 and sinking it with all hands. Taking stock of the damage it was realised that as well as the navigator/air bomber, four of the crew had been injured including Cruickshank himself. The flying officer had sustained ten penetrating wounds to the legs and serious wounds to the lungs. There were fires onboard and the aircraft had been peppered with enemy fire meaning that the crew had to stuff Mae Wests and engine covers into the gashes to make the flying boat seaworthy. There was a petrol leak and the radio had also been damaged and despite briefly passing out Cruickshank remained at the controls until he was sure that the damage had been rectified, signals had been sent and a course for home set. Fainting once more Cruickshank was carried back to the one surviving bunk (the others had been burnt) by the wireless operator/air gunner Flight Sergeant John Appleton. The young Flight Sergeant dressed his pilot's wounds but Cruickshank refused to have morphine as he realised it would cloud his judgement. Meanwhile, the second pilot, Flight Sergeant Jack Garnett (who was also wounded), took the controls. When Appleton went back to check on his skipper towards the end of the five and a half hour return flight the pilot asked about the condition of the navigator/air bomber but guessed from the expression on the wireless operator's face that his friend had been killed.[11] Cruickshank insisted on being taken back to the cockpit as he was aware that his wounded and relatively inexperienced co-pilot might require help in making what would be a night landing with severe damage. Being propped up in the cockpit Cruickshank ordered his co-pilot to circle base until light conditions improved as he judged it too dangerous to attempt a landing straight away. After circling for an hour and with Cruickshank weakening due to blood loss and having trouble breathing, the two pilots brought the Catalina in on the water and taxied to a place where the aircraft could be beached. A doctor boarded the seaplane and gave Cruickshank a blood transfusion on the scene. After being stabilised and taken to hospital it was discovered that Cruickshank had suffered 72 separate injuries and the RAF offered to fly his father from Edinburgh to Shetland so that he could be by his son's side. The fact that his father had flown (for the first time in his life) despite his fears amused Cruickshank but he remained in a poor physical condition

*Flight Lieutenant
Cruickshank VC
(Daily Record)*

with his breathing laboured and his father was only allowed to visit for short periods during the rest of the week. His father commented that he had done a fine job, but his son replied, 'Do you think so? I don't. Do you realise that I have lost my navigator and friend?' On 1 September it was announced that Cruickshank had been awarded the Victoria Cross for setting 'an example of determination, fortitude and devotion to duty in keeping with the highest traditions of the Service'.[12] After his father had congratulated him Cruickshank remained modest saying only that he was glad that Flight Sergeant Garnett had been awarded the DFM and he hoped that the rest of his crew would also be awarded medals.[13] Flying Officer Cruickshank's VC was the 101st of the war.

News of the VC for Flying Officer Cruickshank was met with enthusiasm by the people of Edinburgh and there was to be an investiture ceremony, along with other awards, at Holyroodhouse when the King, Queen and Princess Elizabeth visited. This set a new precedent as it was the first such investiture by the King to be held at Holyroodhouse within memory. Word spread quickly and by mid-afternoon large crowds had assembled along the route that the royals would be taking.

On their way to Edinburgh, the Queen and Princess Elizabeth inspected a large gathering of the ATS Training Centre at nearby Newbattle Abbey. The centre had been responsible for the initial training of thousands of ATS recruits and many others returned for advanced courses. For the visit the Queen wore a powder blue dress and matching coat upon which was pinned a Canadian maple brooch, a triple rope of pearls and an upturned hat which bore a diamond thistle. Princess Elizabeth wore a long grey coat and a hat of mixed flowers with a crown of navy straw.

After being greeted by a guard of honour their Majesties made a tour of the facilities which took over an hour and a half. They visited the sick bay where a 'remarkably healthy collection of invalids' from all over the country welcomed the royal visitors. The Queen spoke to each one and expressed her admiration for the bed covers and jackets and was told that they had been brought to the camp by her own sister Lady Elphinstone as part of her role with the Red Cross.[14]

They then visited the facilities where the trainees underwent the nine-week emergency cooking course. It was explained to the royal visitors that the course began with three weeks of cooking for just three in a small cookhouse before moving on to the larger cookhouse catering for larger numbers and finishing with a short course on field cooking. Princess Elizabeth took a particularly keen interest in the course, going through the cookery books and inquiring whether it involved the study of high-class cookery. The royal visitors asked the trainees what they intended to do after demobilisation and while one answered that she would be going back to her husband several others expressed an interest in serving with the Army of Occupation.

A member of his crew took this picture as the m··ch wounded pilot, Flying-Officer Cruick-shank, finished the second dive over the sinking U-boat. Cruick-shank had to reach back 'o release the jammed

Above: *U-361. Photo taken by member of F/L Cruickshank's crew during the attack (Daily Mirror)*

Right: *A Catalina of 210 Squadron (PD)*

Large numbers of girls, eager to see the royal visitors, crowded the windows of the huts they passed. During their tour of the living quarters the Queen felt the beds to check that they were comfortable and asked the girls if they had sufficient supplies and had mirrors. Near the end of the tour the party were shown the cobblers' shop where women repaired the shoes for the unit. Concluding in the HQ living hut, the Queen noticed the picture of her husband which hung over the door, saying that it was a good one of him.

Their Majesties expressed their admiration for the many stately trees which the grounds were famed for, particularly the ancient beech which occupied quarter of an acre and under which Queen Victoria was said to have sat. The head gardener, Mr Brownhill, was working nearby and, when their Majesties were told that because the other gardeners had volunteered for service he was looking after the garden alone, they asked to be introduced to him. Mr Brownhill had been employed at the abbey for over twenty years and, after wiping the earth from his hands, he took the hand proffered by the Queen and spoke at some length about the garden, receiving praise from the Queen for the 'excellent order of the garden'.[15]

Concluding the visit, their Majesties watched trainees drilling on the parade ground before taking in a physical training class and sharing coffee with the officers. They then left for Edinburgh by car with the road lined on both sides with khaki clad crowds of cheering and applauding women.

Upon arriving at Holyroodhouse that morning the King and his entourage were received by the hereditary Keeper of the Palace, the Duke of Hamilton, and a guard of honour provided by the Irish Guards in dress khaki and steel helmets. After the royal salute and the inspection of the assembled troops, accompanied by the commander-in-chief of Scottish Command, General Sir Andrew Thorne, the King and his entourage entered the palace. A crowd had assembled outside the gates, amongst them many American service men and women, some whom were taking photographs. As word of the investiture spread the crowd continued to grow.

The King, in the uniform of a naval admiral, made the presentations from a raised dais at the end of the portrait gallery. Also present were Lord Clarendon (who announced the recipients) and Lord Forteviot. The ceremony began at 11 am precisely when the King entered and the guests stood for the national anthem played by the band of the Royal Dragoons. Before the ceremony a chair was placed at the front reserved for Flight Lieutenant Cruickshank (whose parents were seated in the front row). Cruickshank was the first in line for investiture and his citation was read out immediately following the national anthem. It was clear that the airman was still suffering from his wounds as he moved slowly and carefully forward to receive his medal. When His Majesty presented the medal to Cruickshank the two conversed at some length in quiet voices. The King congratulated Cruickshank, expressed his pleasure that he was recovering from his injuries, and inquired about the other members of the crew. No doubt Cruickshank was able to inform His Majesty that his co-pilot Flight Sergeant John S. Garnett was behind him in the line to receive the DFM, and that there was another member of 210 Squadron present at the investiture, Warrant Officer Raymont J. Henderson, RAAF, there to receive a DFC.

Following Flight Lieutenant Cruickshank VC to the dais were Air Vice Marshal Sturley Simpson who received the CBE and Major Charles Scott Plummer who received the CB (Most Honourable Order of the Bath).[16] They were followed by a lengthy list of recipients of both civil and military awards. Amongst the most noteworthy of these was Rear Admiral Loben Maund, commanding officer of HMS *Ark Royal* during the early years of the war and captain when the aircraft carrier was sunk.[17] *Ark Royal* had played a leading role in many of the early campaigns of the war and won much honour in actions such as the invasion (and subsequent evacuation) of Norway, the hunt for the *Scharnhorst* and the early Malta convoys, but it was for the part played by the ship (or more correctly her Fairey Swordfish aircraft) in delaying the battleship *Bismarck* (making a vital contribution to her eventual destruction) in May 1941 that Maund was invested with the CBE. This must have been an ambivalent experience for Maund as he was also present to collect the DSC awarded posthumously to his son, Lieutenant Michael Maund.[18] It must have also been seen by the admiral as a vindication, as at a court-martial after the aircraft carrier's sinking he had been found guilty on two charges for his failure to ensure damage control parties had remained on board and failing to ensure that the *Ark Royal* was in a fit state to deal with an emergency.[19]

The recipients of awards lined up outside after their presentations to await their friends and families. As well as civilians, members of the ARP and civil defence services (in uniform), there were present representatives from every branch of the armed forces. After the ceremony Flight Sergeant Garnett DFM had managed to find his former crewmate only with difficulty as he was talking inside the palace with his parents. Many harboured hopes of greeting the hero of the hour, but were to be disappointed as the modest nature of Flight Lieutenant Cruickshank VC imposed itself once more. Anxious to avoid recognition, the flight lieutenant did not assemble outside with the others but slipped away almost unnoticed through a side door before making his way by bus to a city hotel where he met up once more with his parents and his erstwhile co-pilot for lunch. It would seem that Cruickshank had not planned this as he had left his parents and Flight Sergeant Garnett in the palace courtyard expecting to meet up with him!

After the ceremony the King, Queen and Princess visited Craigentinny Primary School with the Lord Provost and his wife. No advance announcement had been made of the visit but the streets were lined with enthusiastic crowds. The school had been selected because of its fine record in fund-raising, the pupils' enthusiasm for gardening and the contribution made by the school to the local community. At the nursery section the King asked why the children were not eating as it was their mealtime; he was told they were waiting until the royal visit had finished. Upon hearing this the King said, 'then let us have the grace' and the children 'shyly but beautifully' sang the grace.[20] They then visited the sewing room and were shown some of the skilful work of the girls there (as part of the make do and mend campaign). In the library the King asked a little girl who was reading *The Swiss Family Robinson* who the author was but she was stumped, as were most of the older guests. Princess Elizabeth told one young pupil who was reading *Dr Doolittle* that she had read all of the Doolittle books herself. Concluding the visit the Queen was presented with a bouquet by 8-year-old Nancy Scott and the Royal group was cheered as they departed.

Their Majesties and Princess Elizabeth at the Regional Commissioner's headquarters. The group also includes Lord Rosebery, Regional Commissioner (left); Mr William Quin, Deputy Regional Commissioner; Sir Gilbert Archer, District Commissioner, South-Eastern District; Sir John Phin, District Commissioner, and Lord Provost Sir Robert Nimmo, Deputy District Commissioner, Eastern District.

Above: Royal Party at Holyrood (TS)

Left: King and Queen at Craigentinny Nursery (Daily Record)

After the school visit the royals visited the East Pilton site of Messrs Bruce Peebles & Co. This firm of electrical engineers employed several thousand people producing aircraft parts, electrical equipment for a variety of items of equipment including mobile searchlight units and minesweeping vessels, shells, and parts for submarines and tanks. There were many women there employed on intricate technical work. The royals witnessed an example of electrical gapping and the use

Above: *The King inspects Honour Guard at Holyroodhouse (Daily Record)*

Right: *Princess Elizabeth at Craigentinny (Daily Record)*

of an X-ray machine to detect faults in electrical equipment. The guests frequently stopped at work stations to ask the workers what they were employed on and to ask after their wellbeing. After the successful visit the royal party was again cheered off as they headed for the City Chambers.

Before that, however, they said they would like to meet the district commissioners who had made such a contribution to the civil defence and ARP of Scotland as these services were shortly to stand down and the commissioners resign. This was speedily arranged and the cars took the royals to the Palmerston Place headquarters of the Regional Commissioner where they were presented to the personnel.

Following this the party made its way along Princes Street where, once again, large cheering crowds had formed despite the lack of formal announcements. Noticeable were the large numbers of American soldiers who perched on the window parapets of the American Red Cross Club.

At the City Chambers the royals were introduced to the Town Clerk and the City Chamberlain before taking tea in the dining room. Then they mingled and talked with the town councillors. The King praised the city's wartime efforts and contribution and commented that the city was fortunate to have councillors who were so dedicated to the well-being of the city and its residents. Following the signing of the guest book they were escorted along the passage which featured photographs of the past Lord Provosts. The current Lord Provost raised a laugh when he commented that the Lord Provosts of old had been drawn from peers of the realm but now they were down to choosing drapers. During the goodbyes the Queen remarked on how attractive the Lord Provost's gold chain of office was and how the gold touches in his wife's hat complemented it. She also praised the Lady Provost's interest in the Girls Training Corps.

The success and determination of the Edinburgh branch of the Women's Home Defence movement proved their skill and resourcefulness throughout their existence and when it held its own stand-down ceremony in London in December the Edinburgh ladies won a host of prizes and the local press called them 'WOMEN SHARPSHOOTERS'. In the nationwide rifle shooting championship the Edinburgh women headed the list. Mrs D.G. Thomlinson won a silver rose bowl for her phenomenal score of 298/300. Edinburgh also won first place in the five-woman team shooting (captained by Miss C. Dodds) with a score of 496/500. The awards were presented by Dr Edith Summerskill MP and Dr Summerskill's own cup, which was presented to the winners of a shoot-off between the top eight teams, was also won by Edinburgh. The Edinburgh women agreed they would continue to meet under the name of the Women's Rifle Association.

With the threat of enemy invasion now gone it was announced that the Home Guard would be disbanded. On Sunday, 3 December, Home Guard units from across Edinburgh gathered to hold their stand-down parade. The salute was taken on the steps of the Royal Scottish Academy by the GOC-in-C Scottish Command, General Sir Andrew Thorne. He was accompanied by the Edinburgh Home Guard sector commander, Colonel Drummond, Brigadier C.W. Bayne-Jardine CBE DSO MC (commander of the Scottish Anti-Aircraft Defences), Commander F.P. Frai, RNVR (on behalf of the C-in-C Rosyth), Air Vice Marshal R. Smart, Bailie Colonel Bruce Turnbull who was there on behalf of the Lord Provost, and Sheriff J.C. Fenton (sheriff of the Lothians and Peebles). All arms of the Home Guard were represented including the anti-aircraft crews and the motorcyclists of Scotland's Home Guard 'flying column' (officially the No. 1 Scottish Home Guard Transport Column).

There were an estimated 7,000 Home Guardsmen taking part in the parade with huge crowds packing Princes Street to watch the spectacle. General Thorne commented that the parade was one of the most moving he had ever taken part in and the men of the Home Guard were so fine that he almost wished they had had the chance to come to grips with the enemy. The massed pipe bands of the Home Guard, accompanied by the band of the Royal Dragoons, formed up next to the Academy and played stirring martial music, relayed via loudspeakers set up in the trees along the route. The procession was led by the motorcycle mounted men of the 'flying column' and they were followed by the men of eleven general service Home Guard battalions. Following these battalions were the members of the anti-aircraft rocket batteries (who had helped in the destruction of two raiders in March 1943). The rear of the parade was brought up by a mobile battalion of twenty-four buses under the command of Lieutenant Colonel James Amos.

Commanders of General Service Battalions present at Edinburgh Home Guard stand-down parade

Battalion	Commanding Officer (all lieutenant colonels unless otherwise stated)
1st	D.A. Foulis DSO
2nd	J. Logan-Strang OBE
3rd	R.F. Ker DSO MC OBE
4th	B. Hall-Blyth
5th	H.C.L. Guthrie MC
6th	J. Walker
7th	J. Armour MC
8th	A.H.C. Murray MC
9th	Captain G.C. Thomson
10th	A.B. Mein
11th	J. Tod MC DCM MM

The men of the 'flying column' had come from across Scotland to attend the Edinburgh parade and they were treated to tea at the Balmoral Restaurant following the parade. The meal and following entertainment was presided over by Lieutenant Colonel James Amos who addressed the men saying they could be very proud of their achievements and that if in any way they had helped the country to victory over Germany then 'all the months and years of training we have had will not have been in vain'.

At Dalkeith the 2nd Midlothian Home Guard held their own parade with the Lord Lieutenant, Lord Rosebery DSO MC taking the salute. Despite the fact that some of the men were on duty there was a good turnout. Rosebery gave an impassioned speech in which he praised the contribution of the Home Guard before exaggeratedly

Edinburgh Home Guard Stand-Down Parade (TS)

Edinburgh Home Guard Stand-Down Parade. Men of the 'Flying Column' and General Thorne (TS)

saying that it was possibly the Home Guard's attitude and willingness to 'defend the country to the last inch' that had 'caused Hitler to think again and remain on the other side of the channel'. He went on to say that the Home Guard 'had certainly prevented an invasion' and that the people of Britain would always remember with gratitude the sacrifice of the men of the Home Guard. A similar parade and inspection, again attended by Lord Rosebery, took place at Penicuik with the men of 1st Midlothian Home Guard.

On the same day London hosted a huge parade with Home Guard units from across the country. Amongst the 7,000 Home Guardsmen who took part was a Scottish contingent with detachments of three men from each Scottish county. Amongst the Edinburgh detachment was Captain S.T. Cowe of the 3rd City of Edinburgh Home Guard.

With the sixth wartime Christmas looming there was a shred of good news as it was announced that rationing on biscuits and beans was to be reduced. The points cost of most types of biscuits was to be halved and on some cans and packs of beans it was reduced by more than half. The authorities cautioned people that although supplies of biscuits would be increased they might not reach the shops before the festive period.

CHAPTER 7

1945

As we have seen the war brought an influx of foreigners into Edinburgh with large contingents of Poles and Americans and men and women from the Commonwealth and various allied nations. Although there were tensions, most of the time the people of Edinburgh got along with these guests. One result was an increase in the numbers of local women marrying foreigners. There was sometimes concern expressed over this and the authorities monitored the figures of these marriages. In February the city's registrar general announced that the number of Edinburgh women who during the war had married men who were not British stood at 8,498.

An Edinburgh man lost his life in what was seen by many of those taking part as a forgotten campaign: Burma. Flying Officer Eoghan Lyon Carmichael was another former student at Edinburgh Academy. In civilian life Eoghan had worked for two years as an apprentice factor on the Argyll Estates on the island of Tiree and at Inveraray. Following this apprenticeship he had gone on to the factoring department of J. Anderson of Edinburgh while also studying at both Edinburgh University and the East of Scotland Agricultural College. He worked for two years as a civil defence ambulance driver in Edinburgh before he enlisted in the RAF and was sent to Canada for training as a pilot. Successfully qualifying he was commissioned in 1943 and the following year he was posted to India where he joined 27 Squadron flying Bristol Beaufighters on anti-shipping strikes, operations supporting the 14th Army, and night-fighter duties over Burma. On 26 March, Carmichael and his navigator were killed while in action against Japanese forces.[1]

On 3 April the fighting in Italy had seen an action which led to a further Edinburgh VC. Corporal Thomas Peck Hunter had been born at Aldershot but his parents, Ramsay and Mary, had moved the family to Edinburgh when he was still a baby. Thomas was brought up in the city attending Stenhouse Primary School and Tynecastle High School before becoming an apprentice stationer. Aged 16 when war broke out he joined the Edinburgh Home Guard before he was called up on 8 May 1942 joining the Royal Marines. Like many from a Home Guard background he proved an able soldier and was promoted to corporal in January 1945. Serving with 43 Commando in Italy he fought in that hard campaign and was in charge of a Bren gun section. During Operation Roast on the shores of Lake Comacchio his men came under heavy fire from several enemy machine guns. Hunter quickly realised that his men would be cut down if they did not reach cover and took the decision to charge the enemy positions (the machine guns were lodged in three houses) alone firing his Bren gun from the hip. So effective was his charge that several of the enemy surrendered and the others fled. By this time Corporal Hunter was under fire from at least nine machine guns and from enemy mortars. Seeing that his troop was now making for the cover of the houses which he had cleared but was under fire from machine guns in pillboxes on the north bank he placed himself in a position of great risk atop a pile of rubble in full view of the enemy and began to engage the pillboxes. As he did so he shouted encouragement to those of his men who had not yet reached cover and demanded more magazines. Firing with great accuracy Corporal Hunter silenced several of the enemy guns and enabled his troop to capture their objective but as they did so he was hit in the head by a burst of fire and killed instantly. The VC citation for Corporal Hunter stated that 'Throughout the operation his magnificent courage, leadership and cheerfulness had been an inspiration to his comrades.'

The official and unofficial celebrations of the announcement of victory over Germany on 8 May were in stark contrast to each other. The official celebration consisted of a short meeting of the Town Council at the City Chambers presided over by Lord Provost Falconer. The provost praised the contribution to the war effort made by Scottish men and women and stated that 'We are … nearing the end of a journey which has no parallel in history … we have been engaged upon the greatest task the world has ever seen … The greatest victory of all time has been gained'.[2] After criticising the way the Nazis had behaved, he said how the sacrifice of the British people in fighting for freedom had given hope to the nations once under the Nazi's heel, adding, 'The price that has been paid in sorrow leaves us with a high trust which we must be ready to discharge and to defend … It is now for us to act so that the unity gained in war will re-enforce the determination that the world shall be made worth living in, and that the return of evil and injustice is to be denied.'[3]

The meeting sent congratulatory telegrams to the King and to the Prime Minister. That to Winston Churchill was fulsome in praising his links with Edinburgh and Scotland. Churchill of course had strong Scottish links, having been MP for Dundee and in 1929 was elected a rector of Edinburgh University. During the war Churchill had visited Scotland on several occasions and would do so again in the forthcoming general election campaign.[4]

This meeting was followed by a short ceremony held at the Mercat Cross during which the Lord Provost urged the small crowd assembled to remember those who had given their lives in war and those who continued to fight against the Japanese. The 76th psalm was read by the Dean of the Thistle; it was chosen because it had been read out at a thanksgiving service after the defeat of the Spanish Armada in 1588.

Unofficial celebrations were rather more effusive. Even though there was wet weather, hundreds of service men and women, factory workers and shop girls poured onto the streets to parade through the capital. By the afternoon the focus of much of the crowd was the area around the American Red Cross Service Club and the Register House. Thousands gathered outside the club from where American service personnel threw down chewing gum, chocolates and service caps. In tune with American tradition, torn up paper was also showered down upon the street below. So boisterous were the crowd that extra police reserves had to be called in to ensure safety. One marine on the balcony acted as conductor as the joyful crowd below bellowed out a number of songs, *Roll Out the Barrel*, *The Yanks are Coming*, *Tipperary* and,

Mercat Cross during the Thanksgiving Parade (TS)

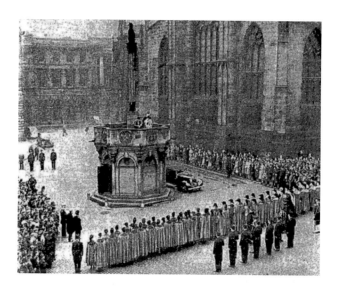

of course, *Land of Hope and Glory*. Demonstrating support for the Soviets, a red flag waved from the balcony received a loud cheer.

At the Register House the statue of Wellington proved a focal point with several servicemen climbing the statue and one even balancing precariously upon the top of the horse's head to catch service caps which were thrown up to him. The crowd once more sang various popular songs with dancing and boisterousness to the fore. Flags were flown from windows and balconies and displayed the favour shown to the nation's allies. Although the Union Jack was predominant there were also numerous Scottish Saltires, Lions Rampant, Stars and Stripes, Red Flags of Russia, French, Belgian and other flags. People had dug out bunting and this decorated many window sills and balconies. The council hoped that the bunting and flags would remain in place for the visit of the King and Queen the following week.

By the evening the weather had improved somewhat and the crowds became even larger and the centre of the city, especially Princes Street, became extremely crowded. The crowds were overwhelmingly younger people and service personnel. In the West End, sailors joined hands in a circle around a policeman and sang and danced around him. When the crowd noticed, they were joined by reinforcements from the naval contingent in the crowd while the police officer stood embarrassed.

The service personnel tended to move about in large groups but there were no reports of inter-service trouble, with the atmosphere described as humorous. The women of the ATS were prominent in the celebrations and a large crowd was assembled at the Wellington statue in the evening. Wellington himself was obscured by those climbing the statue while 'the horse seemed to be struggling with its unwonted load of humanity'.[5] A party of about thirty sailors approached the statue marching down the road in a solemn fashion from the direction of Leith Street, each carrying a pint of beer from a nearby public house. The massive crowd parted for them and when they reached the statue their leader gave the command to halt at which

VE Day. Service personnel on Wellington's statue (TS)

point each man stopped and raised the glass to his lips to drink before, at another command, the group moved off down Princes Street with their glasses raised high.

Indeed, the men of the RN appear to have been amongst the most active celebrants on the night of 8 May. A large group had gathered outside the university and at one point stopped a passing lorry and managed to persuade the reluctant driver to take them for a ride to the post office. One incident here could have resulted in ugly scenes. A loaded dray lorry was stopped by a group of sailors and several barrels of beer removed before being rolled down the street (the sailors made no moves to breach the barrels). But the police took a hand, and the sailors cheerfully assisted the officers and others to reload the lorry so that it could proceed on its way.

In Princes Street Gardens a system for the playing of wireless music had been arranged and large crowds gathered to dance and sing, while at the Ross Fountain a piper attracted a considerable crowd. His eightsome reels proved especially popular with everyone joining in including mothers with young babies in their arms.

Showing a puritanical touch *The Scotsman* seemed to hint that there might have been those who would question the propriety of public houses remaining open later than usual due to the celebrations. However, this was not a problem as the majority of the pubs and hotels were forced to close by 8 pm as they simply ran out of stock. The crowds of younger people were therefore more sober than might have been expected, but the scale of the occasion was intoxicating enough to ensure that good, though boisterous, spirits prevailed. It was presumed that it was this boisterousness that kept the older residents of Edinburgh away from the main celebrations. Another reason given was that perhaps the older members of society were 'more conscious of the shadows of war than the young people, who had good reasons for rejoicing as they did'.[6]

VE Day crowds at the Mount (TS)

Elsewhere children in the High Street, Canongate and Granton areas made full use of the official permission to have bonfires. The largest blaze was next to the entrance to Holyrood Palace at which a loud crowd gathered to sing and dance accompanied by an accordionist. In Granton children were seen carrying blackout blinds to feed the bonfires.

On Sunday, 13 May, a thanksgiving parade was held in the city at which 3,000 men and women from the services, civil defence organisations, war workers and youth organisations took part. The parade along Princes Street was lined by thousands of spectators while others leaned precariously from windows and balconies. Some of the crowd dispersed as rain began to fall but there were still sufficient to cheer the forty-minute procession. The salute was taken on the steps of the Royal Scottish Academy by Lord Provost Falconer who, for this occasion, wore his Lord Lieutenant's costume.

The celebrations continued with crowds proceeding to Princes Street Gardens where the BBC had arranged for the live broadcast of the King's speech to the nation. The atmosphere was both festive and reflective as the band of the King's Own Scottish Borderers played a selection of popular music for the hour leading up to the speech.

Links between Scotland and Norway had remained strong through the war and with the German surrender it was announced that Crown Prince Olav, Commander-in-Chief of Norwegian Forces, along with three Norwegian cabinet members (Oscar Fredrik Torp, Minister of Defence, Terje Wold, Minister of Justice, and S. Nielsen, Minister of Commerce) was to sail from Leith to his homeland on 11 May. The Crown Prince and his party sailed aboard HMS *Devonshire* escorted by a large and powerful British squadron. This was a pointed statement as it had been the same ship which had evacuated the Norwegian royal family and government from Norway in 1941. The party included the future joint commanders of HM Forces in Norway, General Sir Andrew Thorne and Rear Admiral J.S.M. Ritchie.

Women's Land Army contingent pass the saluting stand during Thanksgiving Parade (TS)

Despite the levels of activity around the ships as ammunition and supplies were taken aboard, the workers at the dockyard were largely unaware of the events taking place. Escorted by two naval ratings, the Crown Prince saw his baggage, which included a number of pistols and a small radiogram, taken aboard before the party were taken by tug to the warships which were berthed at a quay a quarter of a mile away. The first warship had its gangplank lowered and a guard of honour of 100 Royal Marines with their band and Major Generals Irwin and McMicking welcomed the Crown Prince as he disembarked from the car which had brought him from London. After inspecting the guard and having a short conversation with a small group of officers including the commander of Rosyth, Admiral Sir W.J. Whitworth, he was piped aboard before HMS *Devonshire* and its two escorts put out to sea passing under the Forth Bridge.

This was not the end of the formalities at Rosyth that weekend as preparations were made for the arrival of the German military delegates who were expected to arrive to relay details of military dispositions in Norway in accordance with the terms of surrender. By the evening of 11 May the delegation, aboard a British warship, was lying off Rosyth. Over the weekend the delegates from the Wehrmacht and the Luftwaffe underwent a series of meetings and interviews at Lord Roseberry's home of Craigiehall. The reports of these early meetings said that the German officers had brought very detailed plans and were co-operative and it was hoped that the evacuation and disarming of remaining German forces would, as a result, only take a few days.

There was an amusing event at Craigiehall when Roseberry arrived to inspect some of his property but was stopped in the grounds by a US Army major and told politely but firmly that unless he had a pass he could not enter. His Lordship pointed out that he had not considered it necessary to obtain a pass to enter his own house and that to do so now he would have to drive fourteen miles to Scottish Command headquarters. The major was unmoved and said, politely, that without instructions to the contrary he could not admit him. Ascertaining that further debate was pointless Rosebery, who saw the humour in the situation, accepted the refusal philosophically and departed from his property.

Despite the excitements of VE-Day, fundraising went on as normal in the city the following weekend. A series of annual 'modified' ambulance competitions were held.[7] They did not have prizes but were arranged at the request of the sections of the St. Andrew's Ambulance Corps in Edinburgh and the east of Scotland to boost interest in first aid skills and training. Sixteen teams took part at the Darrioch Institute. Contests included general knowledge of first aid and a practical test in the transportation of injured persons. The competition was won by the Dysart section with Dalkeith and District LNER No.2 Team second and Waverley No.1 and Portobello No.1 tying for third place.

We have already seen how royal visits were fairly frequent in Edinburgh and were great morale boosts. With victory over Nazi Germany it is no surprise that the city wished to express its gratitude and appreciation to the King and Queen. Eight days after VE-Day the city got its chance. When the day dawned it was overcast with frequent rain showers but this failed to dampen the atmosphere and the enthusiasm of the massive crowds who had assembled in the city. The streets on which the King, Queen and two Princesses were to be driven were all extensively decorated while even those off the route were bedecked with bunting. Reporting on the eight-hour-long visit, *The Scotsman* said that the royals were greeted and 'hailed as just members of the big British family who together have undergone the strain and sacrifice of the war years'. Saying how the war had brought everyone closer, the newspaper described a 'friendlier, less formal, atmosphere than usual'.

Massive crowds had assembled outside Princes Street Station for more than an hour before the scheduled arrival of the royal party. The large traffic island at the west end of the station had been turned into a floral garden at which the band of the Royal Dragoons played a selection of lively tunes, the crowds joining in with gusto. The King's Guard, made up of men drawn from all three services, were assembled where the royals would alight under the command of Lieutenant Commander E.W. Briggs DSC, and it was remarked upon that this was the first time that a combined guard had taken part in a royal ceremony. Alongside the guard were representatives from the services including: Admiral Sir William J. Whitworth KCB DSO, C-in-C Rosyth; Major General N.M.S. Irwin CB DSO MC, Scottish Command; and Air Vice Marshal H.G. Smart CBE DFC AFC.

Shortly before the scheduled arrival, the Secretary of State for Scotland, the Rt. Hon. Thomas Johnston MP arrived on the platform and he was followed minutes later by the magistrates and town councillors in scarlet robes accompanied by a guard of High Constables and City Halberdiers in full dress uniform. The greeting party consisted of Lord Provost Falconer (in the uniform of Lord Lieutenant), the Lady Provost, Mr J.C. Fenton QC (Sheriff of the Lothians and Peebles), the Earl of Rosebery DSO, and Chief Constable Morren.

The royal train arrived on time (drawn by the locomotive *City of Edinburgh*) to loud cheers from the crowds outside. As the King alighted and saluted the commander of the guard the Royal Salute was played by a Marine band followed by the National Anthem as the Queen and two Princesses joined the King on the platform. Following the inspection of the guard and presentation of the keys the greeting party was introduced to the royal party which also included Lady Harlech (lady-in-waiting to the Queen), Sir Eric Miéville KCIE KCVO CSI CMG, and Wing Commander Peter Townsend DFC. As the royal car turned off the platform the Queen, as was her habit, waved to the engine driver (Peter Dempster) and firemen on the *City of Edinburgh*.

The King was wearing the uniform of Admiral of the Fleet while the Queen wore a pale turquoise dress and coat with a felt hat, summer fox furs, a diamond brooch in the shape of a thistle and three ropes of pearls. Princess Elizabeth was also in uniform, this time that of a 2nd lieutenant in the ATS, while Princess Margaret wore a blue dress, grey coat and grey straw hat which was trimmed under the brim with pink and blue posies.

As the royal party progressed towards St. Giles' Cathedral the bells of the many churches in the city pealed and cheering crowds lined the route. Princes Street, Waterloo Place and Regent Road were lined by 1,200 members of the Brigade of Guards in khaki uniform. The windows of buildings along the route were packed with people and an especially loud cheer emanated from the American Red Cross Building where a solid block of American soldiers had wedged themselves onto the balcony and roof over the entrance. The crowds were four or five deep in many places with larger numbers on the Royal Mile where another guard, formed of NFS men and men from a nearby RAF Coastal Command squadron, awaited. The Royal Mile also hosted a crowd of several hundred children who cheered the royal group loudly and were especially pleased when the two Princesses waved back at them.

Reaching High Street the royal group was met with another huge crowd with members of the Women's Auxiliary Police Corps lining the route. The crowds here had been entertained by the frequent arrivals of the various dignitaries including city officials, military representatives, academics, ecclesiastical representatives and several parties of nurses. At the west door of the cathedral the National Anthem was played and the royals were greeted by the Dean of the Thistle and Chapel Royal, the Moderator of the General Assembly of the Church of Scotland, the Lord Lyon King of Arms and various other dignitaries. While the Queen and the Princesses discussed the service with the Dean the King inspected the Guard of Honour which had been drawn up in the square. The guard was commanded by Squadron Leader Adams, RAF, and consisted of a naval party from HMS *Rook* under Lieutenant Jones, Welsh Guards, from the 201st Brigade of Guards under Captain Shuldham, and an RAF contingent under the command of an unnamed New Zealand officer from nearby RAF East Fortune.

The service was described as a solemn service of thanksgiving for victory. Continuing the theme of a large British family the Dean, the Very Reverend Dr Charles L. Warr, said in his address that the congregation was 'a family gathering'. It was noticed that the regimental colours from past conflicts which used to be in the cathedral were absent on this occasion. They had been removed and placed in a safer location for the duration of

*The Royal Party
at St. Giles'
Cathedral (TS)*

The King and Queen talking with the Very Rev. Dr Charles L. Warr, Dean of the Thistle, and the Right Rev. Dr E. J. Hagan, Moderator of the General Assembly of the Church of Scotland, outside St Giles'. The Princesses are standing between Lord Rosebery and Mr Thomas Johnston, Secretary of State for Scotland.

the war and not yet been brought back. Amongst the congregation were representatives of the civil defence services, NFS, voluntary services, police, nurses, Land Army and factory workers who were reminders of the war on the home front. The royal party entered led by the Lord Lyon King of Arms (Sir Francis J. Grant) and the heralds and pursuivants in their scarlet and gold medieval garb. The royals took their seats to Elgar's *Pomp and Circumstance* march before the service was opened by the singing of Psalm 124. Prayers were also offered by the minister of Glasgow Cathedral. A particular highlight of the service was the choral performance of Laurence Binyon's verses in commemoration of the fallen set to Elgar's 'With Proud Thanksgiving'. After prayers of thanksgiving the congregation sung the hymn *God of Our Fathers*. Dr Warr said in his address that the nation should give thanks that the Nazi regime which sought to enslave the world had been defeated so soon as things could easily have been different. He related how a soldier had, only days before, told him of how when he had to go out in the darkness and was fearful, he had remembered the King's words at the beginning of the war and how they had sustained him:

I said to the man who stood at the Gate of the Year: Give me a light that I may tread safely into the unknown. And he replied: Go out into the Darkness and put thine hand into the hand of God. That shall be to thee better than light, and safer than a known way.

The congregation sang *Now thank we all our God* before the benediction, silent prayer, and singing of the National Anthem.[8]

Church was followed by lunch with the Edinburgh Corporation in the City Chambers. A car had been prepared to take the royal party the short distance to the

Chambers but as the rain had eased off the King decided they would walk so as to give the crowds a better view. After lunch the party visited the National Shrine in Edinburgh Castle before they set off on their driven tour of the city. The drive to the castle went along High Street, the Lawnmarket and Castle Hill and was again lined with cheering crowds. The crowds here had been waiting in intermittent showers for over an hour but they remained cheerful and many had standing picnics, eating from hampers which they had brought along.

At the drawbridge the royal car halted and the party alighted to be met by the acting governor of the castle, Major General Irwin. The King inspected the Castle Guard while the Royal Salute was sounded by a bugler. The route up to Crown Square was lined by parties from WRNS, the ATS, the WAAF and various nursing services. At Crown Square the King inspected yet another Guard of Honour before laying a wreath at the base of the Scottish National War Memorial. After this the royal party had a short tour of the shrine and went across to speak to wounded veterans (from both this war and the last) some of whom had been patients at Edenhall since 1918. The royal party visited the room where the Scottish Crown Jewels were stored and signed the visitors book and then set off on an eighteen-mile tour of Edinburgh scheduled to take 1½ hours. The route had been carefully planned to take in every aspect of the city, from leafy suburbs to crowded working-class areas. It ran past every school and many of the churches, hospitals and major factories. The route everywhere was lined with thronging crowds. In many places the crowds surged forward to greet them and progress was along a small lane in between the crowds. Foremost amongst the crowds were the huge numbers of schoolchildren, almost all of whom were waving flags of some description. The crowds remained large right up until the approaches to Leith. Following a sparser patch by the Firth at Annfield the crowds picked up again at Newhaven; here it included girls and fishwives in gala dresses. Driving up Crewe Road the royal party would have noticed a group of ATS girls who were based at a nearby anti-aircraft gun site and a contingent of scholars. There was a large contingent of Polish doctors and nurses from the nearby hospital while at Murrayfield a group of clergy had gathered under a banner proclaiming a warm welcome from Scottish Episcopalians. In Gorgie Road a piper was playing *Hielan' Laddie*. After Gorgie the tour proceeded to Fountainbridge where a large group of rubber workers had gathered, and then through Bruntsfield, Salisbury, Prestonfield, Duddington, Willowbrae and Meadowbank before reaching Holyrood where they were met by the Duke of Hamilton.

The royal party rested at Holyrood Palace where they remained until their departure from Waverley Station at approximately 7 pm. They were accompanied to the station by various dignitaries. While talking on the platform the King told the Lord Provost that he had enjoyed his visit to Edinburgh very much and hoped he would be able to return soon. He commented particularly favourably on the reactions of the large numbers of schoolchildren and praised their obvious patriotism and enthusiastic loyalty. The Princesses meanwhile commented to the Lord Provost that they were disappointed not to have seen the castle when it was floodlit but hoped to return in the future to witness this spectacle.

The visit had obviously been a huge success and an editorial in *The Scotsman* praised the crowds for their enthusiasm in less than ideal weather and for the way the city buildings had been bedecked with bunting and flags to welcome the royal party. The people of Edinburgh had overcome their 'reputation of being rather stand-offish' and had reacted with enthusiasm and warmth. 'The affection for the royal family is something which unites all classes' and one only 'had to mingle with the crowds to sense how sincere were the tributes paid to the King and Queen and to the two Princesses.'

Other sections of Edinburgh society were preparing for the forthcoming general election with the Executive of the Scottish Liberal Federation meeting under the leadership of Sir William Beveridge to arrange the campaign. Sir William said he was determined the Liberals should put up the strongest possible candidates and urged Scottish voters to vote Liberal.

Minor crime continued to be a source of concern for the authorities but in June there was a crime which shocked many in the city. Undoubtedly some people resented the Italian community despite the fact that Italy was now an ally. On 5 June two men, Robert McKenzie Robertson and Timothy John Donoghue, went into a Portobello café, at 78 High Street, owned by an elderly Italian man, Guiseppe Demarco (82), and had begun to conduct themselves in a disorderly and threatening manner, swearing and generally acting in a unruly way, before seizing Mr Demarco by the throat, striking him repeatedly about the head and body with empty bottles and kicking him as he lay on the ground. They then assaulted his wife Mrs Assunta Guiseppe Demarco by hitting her about the head with bottles. Leaving both victims on the floor they made off with two bags of money containing £103 10s 6d. Mr Demarco died of his injuries while doctors described Mrs Demarco's injuries as severe.

Robertson entered a plea of self-defence and the judge directed the jury to reduce the charge of murder to one of culpable homicide. In his summing up the judge said that the excuse given that Mr Demarco would not have died if he had been a healthier man was appalling and that 'it was every bit as criminal to kill a feeble old man or an infant as a person in the prime of life'. He hoped it 'will never go out from this court that people should be entitled to lay violent hands on a very old, very sick, or very feeble person and afterwards say the death had not occurred if he or she had been fit and younger'.[9] The jury took half an hour to return a guilty verdict on Robertson on the charges of culpable homicide, assault to severe injury, robbery and breach of the peace, while they found Donohue not guilty of murder and breach of the peace and not proven on the charges of culpable homicide, assault, assault leading to severe injury and robbery. The judge discharged Donohue but sentenced Robertson (45) to seven years penal servitude. Robertson, a married man from Fife with two children, collapsed when the sentence was delivered and was afterwards led moaning and sobbing down to the cells.

The pre-war housing shortage in Scotland cast its shadow over the anticipation of final victory and plans were feverishly being drawn up to build a better peacetime environment. A sign of the problem was picked up by the press who relayed the story of a former PoW who had been forced, with his family, to take radical, and illegal, measures to house himself and his family. Jack Dempsey, from Cowdenbeath, had been a PoW of the Germans but during a forced march he had escaped and made his way back to Scotland. However, he had travelled around the country in vain in search of a council house. The fruitless search had used up all of his savings and the family were bereft. In his hometown there had been several hundred applicants for just six houses. Finding themselves in the village of Culross (across the Forth from Edinburgh) he noticed a large house which was standing completely empty and was astounded that the front door was open. It was so tempting that he and his family simply moved in. The property was known locally as Bishop Leighton's House and it was presumed that it was owned by the Scottish National Trust. Mr Dempsey wrote to the Trust saying that he was willing not only to pay rent but to restore the property.[10]

By the summer it was clear that Japan was teetering on the brink of defeat, but how soon the fanatical Japanese defenders would acknowledge the inevitable was less clear. The dropping of atomic bombs on Hiroshima and Nagasaki changed things dramatically. The newspapers commented on the 'sober calm' in the capital city but predicted that once the official announcement of victory was made, 'the capital will go gay with dancing, floodlighting, bands and parades, and possibly football.'[11]

A meeting of the Edinburgh Celebrations Committee was held. The official news of surrender would be heralded by the ringing of church bells for fifteen minutes, churches would be opened for prayer, flags would be flown from all civic buildings and major city businesses, and the general public was encouraged to fly their own flags. There would be a two-day holiday (with every business encouraged to observe this fully), food shops were advised to open for a few hours on each day to allow people to buy food. Restaurants would open 'to cope with the influx of visitors', as would the Ministry of Food's 'British Restaurants'. The committee exhorted all licensed premises to remain open for as long as legally allowable, while the magistrates granted late licences on the day of the announcement and during the two-day holiday period. There would be dancing in Princes Street Gardens, and bonfires would again play a major role in both official and unofficial celebrations, but the public were warned not to appropriate building supplies which were needed for the rebuilding of Scottish housing (VE-Day had seen widespread use of such materials in many Scottish communities including Edinburgh).[12]

In the early hours of 15 August, the day before VJ-Day, a Mr George Dickinson (78) fell from the top-floor flat window of his residence at 59 Causewayside. He was rushed to Edinburgh Royal Infirmary but died three hours later.

As the people of Edinburgh awoke to their first day of peace in six long years they were encouraged to remember the sacrifices that had been made on their behalf. In an advert on VJ-Day itself, the RAF Benevolent Fund urged the people of Edinburgh not to forget the RAF personnel who had been lost or maimed, or whose family members who had been left bereft by the loss of a loved one. It informed the public that during the war the RAF had lost 8,697 bombers, and that from D-Day to VE-Day Bomber Command had lost more men than all of the British armies fighting in Europe.

VJ-Day was officially announced by the King at midnight on 15 August and the next day saw rejoicing and celebration amidst 'deep-seated feelings of relief ... and the re-emergence of hopefulness and assurance after the strain and stress of the war years'.[13] *The Scotsman* commented, 'the cost in casualties has been too widespread, affecting practically every family, to make exuberance or noise the proper expression of the predominant feeling'. Some of the younger generation were boisterous, but most felt 'sober satisfaction and relief'.

For many the first notification was provided by the RN as ships in the Forth sounded sirens and lit up searchlights in celebration. This woke people living nearby and they made their way to the coast where they crowded at Granton Harbour to watch a display of coloured lights and rockets along with beams of light played across the water while the sirens wailed the victory signal.

The price was grim...

In 2,900 days of European fighting we lost of bombers alone, 8,697 ; of airmen of Bomber Command the losses were greater than in all the British Armies on the Continent from D-Day to V-Day.

Think of the task of succouring the maimed and broken, assisting the dependants of those who lost their lives.

Help us to make sure that the splendid service of the R.A.F. Benevolent Fund shall not be interrupted.

Send us the means, to the limit of your grateful hearts, to 'finish the job.'

ROYAL AIR FORCE BENEVOLENT FUND

Please send your donation to LORD RIVERDALE, Chairman, or BERTRAM T. RENGLE, Hon. Secretary, Appeals Committee, R.A.F. Benevolent Fund, 1 Sloane Street, London, S.W.1. Cheques and P.O. payable to R.A.F. Benevolent Fund.

(Registered under War Charities Act, 1940)

RAF Benevolent Fund advert which appeared in the press on VJ-Day (TS)

In the morning there were long queues outside bakers and grocers shops. *The Scotsman* described the situation of the Edinburgh housewife on the morning of VJ-Day: 'Peace might be declared in the world at large ... [but] there would be very little on the home front if she did not stir herself to get some food.'[14] Even those who set off before 8 am found themselves having to queue while those who left it too late faced a struggle to get anything. The shops selling staples such as bread, fish or fruit remained open until noon but many shops ran out of stock. The rationing system meant that even when items were available they were already spoken for and the hard-pressed shop assistants were forced to turn customers away telling them that stocks had already been ordered. A reporter witnessed one housewife actually turn down a loaf which was offered, while another could only be sold one despite having a family of seven to feed. Another accepted cake in place of the hoped-for loaf of bread.

Restaurants and catering establishments across the city remained open and became focal points for those planning celebrations who wished to eat without using up their precious ration supply. A small number of canteens in the city decided to mark the end of the war by offering free meals to members of the services, one being the Church of Scotland canteen for the forces on Princes Street. The Edinburgh WVS Centre leader, Mrs Andrews, commented that the canteen had 'had a grand day'. All were extremely grateful for the Church's hospitality and when one serviceman expressed his thanks he was humbly told, 'Well, you did win the victory, didn't you?'[15]

As had been planned, flags were displayed from civic buildings and places of business, more as the day progressed and local communities organised themselves. Men and women in uniform again played the role of leaders of the more boisterous celebrations. Mixed groups from all the services were seen forming impromptu groups to dance and march in carefree celebration. *The Scotsman*, however, said that the members of the forces in the city had demonstrated 'a general slackening in decorum and discipline'. The newspaper was more approving of the morning and evening church services, saying that they 'formed a rallying point for the more serious and responsible attitude to a great historic occasion' and that the services 'expressed more correctly, perhaps, the innermost feelings of the moment'.

The morning had been marked with showers and an overcast sky, but shortly before 1 pm a startling change occurred. The skies dramatically darkened with clouds engulfing the city and turning it to darkness more akin to evening. The shops and offices which had stayed open had to turn on their lights as did the trams. The effect lasted for only five minutes before the skies lightened up again. After this the weather began to clear, although it remained cold for August.

As the afternoon wore on larger crowds were drawn towards Princes Street and the pavements were choked with celebrants. The trams running down the centre of the streets had little difficulty but motor-vehicles were forced to slow down and proceed with extreme caution. Any lorries which inadvertently turned onto the main thoroughfare found themselves quickly engulfed by throngs of celebratory Edinburgh folk and service personnel. Loud cheers and applause greeted the impromptu march-past of the pipe band of the Royal Scots followed by a crowd of sailors, soldiers, airmen and civilians (many of whom had linked arms with women) in a swaying procession which, although undisciplined by military standards, was extremely happy. Many of the side streets off Princes Street became focal points for impromptu dances with eightsome reels proving particularly popular.

In the evening parties and dances were held in houses, in military messes, aboard ships and in other places. At Holyrood Square a children's tea party was held. The district was one of the poorer ones bordering the Great Mile but the children and their parents' efforts in organising the party 'soared above the dingy surroundings'.[16] The local housewives had prepared a tea for sixty children and the repast was enjoyed by all. When it was over the tables and chairs were cleared away and the children danced to the accompaniment of an accordionist and a man playing the spoons.

Back in Princes Street a group of youngsters created some amusement when they marched behind two older boys who had made an effigy of the Emperor of Japan borne upon a dilapidated armchair. The effigy wore a crown at a rakish angle and held aloft a small parasol with a Rising Sun flag attached. Their destination was the nearest bonfire.

As the evening darkness deepened the crowds were left astonished and amazed by the suddenness of the floodlights which snapped on to dramatically illuminate the castle and the Nelson Monument. Everyone approved of this addition to the VJ-Day celebrations.

The first night of the celebration was captured by a BBC unit which broadcast to the nation from Princes Street. Not everyone was happy with the broadcast, with one disgruntled resident writing in to *The Scotsman* to complain that the programme consisted of 'little more than about a dozen words from two tired Sassenachs and one Newfoundlander looking for a bed'.[17]

At the height of the celebrations a party of Dutch children who had been evacuated from the famine-stricken Netherlands were brought by train into Edinburgh (a group of sixty or so had been brought the previous week). The twenty-one girls had been at a camp in the Borders where they received medical supervision and a special diet to recover their strength and were now going to stay with families in Edinburgh and Glasgow. On arrival in Edinburgh the party was fed and entertained by members of the WVS led by the indomitable Mrs Andrews who had earlier been working at the Church of Scotland canteen for the forces. Thirteen of the girls were to be homed in Edinburgh and the leaders of the group spoke enthusiastically of the welcome they had received

Edinburgh Castle illuminated on VJ-Day Night (TS)

Flood-Lit dance floor of Ross Band Stand in West Princes Street Garden (TS)

Revellers march with Pipe and Drum Band on Princes Street (TS)

Crowds listening to bands at The Mound (TS)

and their enjoyment of their stay in Scotland. The Edinburgh District Committee of Young People from Occupied Countries (YPOC) had found homes for the thirteen girls and asked any Edinburgh families who were interested in participating to contact them as 500 more children were expected to arrive every week.

So, that was Edinburgh's war. While Edinburgh had experienced and shared many of the hardships of wartime Britain, it had escaped the worst of the bombing and had been, perhaps, less badly affected than many citizens had feared in 1939 when war was declared: eighteen people had been killed during raids and 200 had been injured to some degree. The constant threat of air raids, however, had resulted in many sleepless nights and much strain.

Many who had volunteered or been ordered into the armed forces had given their lives in the cause, many had suffered physical or mental injury, others had suffered through years of separation from their families.

*Crowds with Nelson Monument
in background (TS)*

For the civilian population the war had left an indelible mark. Edinburgh society had changed in many ways during the war. With the bombings, the blackout, shortages and the black market, the war had altered lives and attitudes. The influx of foreign troops and the evacuation of thousands of children and adults from the city had led to a greater awareness of differences in both class and nationality. Common to all was a desire to celebrate the victory, to commemorate the fallen, and to ensure that the many sacrifices would not be in vain.

The Leith-based Ben Line, as well as assisting the British army in 1939 and 1940, contributed vessels to support British forces during the North African campaigns and the invasions of Sicily and Italy. By the end of the war it had lost fourteen of its own vessels and a further four which had been placed under its control. In all 292 crew of the Ben Line were lost during the war, including many from Edinburgh and Leith.

There were many men from Edinburgh and Leith in the Merchant Service and they had paid a heavy price. Mrs Mary Kay, for example, from Leith, lost two of her sons during the war, both while serving in the merchant fleet.[18]

The yard of Henry Robb Ltd produced naval and cargo vessels and also repaired some 3,000 vessels in what was a major contribution to the war effort. Amongst these were at least six Flower-class corvettes, three Castle-class corvettes, six River-class frigates, three Loch-class frigates, three Bay-class frigates, and three Bird-class minesweepers. The yard had also designed and built the prototype of the Basset-class minesweeping and anti-submarine warfare trawler for the Admiralty. It built and launched several of this class of vessel in the war including the first two, HMT *Basset* and HMT *Mastiff*. The design proved so effective that 180 such vessels were built at various yards during the war.

Thoughts soon turned to how to resolve the many problems facing the city after six years of war. Politicians were aware of the housing crisis which had been made worse by the war. Days after VJ-Day the Scottish Secretary, Mr J. Westwood, announced that he intended to put in place a 'housing speed-up drive' on similar lines to that which had been announced for England and Wales. To this end, building workers were released early from the forces, and it was agreed that roads and sewers would be constructed at the same time.

On 26 September, Edinburgh awoke to much excitement and activity. This was the day the royal family were to arrive on a two-day visit which would include, on the first day, the Scottish Victory Parade. Crowds flocked into the capital where, despite the threatening clouds, there was a party atmosphere. Those who were waiting in the West End received the first indication of the arrival of the royals when the bells of St. Cuthbert's Church began ringing as the royal train pulled into Waverley Station to be met with the now-familiar group of dignitaries. After the Lord Provost had presented the keys to the city to the King (they were always returned with the assurance that they could not be in better keeping) the King inspected the guard and the royal party departed by car for Holyrood Palace with a large crowd cheering and waving.

During this visit, the opportunity for the investiture of Corporal Hunter's VC was taken. Ramsay and Mary Hunter (of Stenhouse Avenue West) were presented to the King at Holyrood Palace where His Majesty was honoured to present to them their son's medal. The King enquired how long Corporal Hunter had served in the Marines and told the grieving parents that he was proud to present them with the VC earned by their son. Afterwards Mr and Mrs Hunter were met outside by Captain J.P. Stevens, Royal Marines. Stevens had been Corporal Hunter's commanding officer and he spoke very highly of his bravery and devotion to duty. The ceremony, in which other Edinburgh men were awarded a variety of medals and honours, took over one hour.[19] Awards were made to people from across Scotland and to some whose connection with Scotland seems to have been tenuous at best. There were a number of posthumous awards made with medals being presented by the King to next of kin.

One of these awards had a particularly interesting and tragic tale behind it. Mrs Margaret Hellen Terry (née Robertson) of Monifieth, Angus, collected the DFC awarded to her late husband Flight Lieutenant Brian Routh Terry. He was an Australian, born in Sydney, and had journeyed to Britain and joined the RAFVR at the start of the war. Posted to 127 Squadron in Egypt flying Hurricanes he was later posted to 601 Squadron flying the Spitfire in 1942. It would appear that Terry was a successful fighter pilot and on 31 October 1942 he landed his Spitfire in the desert to rescue a fellow pilot. He was also recommended for the DFC for his part in an attack on the headquarters of an enemy mechanised division on 5 February 1943. There is some confusion over the death of Flight Lieutenant Terry as the Australian War memorial still lists his unit as being 601 Squadron but by this time the squadron was serving in Italy and the reports of Flight Lieutenant Terry's death say that he was killed in a flying accident in Egypt on 14 August 1944 and is buried in Egypt. What is known is that the Terry family had suffered an earlier loss when his brother Flight Lieutenant Ian Wingate Terry, RNZAF, had been killed on 21 December 1941 while serving as a navigator aboard a Lockheed Hudson of 206 Squadron, RAF Coastal Command.[20]

Another posthumous award was an MC to Major Richard M Campbell, Black Watch (Royal Highlanders), who had been killed in Italy on 6 October 1944 while attached to the 2/6th Battalion, The Queen's Royal Regiment (West Surrey). Major Campbell was the son of Jock Otto and Aimee Dorothy Campbell and was a 32-year-old married man with a young son. His medal was presented to his widow, Beatrice Mary Anna Campbell. Outside she was photographed showing the medal to the young son of the major.

In the afternoon the royal party, again consisting of the King, Queen and two Princesses, took their places to accept the salute of the parade. Flags and bunting decorated the many monuments in the city centre and the greenery of the gardens and trees. The parade, the paper said, was the greatest that Princes Street had ever witnessed and the most important. It was also the first royal parade to be held in the British Empire after the war. From noon the rainclouds which had threatened disappeared and the sun came out, helping to boost the already giddy and happy mood

Above: *His Majesty the King inspects Cameron Highlanders Guard of Honour at Holyrood Palace (TS)*

Right*: Mr and Mrs Hunter with Captain Stevens (TS)*

Left: *Captain Gerard Norton with his wife (TS)*

Centre: *Mrs Terry (Dundee Courier & Advertiser)*

Right: *Beatrice Campbell and her young son (TS)*

of spectators and participants. By 3 pm, when the royal party arrived at the saluting stand which was at Royal Scottish Academy, there were an estimated 200,000 men, women and children. In Hannover Street alone, from Princes Street to George Street, there were over 5,000. The stand was decorated with flags, bunting and masses of begonias and foliage. Loudspeakers had been set up to broadcast the music played by the band which was stationed to the east of the Academy.

The royal party arrived by car at the back of the Academy and the military band alerted the crowd by striking up the National Anthem while the command of the Guard of Honour's commander to present arms could clearly be heard. While the King inspected the Guard, which consisted of men of the Scots Guards, the royal party emerged from the Academy and onto the stand. At this point the Edinburgh crowd again forgot their reputation for standoffishness and 'let itself go … a great cheer rose on the air' as the party took their places. The King and Queen were visibly affected by the warmth of the greeting and the King stepped forward and, while the cheer lasted, stood at the salute while the Queen gave her characteristic royal wave to the crowd. The King again wore the uniform of an Admiral of the Fleet while the Queen wore a blue ensemble trimmed with silver fox fur and a large diamond coat-clip. The royal party then took their seats to await the parade, the Queen and the Princesses on the right of the King along with the Lady Provost and Admiral Sir William Whitworth. On the King's left sat the Lord Provost, the Deputy Secretary of State for Scotland (the Secretary was recovering from an operation), Admiral Sir Henry Moore (C-in-C Home Fleet), Lieutenant General Sir Neil Ritchie (GOC-in-C Scottish Command), and Air Vice Marshal Simpson; other members of the royal party occupied a second row. As a tribute to the nation's allies the ground in front of the saluting base was guarded by two Canadian Military Police and two US Army Police.

Shortly after 3.15 the head of the parade, heralded by *Hearts of Oak*, came into view from the east end of Princes Street led by a Marine band and a large naval contingent. The King, Queen and Princesses stood and remained standing for the half hour that the 5,000 participants in the parade took to march past. The King kept his eyes fixed on the parade except for one or two occasions when he spoke to the Queen.

Marching six abreast the parade was in two distinct sections. It was led by the magnificent sight of the Royal Marine Band followed by a large contingent of the Royal Navy (with fixed bayonets), Royal Marines, followed by the women of the WRNS, and naval nursing sisters. The naval contingent was followed by an oddly assorted group, some in blue, some in civilian dress. These were the men and women of the Merchant Navy, fishing fleet, Sea Cadets and Sea Rangers. This contingent, despite its unmilitary appearance compared to the naval contingent, received huge cheers of gratitude from the crowd. The army contingent followed, with the Royal Artillery, the Royal Scots, the Scots Guards to the fore. This included nurses of the Voluntary Aid Detachments, those of the Queen Alexandra's Imperial Military Nursing Service, and the youngsters of the Army Cadet Force. *The Scotsman* reported that, perhaps, the greatest cheer for the army contingent was reserved for the men of the Home Guard. Notable amongst them were numerous 'white-haired veterans ... men who had served in the First Great War, and some who looked as though they might well have served in the South African War'. The reporter suggested that some had 'forgot the date of their birth when they were supposed to retire at the age of 60'. The army were followed by the Royal Air Force who, it was noted, were carrying the longer sword-bayonets fixed to their rifles. This contingent included the WAAFs, the VAD, the men and women of the Royal Observer Corps, and the boys of the Air Training Corps.

Many in the civilian services section of the parade were from the Borders, the West, Clydeside, the north-east Coast, the Highlands and the Islands. The pipes and drums of the Scottish Police (in their feathered bonnets) played as they passed the review stand. The band was followed by a large contingent of Scottish Police officers but, once again, the crowd reserved its loudest cheers for those who reminded them most of the voluntary sacrifices made during the war. In this case it was the older men and women of the Wardens Service who, at times, struggled to keep pace with the rest of the parade but were, according to *The Scotsman*, 'the soul of National Service'. This section was followed by shipyard workers, war workers, WLA, Post Office workers and then finally the boys and girls of the various youth organisations (many of whom had barely been of school age at the outbreak of war).

The Scotsman wrote that there was something 'joyous and inspiring in the spectacle' and compared it to the parades of the Nazis saying it 'was not an army of drilled automatons doing the goose step and artificially ferocious but an army of free men, united under a common purpose, and rightfully taking its part in the general feeling of a great task successfully accomplished'.[21]

Following the parade, the Royal party had tea at the Academy and then, to cheering crowds, drove off in an open-top car. The night of the victory parade was given over to celebration with the corporation giving permission for bonfires and fireworks displays

*Lord and Lady Provost
welcome the Queen
and Princesses at the
Academy (TS)*

*Royal Party taking the
salute (TS)*

*Band of the Royal Marines
and Naval Contingent
during the Victory
Parade (TS)*

(the Lord Provost handed over ceremonial torches to light numerous bonfires) and many areas of the city were floodlit. The royal party requested that they be conducted on a late-night tour of the city (over twenty miles) with the purpose of making contact with members of the public who had not had the opportunity to see them earlier in the day. The trip was marked by 'crowd-lined streets, bursts of cheering, torchbearers, bonfire glow above Arthur's Seat and at other points on the route, the haunting outlines of the city, floodlit, moonlit and starlit'.[22] The Princesses were said to be particularly excited by the trip and sat in the front seats while the King and Queen sat in the back of the car which was cheered off by crowds, many young, who ran after it.

As the car approached Leith Links a large group of Boys' Brigade and Boy Scouts lined the route holding aloft torches. The celebrants on Leith Links greeted the royal party with wild cheering and dancing. The royal party again noted the Newhaven fishwives in colourful costume. The crowds at Duke Street were so dense that the car had to slow down and at one point stop, at which point detectives had to get out to ease the passage of the royal car. At the west end of Princes Street the crowd broke into exceptionally loud cheering.

The next day the Queen and the two Princesses departed Holyrood shortly before 11.30 am and visited the Aitken, Dott & Son gallery at 26 Castle Street where they viewed a display of Earl Haig's drawings. They were met at the gallery by Lord Haig and Colonel Robertson VC and were shown around by four men who had been injured in the war (the exhibition was in aid of Lady Haig's poppy factory). The royal party was accompanied by the Countess of Minto and her sister, the Countess of Haddington, Lady Mary Herbert, Lady Grant of Monymusk and Lady Caroline Scott. The Queen was much impressed by the exhibition and stayed for much longer than expected. Afterwards she was presented with a picture: *The Orchestra at Oflag 12B*.

The King meantime was attending a second investiture ceremony at Holyrood. Again there were excited scenes with 500 relatives and friends of those being honoured crowding the Picture Gallery of Holyrood Palace. Notable amongst the Edinburgh residents being decorated was Lieutenant (acting Major) Jasper Hugh

Lord Provost hands out torches to youth organisations (TS)

*Floodlit fountain
at Holyrood Palace
with glow of bonfire
at Arthur's Seat in
background (TS)*

F. MacMichael. He was awarded both the MC and the DSO for two acts of bravery. The MC was awarded for an action in 1943 at Syracuse when MacMichael led his company in the capture of an Italian barracks and freed a large number of British airborne soldiers who were being held prisoner. The DSO was awarded for an action on 23 January 1944 while he was attached to the Royal Scots Fusiliers. Major MacMichael had led a bayonet charge to dislodge the Germans from a strong position but when his company was outflanked he then took a platoon around the flank of the German position and launched an attack on several machine-gun posts despite being wounded in the head. He continued to encourage his men and only withdrew after loss of blood forced him to.[23]

The Queen returned to the Palace before she, accompanied by the King and the two Princesses, left (at 2.40 pm) for a ceremony at St. Giles' where Admiral Lord Cunningham was installed as a Knight of the Thistle and where the presentations of the White Ensign of HMS *Warspite* and the Red Ensign of the SS *Queen Elizabeth* were made. At all stages of the journey the royals were cheered by large crowds. Outside the cathedral a Royal Marine band played the National Anthem and the King inspected the naval Guard of Honour. The royal party were met by the Dean of the Thistle and Chapel Royal and Admiral Sir Henry Moore along with heralds, the Lord Lyon King of Arms and the Gentleman Usher of the Green Rod. Several Knights of the Thistle were present in the Thistle Chapel for the ceremony which would see Admiral of the Fleet Lord Cunningham become a member of that order. Their Majesties were greeted by the Earl of Mar and Kellie. The ceremony began with prayers before the oath was read out and the King signified his approval that Lord Cunningham of Hyndhope (his ancestors had owned a farm at Hyndhope near Selkirk) be installed. More prayers were read and the group moved to the royal pew for the main service.

The King inspects Naval Guard of Honour at St. Giles (TS)

The ceremony during which the ensigns were deposited in the cathedral marked the first occasion when flags of the naval services had been placed in St. Giles'. To mark the occasion the pews were occupied by hundreds of men and women associated with service at sea. They included naval officers and men, members of the WRNS, Sea Cadets and Sea Rangers, officers and men of the Merchant Navy, representatives of skippers and crews from the fishing fleet, Ministry of War Transport officials, men from the Cunard White Star Company, stevedores and dockers from various ports and shipyard workers (including nine men from the Clydeside firm of John Brown & Co who had been involved in the building of the *Queen Elizabeth*). More than a dozen admirals and commodores were present including the C-in-C of the Home Fleet, the C-in-C Rosyth and the Duke of Montrose (as a commodore in the RNVR). There were also high-ranking officers from the army and the RAF. A contrast to the predominant navy blue of many of the congregation was provided by the magistrates and councillors of Edinburgh who were dressed in their scarlet robes, and accompanied by the mace and sword bearers and the halberdiers. Splashes of colour were also provided by the robes of members of the university senate. In the course of his lengthy address Dr Warr said that he felt a humble gratitude for the six years in which the nation's seamen had 'by day and by night, from the icy cold of the Arctic to the sweltering heat of the tropic sun, exposed to the lightning and the storm, to fire and shipwreck, and constantly menaced by the bomb, the mine, and the torpedo of the enemy ... guarded our island home, gave battle to our foes, and fearlessly faced the perilous pathways of the sea'. He praised them as a 'matchless breed of men'.[24] As the ensigns were presented the congregation sang Psalm 124. Originally it was to have been chanted but a special note inserted into the order of service said that at the request of the King this had been changed. This was followed by a minute's silence and the playing of the *Last Post* before the congregation turned to the royal pew and sang two verses of the National Anthem.

Between 9 and 10 pm the forecourt of Holyrood Palace was floodlit and the public were admitted for singing accompanied by military bands, pipes and drums and the police pipe and drums. 'Great crowds' gathered to take part in the communal singing, and the loudest cheers of the night were reserved for the appearance of the King, Queen and both Princesses on the balcony.

The following day was the last of the royal visit and the party split for the occasion with the King, Queen and Princess Margaret reviewing the Home Fleet at Rosyth while Queen Elizabeth was to take the salute of the Scottish Cadets of the Girls' Training Corps.

The King, Queen and Princess Margaret were received at Rosyth by the C-in-C Rosyth and were then conducted aboard the C-in-C's barge which proceeded out of

Admiral Lord Cunningham and Lady Cunningham leaving St. Giles (TS)

White Ensign of HMS Warspite and Red Ensign of SS Queen Elizabeth (TS)

The Royal Party leave St Giles'
accompanied by Dr Warr (TS)

The floodlit Palace of
Holyrood (TS)

the dockyard and into the estuary where the sun sparkled on the Firth of Forth. The flagship of the Home Fleet, the battleship *Rodney*, was accompanied by cruisers, including HMS *Birmingham* and HMS Dido, destroyers and smaller vessels. The royal party were piped on board HMS *Rodney* and introduced to Rear Admiral Cunninghame-Graham (commander of the 10th Cruiser Squadron). The Royal Salute was given followed by the running up of the Royal Standard, the flag of the Lord High Admiral and the Union Jack of the Admiral of the Fleet, and there was an inspection of the ship's company which was paraded at divisions. Also aboard *Rodney* were crewmembers from three destroyers which had given notable service: HMS *Orwell* which had taken part in eleven Russian convoys; HMS *Offa* which had served in sixteen Russian convoys; and HMS *Comet* which was one of the latest RN destroyers to join the Home Fleet (she had been launched on the Clyde by Yarrows on 22 June 1944). Representatives of the crews from two of the Home Fleet's oilers (*Black Ranger* and *Mixol*) had been invited aboard and, along with the crew from *Rodney* and the three destroyers, all were spoken to by the royal party. The royals lunched aboard *Rodney* and the King then took a few minutes to privately walk with Captain, R.C. Fitzroy before the royal party took to the barge and sailed for HMS *Birmingham*.

Aboard the *Birmingham* the King inspected the ship's company and talked with the captain, and then boarded the *Dido* and did the same. This cruiser had been launched just before the start of the war and had led an eventful life seeing dangerous service in both the Mediterranean and the North Sea. During the evacuation of Crete *Dido* had been hit by a 1,000lb bomb and fifty of her complement, along with a large number of soldiers, were killed. She had also been at Copenhagen for the surrender and the disarming of the German ships *Prinz Eugen* and *Nürnberg*. When the King asked an officer how many anti-aircraft rounds the ship had fired during the war the officer replied that they had lost count.

Returning to Rosyth Dockyard the King inspected a parade of men from the aircraft carrier *Illustrious* which had recently returned from the Far East. This concluded the royal visit and shortly afterwards Their Majesties departed for Ballater aboard the royal train.

While the three royals were at Rosyth, Princess Elizabeth had remained behind in Edinburgh. The Princess took the salute of over 3,000 members of the SGTC who had come from all over Scotland. The procession was led by a pipe band from Sea Cadet Corps while pipers and drummers from the ATC and the Boys' Brigade accompanied the parade. Following this, Princess Elizabeth, accompanied by the Lord Provost, departed for the Assembly Hall where the SGTC had assembled to hear a speech from the Princess. The SGTC had mounted an exhibition at the hall and when the Princess arrived the hall was packed with members from all over Scotland who gave a rousing and loud ovation to welcome her. *The Scotsman* reported that there was a great roar

Above: *Princess Elizabeth inspects Guard of Honour from the SGTC (Sunday Post)*

Left: *Princess Elizabeth, with Lady Strathearn and Campbell and the Lord Provost, at SGTC Exhibition (TS)*

which greeted her: it 'rose to a long thunderous roll which continued for about two minutes'. After Lady Strathearn and Campbell, the Commandant of the SGTC, had welcomed Princess Elizabeth to the exhibition the Princess gave her speech praising the members of the SGTC for their contribution to the war effort. She said they could be proud of how they had 'acted as messengers, helpers, and canteen workers, have entertained refugees from overseas, and have helped in hospitals and so on'.[25] She went on to say that as the older generation had shouldered the burden of the war it was the younger generation's task to accept the responsibility of rebuilding a world 'where all men shall have freedom of belief and thought'. There followed a chorus of *Jerusalem* and three cheers, before Her Majesty was wished goodbye by the Lord Provost and Lady Strathearn and Campbell.

As the royal party left Edinburgh, the King talked to Lord Provost Falconer and said that the Queen and he had both thoroughly enjoyed their visit. They said that they had enjoyed the 'evident feeling of loyalty exhibited by the citizens' and that they had particularly enjoyed the open air communal singing outside Holyrood Palace.[26] The Queen talked to the stationmaster at Princes Street Station expressing her thanks to all for making them so comfortable during their visit. Again the route of the royals was lined with cheering crowds and a huge crowd assembled at the station long before they arrived.

Endnotes

Chapter 1: 1939

1 *Edinburgh Evening News*, 13 April 1939, p. 15.
2 *Ibid.*
3 *Ibid.*
4 *Edinburgh Evening News*, 2 September 1939, p. 11.
5 The Empire was one of Edinburgh's foremost theatres and hosted a huge variety of performers as well as showing the first moving pictures in Scotland. In 1911 a performance by magician and illusionist The Great Lafayette went terribly wrong and the magician and ten others were killed by a fire on stage. The Empire closed in 1963; it is now the Edinburgh Festival Theatre.
6 The St. Andrew's Square Cinema, in Clyde Street, was destroyed in what was described as one of the most spectacular of Edinburgh fires in November 1942.
7 602 (City of Glasgow) Squadron remained at Grangemouth for only a matter of days before moving to RAF Drem. It moved again, in April, to RAF Dyce for a month before returning to Drem. In August they moved south to RAF Westhampnett in Sussex.
8 HMS *Valorous* had been launched in 1917 and fought through the First World War and the Russian Civil War of 1919 before being refitted in 1938 and recommissioned in 1939 as an anti-aircraft escort destroyer. She survived the war only to be scrapped in 1947.
9 The aircraft was in fact part of a pair from Kampfgeschwader 26 which had been tasked with photographing Rosyth Naval Dockyard.
10 HMS *Hood* was sunk by the *Bismarck* and *Prinz Eugen* at the Battle of Denmark Strait on 24 May 1941 with the loss of 1,418 men (only 3 survived). HMS *Repulse* was sunk by Japanese torpedo aircraft on 10 December 1941 with the loss of 508 men.
11 HMS *Southampton* was sunk off Malta on 11 January 1941 by Stuka dive bombers with the loss of 81 crew.
12 HMS *Mohawk* was sunk by an Italian destroyer on 16 April 1941 with the loss of 43 crew. Commander Richard Frank Jolly was an exceptionally experienced officer having joined the RN in 1914 as a midshipman. He was 43 at the time of his death and was initially awarded the Empire Gallantry Medal (EGM) but this was exchanged for the George Cross (GC) on the inauguration of that medal. Rather strangely this medal is awarded for acts of great courage not in the

presence of the enemy but it seems, surely, that this should perhaps have been the VC as Jolly's injuries were certainly inflicted in the presence of the enemy. Initial reports were that Jolly was awarded the OBE (Military Division).

13 603 (City of Edinburgh) Squadron, for example, had only completed their conversion from Gladiator biplanes to the Spitfire just days before the action of 16 October 1940.

14 So poor was the standard of gunnery believed to be in Fighter Command that the 'Dowding Spread' ordered pilots to fix their guns' harmonisation at 400 yards and use their machine guns in a shotgun, spray, manner. This actually lessened the effect of any hits and made a hit far less likely. With experience, Fighter Command learned and the area attacks were abandoned along with the tight formations they necessitated along with a change in gun harmonisation to the 'spot' principle of 200 yards range. Some pilots who were confident in their marksmanship harmonised their guns to an even shorter range knowing that this would mean greater hitting power.

15 *Edinburgh Evening News*, 17 October 1939, p. 5.

16 *Ibid.*

17 *Ibid.*

18 *Ibid.*

19 *Ibid.*

20 *Ibid.*

21 *Ibid.*

22 *Ibid.*

23 *Edinburgh Evening News*, 17 October 1939, p. 3.

24 *The Scotsman*, 20 October 1939, p. 7.

25 *The Scotsman*, 21 October 1939, p. 7.

26 *Ibid.*

27 *Ibid.*

28 After the war the bodies of Seydel and Schleicher were removed to the Cannock Chase German Military Cemetery.

29 St. Bernard's FC had been formed in 1878 and after a tumultuous early period in and out of the league became an established club playing its fixtures at the Royal Gymnasium Ground (which had a 40,000 capacity and excellent training facilities). By the 1930s St. Bernard's was in the Second Division and had been largely eclipsed by both Hearts and Hibs but during this decade the club attracted large crowds by playing attacking football unlike most other clubs at the time. In 1938 they reached the semi-final of the Scottish Cup before being defeated by East Fife (who went on to win the cup) in a second replay at neutral Tynecastle (a crowd of 35,264 attended the match). St. Bernard's struggled on until 1943 when the death of a director left the club with a huge debt and they were forced to sell the Royal Gymnasium Ground and subsequently disbanded. The club's last match had taken place on 16 May 1942, a 2-3 defeat to East Fife. Local primary schools still play in the St. Bernard's Cup and St. Bernard's Boys Club continues to this day.

30 Englishman Sir Thomas Henry Cotton, the leading British golfer of his generation, had won the Open Championship in 1934 and 1937 and went on to win again in 1948. During the Second World War he served in the RAF and raised a great deal of money for the Red Cross through taking part in exhibition matches (for which he was awarded the MBE). Cotton played in the Ryder Cup on four occasions, captaining Europe in 1947 and 1953. Following his retirement he enjoyed a successful career designing golf courses, as a golfing author and in establishing the Golf Foundation which went on to help thousands of youngsters get involved in the game. Well known for his lavish playboy lifestyle he was inducted into the World Golf Hall of Fame in 1980. The award of knighthood (Knight Bachelor) was announced in the New Year's Day Honour List in 1988.

31 *Dundee Evening Telegraph*, 26 October 1939, p. 3.

32 *Edinburgh Evening News*, 18 December 1939, p. 11.

Chapter 2: 1940

1 *The Scotsman*, 22 February 1940, p. 8.

2 Despite poor arms the British Army of 1939/40 was probably the most mechanised in the world and possessed far more motor transports than either the French or German armies.

3 *The Scotsman*, 26 February 1940, p. 4.

4 William Staton had been a First World War ace (with 26 victories), had remained in the RAF, and had led four 10 Squadron Whitley bombers over Berlin on 1/2 October 1939. He helped pioneer early pathfinder techniques and was the first pilot to drop bombs on German soil during the war – during an attack on the airfield at Sylt on 19/20 March 1940 (the Berlin raid had only dropped propaganda leaflets). After a period commanding RAF Leeming and time acting as ADC to the King he was assigned as senior air staff officer, West Group, Java. After the fall of Java in March 1942 he was taken prisoner by the Japanese. He was tortured but refused to reveal information. After the war he testified against several Japanese officers accused of war crimes. Staton retired from the RAF in 1952 with the rank of air vice marshal. AVM William Staton, CB, DSO and bar, MC, DFC and bar, died in 1983 at the age of 84.

5 *The Scotsman*, 30 April 1940, p. 5.

6 *The Scotsman*, 1 March 1940.

7 *The Scotsman*, 13 May 1940, p. 5.

8 *The Scotsman*, 24 May 1940, p. 7.

9 *The Scotsman*, 24 May 1940, p. 7.

10 *The Scotsman*, 11 June 1940, p. 6.

11 It was estimated that the total Italian population in Scotland at the time was approximately 3,000.

12 *The Scotsman*, 19 June 1940, p. 11. Mr Bosi's case was mentioned in the House of Commons on 4 July when Colonel Burton MP (Sudbury) asked if Bosi had

now been interned and was told by Sir John Anderson that he had indeed been detained as a person with hostile associations. Colonel Burton then inquired how many more such men were at large and Mr Cocks (Broxtowe) raised laughter from the House by asking how such a man could own a pistol and ammunition when MPs were not allowed to have either.

13 There seems to have been some confusion over this officer's death as the CWGC website lists his death as having taken place between 27 May and 2 October but the unit war diary compiled by its temporary commanding officer (Major Bruce) clearly states that he was killed on 27 May. Tragically, the war brought further grief for Mr and Mrs Turcan as they lost another son. Gunner James Prentice Turcan, Singapore Royal Artillery, Straits Settlements Volunteer Force, lost his life while a prisoner of the Japanese in Borneo in 1944. He has no known grave and is commemorated on the Singapore Memorial and on his younger brother's headstone in France.

14 *Edinburgh Evening News*, 14 May 1942, p. 2.

15 Gazetted 18 December 1917.

16 Brian D. Osborne, *The People's Army. Home Guard in Scotland 1940-1944* (Birlinn, 2009), pp. 36-8.

17 Balgone is the name of the hereditary estate of the Grant-Suttie family and has been in existence since 1700. It is situated at North Berwick in East Lothian. The Balgone baronetcy is in the County of Haddington, Nova Scotia. Colonel Grant-Suttie's younger brother, Archibald Ronald Grant-Suttie, had been killed aged 20 on 23 July 1917 as a lieutenant in 'L' Battery, 15th Brigade, Royal Horse Artillery.

18 One of the acronyms the LDV was branded with was 'Look, Duck and Vanish', after their role in spotting and reporting parachutists.

19 It would appear that Jane Lyall Wilson was the final victim of the raid but this has not been confirmed. Wilson was not from Edinburgh, being resident at Montrose.

20 The squadron included several aces during the battle: Flying Officer Carbury (15½ victories); Pilot Officer R. (Rasp) Berry (9 victories during the battle, final total of 17); Flight Lieutenant H.K. MacDonald (8 victories) Pilot Officer Gilroy (who was known as Sheep) (over 7 victories); and the famous Pilot Officer Richard Hillary (5 victories).

21 Pilot Officer MacDonald has no known grave and is commemorated on the Runnymede Memorial. The other pilots lost on this day were: Flight Lieutenant John Laurence Gilchrist Cunningham (23) of Burntisland, Fife (who also has no known grave); and Pilot Officer Noel John Victor Benson (21) of Great Ouseburn

22 *The Scotsman*, 1 October 1940, p. 3.

23 www.edinphoto.org.uk/1_edin/1_edinburgh_history_-_recollections_air_raids. htm#31_anne-baumgartner-brown

24 *The Scotsman*, 29 November 1940, p. 4.

25 *The Scotsman*, 11 November 1940, p. 3.

26 *The Scotsman*, 8 November 1940, p. 3.

27 See measuringworth.com

28 *The Scotsman*, 30 May 1941, p. 3.

Chapter 3: 1941

1   In addition to his Edinburgh and Leith business connections, Mr Thomson's late brother, Sir Frederick C. Thomson, had been an MP and Whip for the Scottish Unionists while his nephew, Sir J.D.W. Thomson, was the current MP for South Aberdeen.

2   *The Scotsman*, 7 March 1941, p. 6.

3   *The Scotsman*, 15 July 1941, p. 5.

4   Days later du Vivier was promoted to flight commander and during this series of raids he destroyed three JU88s (on the 6th, 10th and 28th of May). He finished the war as a Wing Commander, DFC and bar, Croix de Guerre, and later became an airline pilot only to lose his life in a car accident in the USA in 1981.

5   Mr Larmour seems to have been from a prominent family with their roots in Ireland.

6   *Dundee Evening Telegraph*, 8 August 1941, p. 5.

7   *The Scotsman*, 9 August 1941, p. 3.

8   *Ibid.*

9   *Ibid.*

10   *The Scotsman*, 22 October 1941, p. 3.

11   *Ibid.*

12   *The Scotsman*, 25 October 1941, p. 6.

13   *The Scotsman*, 19 December 1941, p. 6.

14   Sergeant Bowie was a career airman and a successful one. He rapidly rose through the ranks and was subsequently commissioned. He tragically lost his life on 25 June 1946 when the Wellington XIII (NC661) in which he was flying on a cross-country training flight crashed at Trusley near Derby. The six people aboard the aircraft were all killed. The dead included two 17-year-old air cadets. Flight Lieutenant David Bowie DFM is buried at Eaglesham Cemetery in Renfrewshire.

15   *The Scotsman*, 30 December 1941, p. 3.

Chapter 4: 1942

1   *The Scotsman*, 3 January 1942, p. 3.

2   The rest of Flight Sergeant McKenzie's crew was: Pilot Officer D.A. Howard, DFM; Flying Officer A.J. Fraser, RCAF; and Sergeant A.H. Gardner. All are commemorated at Runnymede.

3   The crew consisted of Flight Sergeant Stables, F/S R.N. Smith, Sgt C.E. Carroll RCAF, and Sgt A.G. Bockock. The pilot, a Rhodesian, had had a lucky escape six weeks previously when he had been shot down into the sea off Vaagso. The entire crew are commemorated on the Runnymede Memorial.

4   The crew who were killed were F/O R.W. Cooper (pilot), Sgt Mowat, Sgt M.J.C. Cross, Sgt G.W. Dalby and Sgt C. Broad. They are all buried at Smilde

(Hoogersmilde) General Cemetery. The survivors, both of who became PoWs, were Sgt A.F. Key and Sgt G.W. Rex.

5   The fighting at Toungoo was largely between Chinese and Japanese forces but there were several Indian units aiding the Chinese. Moodie's would appear to have been one of them.

6   Sergeant Powrie had joined the RAF in May 1940 and survived the war.

7   *The Scotsman*, 5 February 1942, p. 3.

8   *The Scotsman*, 6 February 1942, p. 8.

9   *The Scotsman*, 14 February 1942, p. 6.

10 Larmour, who had been sentenced to three years in prison in 1941, later launched a petition of right against the War Department but it is not known exactly what this matter pertained to or whether or not it was successful. In 1954 (and then aged 71) Larmour again found himself before the courts when he and a carter he employed were charged at Belfast with having stolen 19 bags of fish meal and 25 bags of bran. On this occasion Larmour, who claimed that he had not been managing his farm for some time as he was battling alcoholism, was acquitted by the judge as there was insufficient evidence to convict.

11 *Liverpool Evening Express*, 26 March 1942, p. 3.

12 *The Scotsman*, 10 June 1942, p. 3.

13 *Ibid.*

14 *The Scotsman*, 20 April 1942, p. 4.

15 *The Sunday Post*, 15 February 1942, p. 2.

16 *Edinburgh Evening News*, 14 May 1942, p. 2.

17 *Edinburgh Evening News*, 8 May 1942, p. 5.

18 *The Scotsman*, 6 June 1942, p. 7.

19 *The Scotsman*, 28 August 1942, p. 4.

20 *Edinburgh Evening News*, 22 July 1942, p. 4.

21 The British Restaurants were a huge success and by 1943 there were 2,160 across the country, serving over 600,000 meals per day.

22 Like many aircraft used by the OTUs this Spitfire had seen active service. In this case the Spitfire had served with at least four front-line squadrons. It had been damaged at least once during its service but this played no part in the fatal accident suffered by Sergeant Forsyth.

23 *The Scotsman*, 27 October 1942, p. 3.

24 At the time, Poon Lim's 133 days adrift were a record. After his return to the UK the King awarded him the BEM and the Royal Navy included elements from his ordeal in a handbook on how to survive at sea. After the war Poon Lim emigrated to the USA but was turned down by the US Navy as he had flat feet! He died in 1991 in Brooklyn, New York.

25 The 10 OTU operational contribution during the war resulted in 63 losses (nine on bombing operations and one on a leaflet raid).

Chapter 5: 1943

1   *The Scotsman*, 8 January 1943, p. 3.
2   This was an experienced and courageous crew with three of the officers having been decorated. They were F/L E.F.G. Healey DFC DFM (pilot), Sgt Dunbar (flight engineer), F/O J.R. Pennington DFC (navigator), P/O D.M. Crozier DFM RCAF (bomb aimer), P/O M.H. Lumley (wireless operator), Sgt C.H. Jurgensen (mid upper gunner), and Sgt F.J. Edwards (rear gunner).
3   The crew consisted of: F/L H.G. Shockley, RCAF (pilot); P/O B.H. Labarge, RCAF (2nd pilot); Sgt C.O. Henderson, RCAF (flight engineer); P/O W.W. Kirkpatrick, RAFVR (navigator); P/O F. Holland, RAFVR (bomb aimer); F/O W.M. Palmer, RCAF (wireless operator); Sgt M.W. MacKenzie, RAFVR (mid-upper gunner); and P/O J. Henderson, RAFVR (rear gunner).
4   The other 103 Squadron crew which failed to return on this night ditched in the sea off Falmouth and the crew were picked up safely.
5   Calder, Angus, *The People's War. Britain 1939-1945* (Pimlico, 1999), p. 344.
6   *Daily Mirror*, 21 January 1943, p. 5.
7   After his release from captivity at the end of the war Milne left the RAF but remained linked with the aeronautics industry playing a role in the development and sale of the Canberra jet.
8   *The Scotsman*, 21 August 1943, p. 3.
9   *The Scotsman*, 21 August 1943, p. 3.
10 *The Scotsman*, 21 August 1943, p. 3.
11 The rest of the crew were: Sgt A. Chibanoff, RCAF (pilot); Sgt D.R. Coe (flight engineer); F/O F.V. Webb, RCAF (navigator); F/O K.B. Begbie, RCAF (bomb aimer); Sgt A.R.J. Gaiger (wireless operator); Sgt E.T. Potts (mid-upper gunner); and Sgt H.W. Frost, RCAF (rear gunner).
12 Amongst the other crews lost on this night were that of the new commanding officer S/L G.W. Holden, DSO, DFC & bar, and the crew which had flown with Guy Gibson on the dams raid, and another of the dams raid survivors, F/L L.G. Knight DSO, RAAF. This raid demonstrated that low-level attacks on German targets were not viable in large heavy bombers and were discontinued as a result.
13 *The Scotsman*, 24 September 1943, p. 3.
14 *The Scotsman*, 24 September 1943, p. 3.
15 Edinburgh Academy produced a roll of honour which detailed the loss of 177 academicals who had lost their lives during the war and of 1,817 academicals and eight masters who had served in the armed forces during the war.
16 *The Scotsman*, 16 November 1943, p. 6.
17 The crew consisted of F/L D.M. Moodie DFC, RCAF (pilot); Sgt E.L. Melbourne (flight engineer); F/S J.T. Bundle DFM (navigator); F/S H.W.N. Clausen DFM (bomb aimer); F/S T.E. Stamp (wireless operator); F/S L.A. Drummond (mid-upper gunner); F/S F.A. Hughes (rear gunner).
18 *The Sunday Post*, 31st October 1943, p. 2.
19 *The Sunday Post*, 26 December 1943, p. 13.

20 *The Scotsman*, 27 December 1943, p. 6.

21 From *Scharnhorst*'s crew of 1,968, only 36 survived to be taken prisoner. Much of the action took place in darkness.

Chapter 6: 1944

1   All seven are buried at Hannover War Cemetery, they were: F/O G.E. Sharpe, RCAF (pilot); Sgt B.G. Imber (flight engineer); F/O E.A. Willard (navigator); F/O A.V. Shirley (bomb aimer); Sgt A. Ross (wireless operator); Sgt W.J. Churcher (mid-upper gunner); and Sgt H. Patrick (rear gunner).

2   Mooney's crew were all buried at Rheinburg War Cemetery. They were: F/O Robert Leo Mooney, DFM (pilot); Sgt Felix Bernard Grey (flight engineer); Sgt George Albert Johnson, DFM (navigator); F/S Jack Worsdale, DFM (bomb aimer); Sgt Norman Davidson Cameron (wireless operator); F/S Godfrey Woolf, RAAF (mid-upper gunner); F/S George Edward Smith (rear gunner).

3   *The Sunday Post*, 14 May 1944, p. 2.

4   www.edinphoto.org.uk/1_edin/1_edinburgh_history_-_recollections_edinburgh_ at_war_ed_thomson.htm#crates_for_garden_shed

5   Captain Cowan is buried at Orvieto War Cemetery.

6   Originally conceived as a day school converted from the Merchant Maiden Hospital and named the Edinburgh Educational Institution for Young Ladies this was changed to the slightly less formidable Edinburgh Educational Institution Ladies' College. This was again simplified in 1888 to the Edinburgh Ladies' College before, in 1944, changing its name again to the Mary Erskine School for Girls.

7   *The Scotsman*, 6 June 1944, p. 4.

8   The crew consisted of: P/O S.A.D. Walker (pilot); Sgt N.J. Neal (flight engineer); Sgt M.C. Murray, RCAF (navigator); P/O I.R. Draper (bomb aimer); Sgt D.W.H. Edsall (wireless operator); Sgt P. Craig (mid-upper gunner); and Sgt T.A. McRobbie (rear gunner). Six of the crew are buried at Bayeux War Cemetery while Sgt Murray is buried at Beny-sur-Mer Canadian War cemetery.

9   All were buried at Ranville.

10 Sub-Lieutenant Roney is buried at Hermanville War Cemetery.

11 F/O J.C.Dickson was 30 years old and a married man who lived at Plumpton, Ulveston, Lancs. He left behind his widow Mary and parents Andrew and Martha. He was buried at Lerwick New Cemetery.

12 *London Gazette* (Supplement), 29 August 1944, p. 4073.

13 Flying Officer Cruickshank's injuries were so severe that he never flew again and after finishing the war with the rank of flight lieutenant he went back to his banking job in Edinburgh. He retired in 1977 and is currently vice chairman of the Victoria Cross and George Cross Association. After attending the unveiling of the first national monument to Coastal Command in 2004 he was asked about his experiences and modestly answered, 'When they told me I was to get the

VC it was unbelievable. Decorations didn't enter my head.' He is the last living recipient of the VC awarded during the Second World War.

14 Lady and Lord Elphinstone resided at nearby Carberry Tower.

15 *The Scotsman*, 22 September 1944, p. 4.

16 AVM S.P. Simpson MC CB CBE had served in the First World War and throughout the interwar period in the RAF and during the war had been commanding officer of RAF forces at Gibraltar before taking over as commanding officer of No.18 Group which was the Coastal Command reconnaissance group responsible for Rosyth, Orkney and Shetland and as such was F/L Cruickshank's senior commanding officer. He retired from the RAF in 1947 and died in 1966. Major Charles Henry Scott Plummer was the president of the Territorial Army Association of the County of Selkirk and lived at Sunderland Hall, Selkirk.

17 *Ark Royal* was sunk by U-boat U81 while ferrying aircraft to Malta from Gibraltar as part of Force H. All but one of the 1,488 crew of the aircraft carrier were safely taken off the ship.

18 Maund was a Fleet Air Arm pilot who had been previously mentioned in dispatches twice (once for his courage in 1940 while aboard HMS *Eagle* as part of 813 Squadron and then for the part he played in the attack on Taranto). He served at HMS *Jackdaw* (RN Air Station Crail) with 786 Squadron before transferring to HMS *St. Angelo* (RN Base, Malta) in March 1942 with 828 Squadron. At some point he was posted to 821 Squadron (still at Malta) and was killed in action on 11 January 1943. Lieutenant Maund was aged 28 at the time of his death and is commemorated on the Lee-on-Solent Memorial to those from the Fleet Air Arm with no known grave.

19 This was a harsh verdict but tempered by the realisation that during the crisis Maund had been more involved with safeguarding his crew. It was revealed later that the ship's reliance on electrical power played a far greater role in her loss than any decisions made by Maund and he had in fact done all possible. Clearly, the authorities had not taken altogether seriously the verdict found against Maund as he had immediately been made Director of Combined Operations in the Middle East before becoming aide-de-camp to the King and then Director of Combined Operations, India.

20 *The Scotsman*, 22 September 1944, p. 4.

Chapter 7: 1945

1 Both Flying Officer Carmichael and his navigator Flying Officer James Leonard Halcrow are buried at Taukkyan War Cemetery. Halcrow was a native of Northern Ireland and at 42 years of age was considerably older than most aircrew.

2 *The Scotsman*, 9 May 1945, p. 2.

3 *Ibid.*

4 After seeing the poor preparations for war during an early visit to Scapa Flow he had voiced his concerns and was reported to have openly wept after hearing the news of the sinking of HMS *Royal Oak*.

5 *The Scotsman*, 9 May 1945, p. 2.

6 *Ibid.*

7 *The Scotsman*, 14 May 1945, p. 3.

8 *The Scotsman*, 17 May 1945, p. 4.

9 *Dundee Courier*, 31 August 1945, p. 3.

10 Unfortunately I have been unable to find out if Mr Dempsey was successful in his appeal to the Scottish National Trust.

11 *Sunday Post*, 12 August 1945, p. 2.

12 The worst example, however, was in Glasgow where tens of thousands of pounds of damage had been done.

13 *The Scotsman*, 16 August 1945, p. 2.

14 *Ibid*, p. 7.

15 *Ibid.*

16 *The Scotsman*, 16 August 1945, p. 2.

17 *Ibid*, p. 4.

18 Richard Kay (28) was an assistant baker aboard the ocean liner MV *Dunbar Castle* which was sunk by a mine on 9 January 1940. His brother Alexander (also 28) was a baker aboard the SS *Walmer Castle* which was sunk by enemy aircraft on 21 September 1941 while part of a Gibraltar convoy.

19 A second VC was also awarded at the investiture. This was to Captain Gerard Norton of the South African Military Forces.

20 F/Lt I.W. Terry is buried at Nantes (Pont-du-Cens) Communal Cemetery. He had already flown at least 32 operations with 206 Squadron before his death. The crew, P/O E.D. Rawes (pilot), Terry (navigator), Sgt J.W. Durrant (wireless op/air gunner), and Sgt R.L. Watts (air gunner), took off from their base at Chivenor aboard Hudson V (AM837, VX-N) to raid an oil refinery at Donges. The pilot was from Lisbon, Portugal.

21 *The Scotsman*, 27 September 1945, p. 4.

22 *Ibid.*

23 Major MacMichael's father, Pilot Hugh MacMichael, had been drowned on 2 January 1941 while serving aboard the pilot cutter *Queen of the May* at Methil. Major MacMichael's grandfather was Bailie John MacMichael.

24 *The Scotsman*, 28 September 1945, p. 4.

25 *The Scotsman*, 1 October 1945, p. 4.

26 *The Scotsman*, 29 September 1945, p. 4.

Index